'CHRISTIAN'
ENGLAND

'CHRISTIAN' ENGLAND

What the 1989
English Church Census
reveals

Peter Brierley

All royalties from this book will go
towards the cost of further research for the church

MARC Europe
London
1991

British Library Cataloguing in Publication Data

'Christian' England: results of the English Church Census.
    1. England. Churches. Attendance
    I. Brierley, Peter *1938-* II. MARC Europe
    306.6

ISBN 1-85321-100-1

Copyright © Peter Brierley, 1991

First published in the United Kingdom 1991

All rights reserved. No part of this publication may be
reproduced or transmitted in any form or by any means,
electronic or mechanical, including photocopying,
recording, or any information storage and retrieval system,
without either prior permission in writing from the
publisher or a licence permitting restricted copying.
In the United Kingdom such licences are issued by the
Copyright Licensing Agency, 33-34 Alfred Place,
London WC1E 7DP.

MARC Europe is a registered charity.

Published by MARC Europe
Vision Building, 4 Footscray Road
Eltham, London SE9 2TZ

Photoset and printed in the United Kingdom
by Stanley L Hunt (Printers) Ltd,
Midland Road, Rushden, Northants NN10 9UA

To my special colleagues, Kemi Ajayi, Suzanne Wardall,
David Longley and Phil Back
without whom the English Church Census
simply would not have been possible
and who bore the load in the heat of the day.

Also to Alan Rogers, Michael Turnbull, Ed Dayton,
John Malcolm and Chris Radley,
the initial Board members who gave the support
necessary for the project to succeed.

Also to Clive Calver and Peter Searle who
both sponsored the study and encouraged
it forward for the sake of the Kingdom.

CONTENTS

	Page
Forewords	9
Acknowledgements	13
1. A Census — Whatever for?	**17**
Change in the 1980s 18	
Religious, structural, resource, social	
How the Census can help 21	
Census Sunday 23	
Census programme, publicity, the form, the response, accuracy	
Summary 27	
2. The overall results	**29**
Adult churchgoers 30	
Reasons for decline, major groups	
Free Church adult churchgoers 37	
Independent churches	
Congregational size and service frequency 47	
Size of congregation, frequency of attendance, morning and evening services	
Child attendance 51	
Church membership 54	
Membership and attendance	
Comparisons 58	
Population, opinion polls, international	
Summary 60	
3. Where do people go to church?	**61**
Churches and churchgoing by region 62	
Areas of strength, non-attenders	
Denominational strengths 67	
Application 72	
Assessing strengths and weaknesses	
Afro-Caribbean case study	
Summary 77	

Page

4. Churchgoers by age and gender   79
   Gender   79
     Geography, denomination
   Gender, denomination and age group   86
     Age group and denomination
   Special groups   93
     Mothers, families, 'baby boomers', non-churchgoers
   Age groups   97
     Afro-Caribbeans, churchmanship by region
   Sunday School   100
   Application   103
   Summary   105

5. Which soil is the best?   107
   Overall results   108
   Environment by denomination   111
   Environment by churchmanship   115
   Different environments   116
     The rural church, ideas for growth,
     urban advance, separate towns
   Environment by region   121
   Application   124
   Summary   125

6. Growth, decline and staticness   127
   Overall growth   128
   Growth by region   129
   Growth by denomination and churchmanship   131
   Growth by environment   133
   Growth by size of church   137
   Growth and decline by church people   142
   What makes churches grow?   145
     Church location, life, leaders, values
   Application   151
   Summary   153

	Page
7. How our beliefs are practised	**155**

    The terms used for analysis 155
    Analysed categories, evangelicals
    Churchmanship strengths 158
    Churchmanship growth
    Churchmanship by denomination 161
    Adult churchgoers, churches
    Churchmanship by region 167
    Counties
    Application 172
    Summary 175

8. How old are our churches?   **177**
    Overall results 177
    Free Churches, Roman Catholic and Orthodox
    Anglican Churches 182
    Churchmanship 185
    Region 188
    Summary 190

9. Giving to the Third World   **191**
    Overall results 192
    Combinations of support
    Support by church environment 194
    Support by churchmanship 197
    Support by region 198
    Summary 200

10. Towards a Christian England   **201**
    Nominal Christianity 201
    Future attendance by denomination 207
    Future attendance by church environment 209
    Future attendance by churchmanship 210
    What then of the future? 211
    Quality leaders, willing pioneers, bullseye priorities, change motivators, committed visionaries
    Conclusion 214
    Summary 215

		Page
Notes		**217**
Appendix — The Census Programme		**229**
	Who supported the Census? 229	
	Council of Reference 230	
	Finding all the Churches 231	
	Ascertaining addresses 232	
	Testing out the Form 232	
	Who is included? 233	
	Why not just a Sample? 234	
	What is a Church? 234	
	Processing the data 236	
Alphabetical Index		**239**
Map Index		**251**
	Map showing counties of England 254	
	Maps showing strength and change 255-278	

Abbreviations

E	Estimate
m	million
N/a	Not available or not known

FOREWORD

Most Rev Dr George Carey
Archbishop of Canterbury

Without any question the survey undertaken by MARC Europe is the most thorough and comprehensive ever done of English churchgoing. It is therefore a significant sociological "map" of the Christian presence which still continues to make an important contribution to the life of our nation.

The importance of this analysis for the Christian churches is self-evident. We are talking of this decade as a decade of evangelism and the research study reveals the reality of the task facing the many Christian Churches. First it gives us a picture of the challenge facing us. Even though such an analysis does not and cannot give us statistics concerning quality of Church life or good work done in the name of the Church, it does show that decline in attendance continues. One area I looked at first of all, was our ministry among young people and we see that we are not holding our youngsters in the faith. This and other data constitute serious and uncomfortable realities for us all.

Second, the challenge is there to be met and addressed. Far from presenting with hopeless conclusions, the study presents us with interesting data concerning sections of the church where growth has taken place and there are possibly clues here for other bodies to consider. It may well be the case, for example, that this survey will act as a stimulus to our growing ecumenical convergence as we share insights into those factors that make for growth and decline.

I am personally clear that MARC Europe has given us in this

volume a most important tool to guide our thinking and confound our complacency. It will provide not only the catalyst for the urgent task of sharing faith today, but I believe that it gives us crucial data for strategic planning as we seek to find ways of meeting the spiritual needs of our fellow countrymen and women and to show the true relevance of worship.

FOREWORD

Sir John Boreham
Former Head of Government Statistical Service

Condorcet, the eighteenth century French philosopher, believed that laws should not be judged by the intentions of legislators nor religions by texts, but by their real effects, as social institutions modified by the practices and beliefs of the people. It is taking quite a time, but we are moving towards his conception of an informed democracy.

On the ancient foundations of broad but shallow demographic and census information we have, in the last hundred years, added, successively, more probing sample surveys of family expenditure, general household characteristics, travel, readership, criminal activities, voting intentions, social attitudes and what-have-you. It is now possible to compile the annual book, *Social Trends,* which would have pleased Condorcet by offering a portrait of contemporary British life.

We are still, however, miles or decades away from being an informed democracy. Not enough statisticians talk or write in a way that makes listening or reading a pleasure, not a duty. And since more than half the people left school before they were 16 years old it is the spiced and over-dramatised mass media that get read, not *Social Trends,* still less the *Journal of the Royal Statistical Society.*

However, measurement goes on and the English Church Census of 1989 falls in to the onward march of Condorcet's survey soldiers. (Could we have a social scientists' anthem, words by Hughes, music by Williamson?)

The Christian churches have declined in membership and influence. It is easy but wrong to think that they don't matter any more. Of course, we all say, Christian ethics are deeply diffused through all our beliefs. Five out of every six adults say that they believe that extra-marital sex is wrong. Two out of every three say that they believe that fiddling expenses or pocketing too much change is wrong.

It's not so easy to know how widely those claimed beliefs are bodied forth in action. Present rates suggest that divorce will be the end of one marriage in every three and in about a third of divorces adultery is the named ground. There is one adult per 200 adult population found guilty or cautioned for burglary, robbery, theft or handling stolen goods.

However actions and beliefs are related, the English Church Census of 1989 shows that 10 per cent of adults went to church on that Sunday in October 1989. The Christian churches are unquestionably a major social institution. Together with the practices and beliefs of the people they continue to affect the lives of all the population.

This volume of statistics from the English Church Census is a source that social statisticians cannot ignore. Roll on the day when *all* the members of an informed British democracy will know and understand the figures.

ACKNOWLEDGEMENTS

A small army of people have helped in various ways with the English Church Census. The key players have been mentioned in the dedication and a huge debt is owed to them all.

Behind the original Board members stood those who came later and supported the decision that had already been taken: Viscountess Brentford, Brian Quick, Dr Harri Heino, Bryant Myers. Within MARC Europe the project owes much to the helpfulness of Mary Lawson, Research Department Secretary, who kept numerous ends tied together. Others in the department helped at various stages including Research Assistants Angela Johnson and Cate Partridge, but a special load fell on Jon Blake, Senior Research Manager, in the early part of 1990 when the computerisation programme was at its height. Later members of the Research Department, Boyd Myers and Lindsey Marshall, have helped with the interpretation and the writing of the Regional commentaries. Our former Director of Research, Phil Back, also kindly helped with these, as did Stephen Brierley and Greg Smith.

Enormous thanks are due, too, to John Marcus who computerised some 16 pages of equations to ensure that the estimates were as reasonable as possible, and who coped at short notice with numerous requests for extra printouts. Many people helped put data into the computer in the first place and we are grateful to Arthur Richards for helping to organise our computer to allow this to happen easily. Betty Reed was one who did much herself and helped to organise others such as Patricia Dyer, Doreen Dewar, Yvonne Parfett, Val Hiscock and those who worked with them — Foluke Ajayi, Gboyinwa Ajayi, Rose Atfield, Pam Bell, Linda Bloomfield, Funlola Craig, Philip Elledge, Jeremy Longley, Angela Major, Dorothy Mayhew, Titi Onigbode, Kaye Stewart, Celia Thomas and Carol Upton (née Davies).

But before the results could be computerised, they had to be collected, and that collection meant sending out 38,600 forms and two reminders. It was not a simple process. Many ministers look after more than one church, and so the forms were grouped together in suitable multiples of two, three, four, even up to ten or more. Many helped get the forms ready for posting including Bukola Adesola, Moniye Christos, Julie Evans, Margaret Evans, Ruth Evans, Gene Fellows, Peggy Hale, Laurence Hobbs, Allen Milner, Joan Milner, Tim Murdoch, Pat Pellet, Steve Rawcliffe, Harriet Rowbottom, Jonathan Southby and Keith York.

The forms had to be sent out, and some people were exceptionally helpful in aiding the identification of all the individual churches. Commissioner Harry Read of the Salvation Army and Pastor John Arthur of the Seventh-Day Adventist Church made sure we had complete lists. Douglas Fryer at Church House graciously guided us in the labyrinth of Anglican Churches and helped us secure extra data at short notice. Bryan Tolhurst at the Methodist Conference Office and Carole Rogers of the United Reformed Church gave good help, too. The excellent response from these churches reflected their co-operation for which we are most grateful.

Many others also helped us get as complete a list as possible. Graham Fisher for the Gospel Standard Baptist Churches, Chester Woodhall of the Churches of Christ, Rev Milum Kostic of the Serbian Orthodox Church, Dr John Boyes for the Christian Brethren (Open), Mike Stockdale for Bristol Churches, Joel Edwards of the Afro-Caribbean Evangelical Alliance, Evan M Lisbund of the Pentecostal Help Organisation, Rev Rocky Scott of Redemption Church for black-led churches and Molly Porter, ex-Administrator of the Zebra Project, all gave advice. Likewise did Robert Beckford help with the Wesleyan Holiness Churches, Pastor Abraham Oshuntola of the Pentecostal Gospel Faith Chapel, and Mike Clarke with the Bibleway Group. We also received advice from the Evangelical Missionary Alliance, World Vision of Britain, Hampstead Bible School, Church Army and the major House Church groups — Harvestime, Pioneer, New Frontiers, Ichthus Fellowship — and Tankerton Evangelical Church, the Coign Fellowship, Zion Baptist Church at Creech St Michael and many, many others who telephoned or wrote.

I am grateful for the excellent work by Dee Frankling and Lois Pratt on the regular staff of MARC Europe who helped in typing this commentary on the results, and to Betty Reed and Rachael Wickington who helped when Suzanne Wardall broke her arm at the critical time. Books and tables had to be proofread and Lesley Reynolds and Allen Milner did a very good job on this as well.

Alec Hitchins put in hours upon hours of both creative thinking and detailed art direction into the illustrations. Roland Pearson helped with all the *Prospects for the Nineties* diagrams, managing to cope despite the tedium of doing so many similar items one after the other.

Philippa King, David Longley and Chris Radley all had major inputs in the critical area of publicity for the venture. I am grateful, too, to Tony Collins for suggesting the title *'Christian' England.*

Without the contributions of 27,000 who kindly completed the forms, however, all would have been in vain, and to these thousands who thus helped make the Census a success many, many grateful thanks. It was clear that a good number went to much trouble to give accurate figures.

Special thanks are due to the great patience of the printer, David Hunt, who not only sorted out all the mass of paper but took a personal interest to ensure it was as accurate as it could be. Likewise thanks are due to his incredible typesetter who has set in *Prospects for the Nineties* approximately 250,000 numbers at an error rate of less than 1 in 1,000. Such attention to detail is the hallmark of quality and for this precision we are most grateful.

All the responsibility for the final version of the text is mine, but the editing of it at very short notice and in a short time span was willingly undertaken by Jenny Rogers, whose willingness to contribute and help in the expert way in which only she can, encouraged me enormously. Likewise we are grateful to those on the Council of Reference who kindly gave advice and supported the project in key ways, gallantly reading the draft of this book in a short period of time. We especially respect the hours taken by Eileen Barker, Richard Bewes, Sir John Boreham, Bernard Green, David Jackman, Stuart Murray, Alan Rogers, Peter Searle, Michael Hornsby-Smith, Basil Varnam and David Winter and to several of these and to Roger Forster, Malcolm Laver, Michael Lawson and Keith Roberts for subsequent discussions. Thanks are due too to Valerie Passmore for copy-editing the book, also at short notice.

The printed book may bear my name but it is clear from this list of people that this is above all a team project. A body has many parts and each part is important for the fulfilment of the work of that body. In the English Church Census many people have played a role and each has contributed to a vital element in the whole. Long hours worked, evening after evening, enthusiasm shown and sheer willingness to help in any way that was necessary, made this an exercise which we all sincerely hope will help the Church in this country move forward, which has also challenged and inspired us to give, and having done all, still to give, for the good of the Kingdom.

Peter Brierley
February 1991

1. A CENSUS – WHATEVER FOR?

'Would all those men aged between 20 and 29 now please put their hand up?' They did so and were duly counted.

'Thank you. Now would all the women aged 30 to 44 years of age do the same?' Another group duly responded. The English Church Census was under way.

In another church many miles away small strips of paper were being handed out as people came into the church. 'You'll be told what to do with these,' was the comment. During the service the congregation was asked to write down their gender and age group and then put the piece of paper into the collection bag – specially distributed for the purpose. The normal offering was taken separately! The strips of paper were then all counted to enable the relevant Census question to be completed as accurately as possible. Many church leaders went to considerable trouble to ensure correct answers were given.

In an altogether different setting in a large Anglican church, a churchwarden surreptitiously stood at the back of the steps in the choir quietly counting the congregation he had come to know well over the years. He went to each side – he didn't want to miss anyone. Then he toured the Sunday Schools to count the teachers and children. He repeated the exercise at the second morning service and at the evening service too. Here too was proficiency at work. No one realised what he was doing, but he was completing the questionnaire for the English Church Census and his concern too was for comprehensiveness and professionalism.

Why all this activity? On Sunday, October 15th, 1989, tens of thousands of churches across England contributed to the English Church Census. Essentially this was an attempt to measure as precisely as possible the number of people attending church that Sunday. The Census was carried out against a background of dramatic change in the 1980s. The following simplified description sets the scene for the results.

CHANGE IN THE 1980s

Religious Change

Many opportunities were taken in the decade to reach out to British people. A major effort to bring the Gospel to those in Southeast England took place with 'Mission to London' in 1983 and 1984 under the evangelist Luis Palau, when nearly 24,000 people went forward, 56% of them to accept Christ.[1] Mission England with Billy Graham visited Bristol, Sunderland, Norwich, Ipswich, Liverpool and Birmingham in 1984 and Sheffield in 1985 when over 1.1 million attended and nearly 10% went forward.[2] Billy Graham returned in May and June that year with Mission 89, based primarily in London but broadcast to over 220 'Livelink' centres throughout the country. To these special events must be added the scores of missions conducted by over 200 British evangelists and the activity of hundreds of Christian organisations.

The regular evangelistic work of thousands of local churches of all persuasions operating in all parts of the country must also be added. Many small streams can make a mighty river.

The 1980s also saw the burgeoning of the so-called 'House Church Movement'. Initially these were groups of people from established churches meeting in the home of one of their members, but their growth meant that by 1986 98% were meeting in halls, hired buildings, cinemas or redundant churches.[3] The name still sticks, however, although today many prefer to call themselves 'New Churches'.[4] The House Church Movement began with about 190 churches in the 1970s, and established over a thousand more in the 1980s. In 1980 they attracted 40,000 people: this more than doubled over the next ten years.[5] Their example has inspired others to start individual churches which are not part of one of the main House Church streams. Another 600 such non-denominational churches were known in 1990.[6] Further streams were founded as groups of these individual churches came together.

In the 1980s a number of conventions, Bible Weeks and like gatherings grew in popularity although some, like Royal Week, lasted only a few years. Greenbelt and Spring Harvest flourished in this decade, with the latter seeing over a quarter of a million attend in the period.

At the same time there was a resurgence of other religions. The Salman Rushdie book, *The Satanic Verses,* revealed the strength of the Muslim community in Britain and their outrage at being so blatantly misrepresented. Outside organised religion the strength of the New Age Movement grew, fanned by many publications and much (often subtle) reflection in the media of its viewpoint.

Structural Change

The Church of England through its *Faith in the City* Report[7] encouraged churches to start thinking strategically through undertaking Mission Audits. The Baptist Union's *Action in Mission* programme and booklet urged its churches to follow a similar path. Methodist Church studies of its church life resulted in reports like *The Missionary Shape of the Congregation.* All these aimed to help leaders focus on key areas of change so that appropriate strategies for evangelism could be developed.

The decade had begun with two influential conferences. The Roman Catholic 'National Pastoral Congress' looked at the life and work of their church. The Nationwide Initiative in Evangelism (NIE) Conference also in 1980 focused on the needs of the country from an across-the-board perspective. Both conferences helped to change the ecumenical structure. The British Council of Churches where the Roman Catholics had had observer status only was disbanded in 1990. A new body, Churches Together in England, was launched on September 1st with a commissioning service in St George's Cathedral, Southwark, with the Catholics as full members. Similar national bodies were established in Scotland and Wales, with the Council of Churches for Britain and Ireland as the new umbrella organisation.

Structures also changed locally. Many Local Ecumenical Projects (LEPs) were started in the 1980s whereby two, and sometimes more, different denominations came together to share a building, a ministry, or a congregation. These Projects bring joint resources to resolve common church pressures. *Faith in the City* looked especially at urban church life while rural life is the concern of the Archbishop's Commission on Rural Areas under the chairmanship of Rt Rev Peter Nott, Bishop of Norwich.

Resource Change

Canon John Tiller's 1993 report on Anglican clergy, *A Strategy for the Church's Ministry,* brought new thinking on a vexed question of how best to apportion the scarce human resources of clergy. Rev Ian Bunting's survey of theological training establishments[8], *The Places to Train,* showed the necessity to think afresh about what ministers are being trained for. These Anglican concerns were also mirrored in other denominations. Although there were 39,300 clergy in 1990 against 40,900 in 1980 (a drop of 160 per year)[9] many felt their numbers could decline much more, and dramatically, in the 1990s and the decade beyond.

The Afro-Caribbean (so-called 'Black') Churches grew rapidly in the 1970s and were more willingly accepted by the white churches in the 1980s. Church members generally were ageing; 31% of those aged 65 or over in 1980 died during the decade.[10] Figures from the *UK Christian Handbook*[11] show the numbers of nominal Christians decreased: 68% of British people claimed some allegiance to Christianity in 1980 but this dropped to 65% in 1990. This high residual strength is reflected in the six million audience of popular religious television programmes such as 'Songs of Praise':

Church finances were not so strong as they used to be, partly because of the multitude of new Christian organisations being started (over 1,000 began in Britain in the second half of the 1980s) each requiring funding, and partly because churches are generally smaller than they were.

Social Changes

It may be an over-simplified generalisation to state that the actual lifestyle of many Christian people became less dynamic, with fewer willing to reflect their beliefs in their behaviour,[12] but there is sufficient truth in it to account for some of the changes seen through the Census.

What people want from life is changing. Crime, abortion, cohabitation, divorce, pornography, and debt have increased. We have become more concerned about the environment and about ethical problems in health care. We have become a nation of slightly older people. Women may much more easily choose a career and return to it after having a family. Fertility rates have declined. Women report generally less satisfaction with marriage. Britain has become more multi-racial.

A major new Education Act in 1988 gave greater financial responsibility to local schools as well as instituting a national curriculum on stated subjects. We had government by one Prime Minister and one party in power. The transitory nature of life has been brought home through major disasters like those at the Hillsborough Stadium, the Zeebrugge ferry, the Piper Alpha oil terminal, the Lockerbie aircrash, and the Kings Cross and Clapham rail accidents.

Britain became more prosperous: the average weekly wage for a man has increased from £125 in 1980 to £265 in 1990, in line with inflation. 72% had a telephone in 1980 — 88% in 1990. 57% had full or partial central heating in 1980 with a projected increase up to 80% by the end of 1990. 58% had a car in 1980; 66% have one in 1990. 55% owned their homes in 1980; 68% did so in 1990.[13]

HOW THE CENSUS CAN HELP

It was against such a background of change that the MARC Europe Board decided to launch a further English Church Census in 1989. They hoped as a consequence that it would:

● *Measure decadal change.* We conducted the first such study in 1979. *Prospects for the Eighties*[14] gave details of church attendance by broad denominational grouping by county for 1975 and 1979. A second volume published three years later gave further analyses of growth.[15] These studies generated similar exercises in Wales in 1982[16] and Scotland in 1984.[17] All copies sold out, including a reprint of the English report. The data in them has been used in scores of places in further studies. The proposed 1989 study was 'an historic opportunity not to be missed' said one church leader. Trend information often allows critical insights into developing situations, and the 1989 Census would provide links with 1975 and 1979 data in key areas.

● *Motivate the churches.* Several major denominations in England have declared the 1990s the 'decade of evangelism'. But simply to say, 'We've got to evangelise Southampton!' is not a great deal of help. Where do you start? To say, 'There are 195,000 adults in Southampton who are outside the churches' gives the task some dimension.

● *Help leaders plan.* Church leaders need to plan their churches' strategy for the year, and years, ahead. Hard information on the needs in their area will be an invaluable guide to thinking and decision-making. Data is not everything, of course, but it is something. As Florence Nightingale once put it, 'To understand God's thoughts, we must study statistics, for these are a measure of His purpose.'

● *Confirm Christianity is still very much alive.* The 1979 Census showed 11% of English adults went to church every week, along with 13% of Welsh adults and 17% of Scottish. How had that figure changed 10 years later? 'Let's help MARC Europe to give the facts to those who wish Christianity would roll over and die,' wrote Richard Bewes, Rector of All Souls' Church in the heart of London. There are many sociologists, academics, educators and professionals who sometimes imply Christianity is a religion of small allegiance in Britain. Any organisation which can mobilise such a large proportion of British people every week cannot be dead. But we need to see how alive it is today and not rest on the results of yesterday, however important they were.

● *Focus on activity not belief.* Belief is critically important but it must be translated into activity if it is to mean anything. Counting church attendance is like taking a photograph which shows one moment in time and reflects what action people are taking. This helps give credence to statements about what people believe. 70% of people may believe in God, but how many actually go to church?

● *Affirm that people matter more than things.* Church membership may be a formal qualification, a baptismal certificate only a piece of paper. They have value, but what people do is more important ultimately than what they have. Church attendance focuses on a major element of the 'leisure' market — and shows people who will not be at a DIY store on a Sunday morning! The Census focuses on people's habits. It gives vital information on age, gender, county, and environmental variations. Ultimately people have needs, and these have to be highlighted and handled. 'In every church I have visited I observe a very high degree of personal need matched by a very low expectation of the need being met,' John Wimber once said.[18] This is a subjective judgment, but if people matter, we need to know something about the volume of those needs.

The Census is also important because *current church data is not uniform* and it is therefore difficult to get an accurate overview of the situation. The Church Censuses so far conducted focus on attendance. Such figures are not collected by every denomination, and church membership figures, which usually are, suffer from the fact that each denomination defines membership differently. Apart from such *definitional* variations, there are also *timing* variations. The Roman Catholics collect their data in October, the Methodists in December, the Anglicans in May for example. Whilst the major denominations collect and publish membership figures regularly, and attendance figures more sporadically, these do not cover the entirety of national church life. The fourth largest group in church attendance terms (after the Roman Catholics, Anglicans and Methodists) — the Independents — never publish collective figures because they are made up of so many composite groups.

Although this project is called the *English* Church Census, opportunity was taken, as in the 1979 Census, to also collect information for the Isle of Man and the Channel Islands. We recognise the special nature of these territories, even if their totals are included in the appropriate region in England.

CENSUS SUNDAY

The Census Programme

Details of exactly how the Census was carried out are given in the Appendix, together with a full list of the Council of Reference. For the purposes of the Census a church was defined as *a body of people meeting on a Sunday in the same premises primarily for public worship at regular intervals.* How this definition was applied is described in the Appendix. Details of the many Local Ecumenical Projects which required special classification are given in the companion volume to this book, *Prospects for the Nineties,* which gives tables of adult and child attendance and membership broken down by county, church environment (whether a church is in a city centre, suburb or rural area), denomination, and churchmanship. Full results of all other features, such as age, gender, age of church, Third World aid and church growth are included.[19]

Publicising the Census

Publicity was important. It was critical that the Census form did not come as a surprise to ministers and clergy. A leaflet describing what the Census was, and how it would be conducted, was sent in May 1989 to every Anglican and Roman Catholic Bishop, Methodist Chairman, Baptist Superintendent, United Reformed Church (URC) Moderator, Salvation Army Divisional Commander, and others of equivalent status in other denominations. Several of these then wrote to the clergy under them asking for their support.

Six weeks before Census Sunday every minister in England was sent a copy of a special issue of MARC Europe's quarterly bulletin, *LandMARC,* devoted to the Census. Advertisements in the major religious press three, two and one week before effectively announced 'Census Sunday is coming — you count!' Two weeks before an article by the Bishop of Rochester, Rt Rev Michael Turnbull, appeared in the influential *Church Times.* Another was published the Thursday before Census Sunday in *The Times,* and an article in the *Sunday Times* on the day itself briefly mentioned MARC Europe. On Census Sunday itself a quarter of the BBC and Independent radio stations in England carried interviews.

The Form Arrives

Two weeks before Census Sunday, every minister received a form for every church for which he was responsible, a covering letter and reply envelope. Forms were printed in two colours and carried the name and address of the minister followed by the words 'or successor' in case some had moved in the interim between updating the address list and posting. One minister replied, 'How could you possibly know I was moving on? I only decided to go last week and haven't told my church yet!'

The publicity raised awareness of the study, and generated a brief rush of correspondence much of which criticised the Census on the grounds that *data collecting was unscriptural*. For instance, some leaders pointed out that David was punished for holding one in Israel. Our replies commented that David was punished not because of the act of collecting data but because of David's pride in wanting to know how large was the number of his subjects. In 1 Chronicles 21 we are told the idea was prompted by Satan. 'The numbering was a sin because it was self-glorification'.[20] Two censuses had been carried out before at God's specific request — before and after the Israelite's forty years in the wilderness. The result? A book in the Bible called Numbers!

Some people felt that *the emphasis should be on quality not quantity:* 'Not how many we are, but how holy we are'. It is certainly wise to guard against excessive dependence on one type of data — in this case quantity — but we believe it equally unwise to look only at quality. Quantity statements are useful when the same phenomenon is measured later, as the trend gives valuable information. Measuring growth or decline can be critical in determining our direction. After one presentation in which a number of graphs all showed a downward movement, one church leader prayed, 'O God, move so that those graphs don't become true'. Quantitative information can stimulate prayer, give encouragement, and act as a firm basis for decision-making.

Some of the objectors felt that *data collection was unnecessary*. If you belong to a small church that might be true, but many small churches grow, and there may come a time when everyone does not know everyone else. It is useful to know that you've grown from say 30 people in 1985 to 150 by 1989. If you've added 120 people in four years, will your present building or meeting place be big enough if a further 120 are added in the next four years?

Collecting such simple information gives a realistic basis for planning in the future, as important locally as nationally. After the Scottish Church Census in 1984 one church elder wrote that the idea was so effective and helpful that they planned to repeat the exercise voluntarily every year.

An important part of the publicity was to stress that we would not divulge information on individual churches. Each response was guaranteed confidential treatment.

Response

Census Sunday was a success. In the immediate aftermath of Census Sunday 45% of churches returned their forms. We sent out two reminders in mid-November and early December for non-Catholics and in December and January for the Catholics (because of their official counting day on October 29th). The Church of England Statistical Office in addition allowed extracts to be made from 500 of their church records to supplement Anglican returns.

Almost 27,000 forms returned gave an overall response rate of 70%. The Government holds that a return of 60% is sufficient for normal accuracy, so this high response rate validates the reliability of the overall figures. The overall response of 70% breaks down by broad denominational groupings as follows:

United Reformed Church	77%
Methodist Churches	76%
Anglican Churches	75%
Baptist Churches	73%
Other Free Churches	65%
Independent Churches	58%
Pentecostal Churches	57%
Roman Catholic Churches	51%
Afro-Caribbean Churches	47%
Orthodox Churches	35%

Accuracy of the data

It is important that the data is as reliable as it can be. How it was processed is described in the Appendix, but the overall accuracy was partly verifiable from existing published data. Although few 1989 figures of attendance had been published in early 1991 by those churches which do collect them, such figures as were available are given in Table 1. Methodists only count attendance every three years.

It is clear that the Census estimates are fairly close to the attendance figures internally collected by these churches. The Census figures in this Table differ from those used later because in each case the church concerned is only part of a slightly larger group incorporated under the general title of that Church.

The accuracy of the data is good, and we can be confident of the

Table 1: Church attendance figures as already published and from the Census 1985-1989

	Denomination		
Year	Church of England[21]	Methodist	Roman Catholic
1985	1,179,300	N/a	1,457,800
1986	1,167,000	413,600	1,411,500
1987	1,161,300	N/a	1,358,700
1988	1,165,100	N/a	1,328,200
1989	N/a	388,200	N/a
Census 1989	1,142,400	387,900	1,302,000

results. The next chapter provides a summary of these, and Chapters 3-9 give more detailed analyses of the key questions — geographical variation (Chapter 3), age of churchgoers (Chapter 4), church environment (Chapter 5), church growth (Chapter 6), churchmanship (Chapter 7), church age (Chapter 8) and Third World Support (Chapter 9). Chapter 10 takes a look at the future.

Chapter 1: Summary

- The English Church Census form was sent to 38,607 churches in 1989.
- A church for this purpose was defined as 'a body of people meeting on a Sunday in the same premises primarily for public worship at regular intervals'.
- There was extensive publicity.
- 70% returned the questionnaire, after two reminders.
- The overall figures were generally close to those published by denominations collecting attendance figures.

2. THE OVERALL RESULTS

The English Church Census primarily looked at people going to church. An England which is Christian will be visibly so. The American researcher, George Gallup, has concluded that 'The gulf between what we believe in our heads and what we feel in our hearts and practise in our lives is growing wider'.[1] That is doubtless true of England as well as America. Church-going is one measurable component of Christian practice.

The *UK Christian Handbook* lists well over one hundred denominations in the United Kingdom. For Census purposes these are grouped in the four main historical streams — the Roman Catholics, the Anglicans, the Orthodox and the Free Churches. The

'I hope that's the hymn number and not the local result of the church attendance census.'

Reproduced with permission of
'Church Times'

first two have few additions to them outside the main Roman Catholic Church and the Church of England. The Orthodox are a composite group of many traditions but in church-going terms they are collectively very small in England (under 10,000 out of a total of 3.7 million) and are always kept together as a unit. The Free Churches are broken down into seven major components — the Methodists, Baptists, United Reformed Church, Independents, Afro-Caribbeans, Pentecostals and Other Free Churches; sometimes these different denominations are looked at separately and sometimes the Free Churches are taken in their totality.

ADULT CHURCHGOERS

The 1979 Census asked for information for both 1975 and 1979. The 1989 Census likewise asked for data for 1985 as well as for 1989 in order to go back as far as reasonable without going beyond the average incumbency length of five to seven years. Memory of comparative numbers for four years previously is not completely reliable, but in the event the results were not too different from what we expected given the 1979 figures.

Between 1975 and 1979 adult church attendance dropped 2% from 4.1 million to 4.0 million. Between 1979 and 1985 it dropped 7% from 4.0 million to 3.8 million — a six-year difference rather than four but even so a much bigger drop. Between 1985 and 1989 it dropped a further 1% from 3.8 million to 3.7 million. In 1851, church attendance was 40%[2] of the English population; in 1979 adult church attendance stood at 11%[3]; in 1989 it was 10% of the adult population. More exact figures are given in the following table:

Table 2: Total adult churchgoers 1975-1989

Year	Adult churchgoers	Percentage change	Percentage of adult population
		%	%
1975	4,093,000		11.3
		−2	
1979	4,025,000		11.0
		−7	
1985	3,755,000		9.9
		−1	
1989	3,706,900		9.5

These 1989 figures are the numbers of different people going to church. Some went more than once on October 15th (14% overall) but second visits are not included in the number of attenders. They are included when the size of the congregation is discussed.

For those concerned with the church these results are not good news. But the actual size of the drop is small, as Table 3 indicates. The average numbers who stopped going between 1975 and 1989 are 28,000 adults each year and 19,000 children.

Table 3: Numbers who stopped going

Years	Number who stopped per year	
	Adults	Children
1975 to 1979	17,000	17,000
1979 to 1985	45,000	23,000
1985 to 1989	12,000	15,000
Average 1975 to 1989	28,000	19,000

The 1985-89 figures represent two people per thousand in the population who no longer attend. That is hardly a rapid decline: the church is not going to roll over and die.

Why are the numbers declining and why the nearly threefold increase in adults between 1979 and 1985 from the previous four years? The figures do not suggest a major fall away from faith. There are always exceptions, but people, once converted and incorporated into a church, typically continue to be associated with it for most of their lives. The adult decline is caused by death: there are proportionately more elderly people (65 and over) in the church than in the population as a whole (19% against 15%) and they are not being replaced by younger people. One major reason for the decline in children is the reduced birth rate especially in the early 1980s.

That means there is a massive job to do. Many elderly people currently going to church will 'be promoted to glory', as the Salvation Army puts it, in the next decade. That will depress numbers further unless more people are added to the church. The church needs a critical mass, a sufficient basic core, to survive. Current numbers appear in excess of that but we dare not be complacent: if 10% attend church, 90% do not.

Why the large decline between 1979 and 1985?

This was primarily due to two factors, and would have been much worse without a third.

(1) *Fall in Roman Catholic mass attendance.* This was especially severe in this period — from 40% of adults and those children taking mass in 1979 to 31% in 1989, a 9% fall. The comparable drop over the preceding ten years was 7%, and if present trends continue the present 31% could drop another 7% in the 1990s. As a major church a drop of this magnitude makes a big impact. Of the 45,000 loss per year between 1979 and 1985 for all churches 30,000 were due to the decline in Catholic mass attendance. The figures are given in the following table:[4]

Table 4: Adult Roman Catholic Mass attendance 1975-1989

Year	Adult churchgoers	Percentage of Catholic population	Percentage of national adult population
		%	%
1975	1,576,000	42	4.3
1979	1,515,000	40	4.2
1985	1,335,900	35	3.5
1989	1,304,600	31	3.4

This information is not new to the Catholic authorities who are already taking steps to reverse these trends. One Diocese is following through the 'Renew' programme, a major reappraisal of their churches which challenges people to be closely involved in evangelisation, especially among lapsed Catholics. 'Messengers' are recruited, trained in visiting and Bible study, to visit those who no longer regularly attend.

They are also involved in a church building programme. They have seen their support wane in the inner cities where they have been traditionally strong but increase in suburban areas. Between 1975 and 1990 over 150 new churches were opened and some of their existing premises, including convents, have been opened for public mass.

(2) *Significant decline in attendance among Other Free Churches.* There was an especially rapid fall in Salvation Army numbers which primarily occurred between 1979 and 1985, and accounted for a drop

of 3,000 people per year between 1979 and 1985. 'Other Free Churches' is an important composite group, consisting of the Salvation Army, the Religious Society of Friends (Quakers), the Lutheran Church, the Moravian Church, the Seventh-Day Adventists, the Countess of Huntingdon's Connexion, Chinese and other churches for overseas nationals (outside the Afro-Caribbean area), Mission Centres responsible to the various City Missions or the Shaftesbury Society, and other smaller churches. Collectively, they stood at 112,000 attenders in 1975, dropped to 98,000 in 1979 (a decrease of 12%), fell further to 81,400 in 1985 (a decline of 17%), but increased slightly to 83,000 in 1989 by 2%. The key denominations in this group are given in the following table.

Table 5: Components of Other Free Churches 1979-1989

Denomination	Adult churchgoers 1979*	1985	1989	Percentage change 1979-89	1989 as percentage of adult population
				%	%
Salvation Army	74,700	58,300	57,300	−23	0.15
Seventh-Day Adventists	9,800	10,500	12,300	+26	0.03
Lutheran Church	5,800	4,800	4,700	−19	
Moravian Church	2,000	1,900	1,800	−10	
Religious Society of Friends	1,600	1,500	1,500	−6	0.03
All others	4,100	4,400	5,400	+32	
Total	98,000	81,400	83,000	−15	0.21

* Estimate based on membership figures

The biggest change shown in this table is the Salvation Army decline. This was partly because of a change in definition of membership — recruits had been earlier included but were now excluded until they became full soldiers or members. This was known to Commissioner Harry Read (now retired), who introduced the concept of Adherents into the Army whereby those who attend fairly regularly are encouraged to have a badge and certificate. They find this relatively small identifier with a local group increases commitment to that congregation and encourages some to go further and become full Salvation Army soldiers. The same concept has worked well in the Salvation Army in Canada and Australia. In a day when many people move from one congregation to another to suit their tastes, this simple concept might be adapted elsewhere to encourage a stronger commitment to one particular fellowship.

(3) *Significant growth in the Independent churches.* This is such a major item that it is considered in detail later in this chapter. It is worth noting here, however, that without this growth, then the decline in total adult church attendance between 1979 and 1989 would have been much greater than 318,000. Had the Independent Churches only grown, say, 2%, between 1979-1989, adult church attendance would be 9.3% of the population instead of 9.5%. The decline in church numbers would have then been an extra 8,000 people per year in that decade.

It may also be noted that the annual rate of decline for adults between 1985 and 1989 was less than between 1975 and 1985. Why is this? Part of the reason will be the people added to the church from the Mission England, Mission to London and Mission 89 campaigns. A survey of those who went forward at Mission England[5] found that eighteen months later over half were regularly attending a place of worship. Going forward had strengthened their commitment even if they had been associated with a church before the campaign. These major initiatives may not have changed the face of British Christianity but they have certainly at least dented the surface.

The major streams of attenders

If 3.7 million adults were at church on Sunday October 15th 1989 what does that say about the regularity of church going? Surveys have shown that 88% of those who go to church at least once a month go to church every week. It is assumed that the 3.7 million present that Sunday were regulars and, in absence of other data, that regulars not present that Sunday for whatever reason were matched by visitors or other 'irregular' attenders. There are always likely to be a number of nominal churchgoers who go on Sundays other than the major festivals. The Scottish Lifestyle Survey[6] found that non-church members in Scotland reckoned on going to church on average nine times a year. English people probably attend less but nevertheless some can be counted on to come any particular Sunday.

These 3.7 million are in three main streams: Free Church, Anglican and Catholic. The proportion in each category are given in Table 6.

THE OVERALL RESULTS

Table 6: Proportions of adult churchgoers by major groups 1975-1989

Church	1975	1979	1985	1989
	%	%	%	%
Free Church	30	31	33	34
Anglican	32	31	31	31
Roman Catholic	38	38	36	35
Total (= 100%)	4.1m	4.0m	3.8m	3.7m

The Anglican proportion was holding firm in 1989, the Free Church proportion increasing, and the Catholic proportion decreasing. The Catholic group is still the largest, though if present trends continue the Free Church numbers could overtake Catholic Church attendance during 1995. The detailed figures behind these percentages are given in Table 7.

Table 7: Changes in adult churchgoing by major groups 1975-1989

Church	1975	C	1979	C	1985	C	1989
		%		%		%	
Free Church	1,209,000	+3	1,247,000	−1	1,229,700	+2	1,249,000
Anglican	1,302,000	−4	1,256,000	−6	1,181,000	−3	1,143,900
Roman Catholic	1,576,000	−4	1,515,000	−12	1,335,900	−2	1,304,600
Orthodox	6,000	+17	7,000	+20	8,400	+12	9,400
Total	4,093,000	−2	4,025,000	−7	3,755,000	−1	3,706,900

C = Percentage change

Apart from the Orthodox Church, included for completeness, but whose percentages are based on much smaller numbers than the others, the only growing group is the Free Churches. They had fewer attenders than the Anglicans in 1975 and 1979, but more in 1985 and 1989. Table 7 is illustrated in Figure 1; note the relatively slow rate of change.

The **Orthodox Church** is a small but distinctive group in the United Kingdom, and has much larger representations elsewhere. It has established many national groups since breaking with the Catholic Church in 1054. Churches from nine different Patriarchates have been established in Britain, as well as representative congregations from eleven other countries. A full list

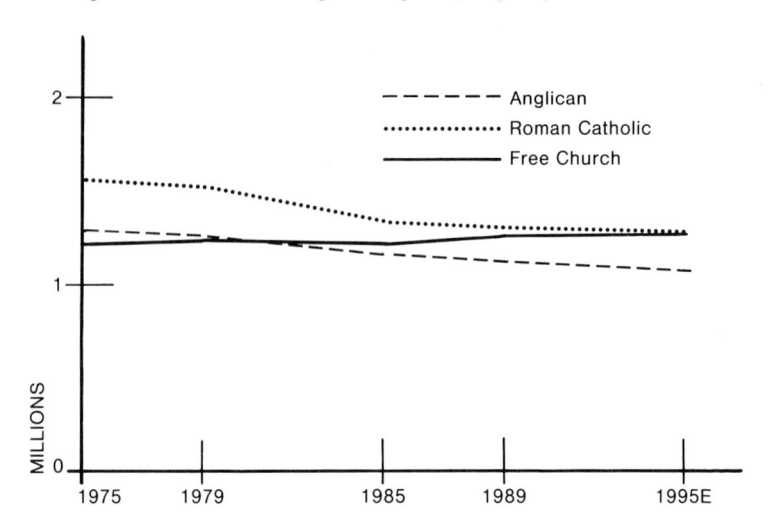

Figure 1: Adult churchgoers by major groups 1975-1989

is given in the *UK Christian Handbook*. At 232,100 in 1989 their membership considerably exceeded their 9,400 attenders.

The **Roman Catholic Church** reflects the Church by that name in England and also churchgoers connected with the Old Roman Catholic Church, the Tridentine Institute of Our Lady of Walsingham, congregations of over eight different Roman Catholic overseas nationalities meeting in England (Croatian, German, Hungarian, Latvian, Lithuanian, Polish, Slovene, Ukrainian and others), and other related bodies. The institutional Roman Catholic Church accounted however for 99.8% of all Catholic mass attenders in 1989, that is, all but 2,600 who attended mass in these other churches.

The **Anglican Church** group reflects the main State Church of England Church, plus the Free Church of England, Protestant Evangelical Church of England and like bodies. As with the Catholics, the institutional church dominates, and accounted for 99.9% of all Anglicans going to church in 1989, that is, all but 1,500 attending elsewhere. The Census includes all the various churchmanships (Low Church, Liberal, Anglo-Catholics, Evangelical etc) within the Church of England. Churches such as All Saints, Margaret Street in West London whose Vicar, Rev D H Hutt, describes as having 'a distinctive presence and distinguished ministry'[7] through preservation of a sacramental service are included as much as his near neighbour, the evangelical All Souls in Langham Place.

The *Free Churches* are however composed of many groups.

FREE CHURCH ADULT CHURCHGOERS

The combined Free Church attenders have increased by 3% in the fourteen years 1975-1989 but this overall growth hides several conflicting movements. The changing proportions of the major groups is given below.

Table 8: Proportions of Free Church adult churchgoers by denomination 1975-1989

Denomination	1975	1979	1985	1989
	%	%	%	%
Methodist	38	36	34	32
Baptist	16	16	16	16
United Reformed	12	11	10	9
Independent	14	17	21	23
Afro-Caribbean	5	5	5	5
Pentecostal	6	7	7	8
Others	9	8	7	7
Total (= 100%)	1.21m	1.25m	1.23m	1.25m

The Baptist and Afro-Caribbean proportion remained constant over these years, but the Methodist, United Reformed and Other Free slowly declined. The Pentecostal increased gradually, but there was explosive growth in the Independent group of churches. If present trends continue, the Independent Churches could exceed the Methodists during 1998. The actual numbers behind Table 8 are given in Table 9.

The Baptist and Pentecostal Churches show a curious pattern in Table 9: they both grew between 1975 and 1979, both declined between 1979 and 1985, and both grew again between 1985 and 1989. At the time of their decline the Independent Churches grew especially fast. Almost certainly these are interlinked since a number of Baptists joined the House Church Movement in the

Table 9: Changes in Free Church adult churchgoing by denomination 1975-1989

Denomination	1975	C	1979	C	1985	C	1989
		%		%		%	
Methodist	454,000	−2	447,000	−6	420,800	−6	396,100
Baptist	193,000	+5	203,000	−3	196,200	+2	199,400
URC	150,000	−7	139,000	−13	121,400	−6	114,000
Independent	167,000	+23	206,000	+25	257,500	+14	292,800
Afro-Caribbean	55,000	+20	66,000	+2	67,500	+1	68,500
Pentecostal	78,000	+13	88,000	−4	84,900	+12	95,200
Others	112,000	−12	98,000	−17	81,400	+2	83,000
Total	1,209,000	+3	1,247,000	−1	1,229,700	+2	1,249,000

C = Percentage change

early 1980s and several Assembly of God Pentecostal Churches left their formal association and became House Churches. Such fluidity reflects the commonality found between House Churches and, say, non-Baptist Union Baptist Churches, which is sometimes a stronger link than between the different groups together here labelled Independent Churches.

This table suggests a definite transfer of churchgoers from two denominational groups to a third, although, of course, it is not possible to prove it from this data alone. Lest the House Churches should be accused of 'sheep-stealing' as this type of transfer is very often called, it should be noted that the *total* decline of the Baptists and Pentecostals between 1979 and 1985 was only 9,900 attenders whereas the Independent group grew by 51,500, five times as many.

The decline of the **Methodist churches** is considerable. It is matched by falling membership, and continues to be a concern to their senior leadership. The *rate* of decline of their members is slowing down, but, unfortunately the rate of decline in attendance is increasing, −0.4% per year between 1975 and 1979, −1.0% per year between 1979 and 1985, and −1.5% per year between 1985 and 1989. Against this drop, their number of workers (not shown here) is increasing. 'It is clear that the Church is good at attracting people to the work,' said Rev Brian Beck, Secretary of the Methodist Conference. 'This is also a reflection of the care and training given in a wide variety of skills.' On the falling numbers however, he acknowledged, 'There is some hard thinking to be done throughout the church.'[8]

The **Afro-Caribbean Churches** grew between 1975 and 1979, partly because of current immigration, and partly because of the ostracism by white church leaders during that period. This began to change in the 1980s, with the result that black people were more easily able to integrate into white congregations. Also the number of immigrants fell greatly in the 1980s so the natural growth of such churches was curtailed. Now there is some flow in the opposite direction with older black people returning to their original country on retirement. These trends have meant a much reduced growth since 1979, and might even lead to decline in the 1990s. The challenge for their leaders is not only to try and hold their many groupings together, but to find a new vision for their churches as a whole.

Free Church attendance is graphed below; with more detailed figures some rates of change are seen to be faster.

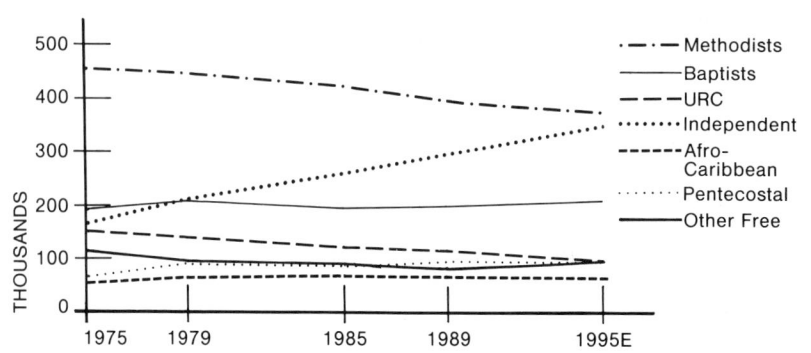

Figure 2: Adult churchgoers in the Free Church denominations

The **Methodist Church** group consists mainly of the attenders in English, Isle of Man and Channel Island churches in the 28 relevant provinces of the Methodist Church in Great Britain. The numbers attending the Wesleyan Reform Union, Free Methodist Church, Independent Methodist and other Methodist Churches are included, but the institutional church accounts for 97.9% of attenders, that is, all but 8,200 Methodists attending other churches not united to the main body.

The **Baptist Church** group includes the main Baptist Union of Great Britain attenders in the Associations in the eleven Areas in England. It excludes English speaking churches in Wales, but the figures do include the returns received from a handful of Welsh-speaking churches in England. The Union accounted for 83% of Baptist churchgoers in 1989 — five in every six. The Gospel Standard Strict Baptist, the Grace Baptist Assembly, the Old Baptist Union, the Jesus Fellowship (also called Jesus Army) and other (free) Baptist Churches are included. A breakdown by these denominations is given in Table 10.

Table 10: Components of Baptist churches 1979-1989

Denomination	Adult churchgoers 1979*	1985	1989	Percentage change 1979-89	1989 as percentage of adult population
				%	%
Baptist Union	174,300	164,800	166,100	−5	0.43
Grace Baptist	12,000	12,100	12,500	+4	
Gospel Standard	6,000	5,600	5,000	−17	
Old Baptist Union	1,000	900	800	−20	0.08
Jesus Fellowship	300	600	900	+200	
Others	9,400	12,200	14,100	+50	
Total	203,000	196,200	199,400	−2	0.51

* Estimate based on membership figures

The Grace Baptist Assembly and the Jesus Fellowship Church (Baptist) both grew between 1979 and 1989 in quite small numbers, though a large percentage for the Jesus Fellowship Church. The Gospel Standard Strict Baptists and the Old Baptist Union declined in the same period by one person in five or six. The Baptist Union declined between 1979 and 1985 but slightly recovered between 1985 and 1989, whereas the Other Baptists grew rapidly in the same period.

The variations in the Baptist Union attenders suggest that it would be strongly worthwhile for the Union to collect attendance figures regularly as well as the membership data they now routinely gather. The Other Baptists are much more akin to the Independent sector churches although they are specifically Baptist in doctrine and, in most cases, in church government.

Of those who responded accepting Christ in Mission to London and Mission England, 13% were referred to Baptist Union Churches, so that some of the 1985 to 1989 increase probably came in this way. Baptist Union growth in these years was hindered by the ill health, and ultimate death in office after only two years, of the then Baptist Union Secretary for Evangelism, Rev Tom Rogers, who could not realise his vision for the job, and which delayed the launching of their *Action in Mission* programme. There was a team of Baptist Evangelists at work, however, and many Associations appointed regional missionaries helping urban experiments and starting new churches.

The **United Reformed Church** (URC) is the main institutional church included under this heading, and accounted for 98.6% of churchgoers in 1989. The residual 1,600 were from the Presbyterian Church in England, and those Fellowship of Churches of Christ which united with the URC in 1981.

The **Afro-Caribbean Churches** comprise a heterogeneous collection of 164 specific churches, each a mini-denomination, some with many congregations, and most with just one. The largest two of these, the Church of God of Prophecy and the New Testament Church of God (with 9,200 and 8,500 attenders respectively in 1989) together account for about a quarter of the total attenders. Other groups such as the First United Church of Jesus Christ (Apostolic) UK, the New Testament Assembly, the United Pentecostal Church and the Wesleyan Holiness Church had over a thousand churchgoers each in 1989.

This still leaves a very large number of smaller churches in this sector. The average number of adult attenders in 1989 was 82 for the Church of God of Prophecy, 71 for the New Testament Church of God, 89 for the other large churches. The remaining 622 further churches are across 157 'denominations' with an average of 68 attenders in each. Some of these churches (such as the United Pentecostal Church of God, the Bible Way Church of Our Lord Jesus Christ) are 'oneness' churches in that, while believing in God the Father and the Holy Spirit, they focus almost exclusively on the one redeemer, Jesus Christ. Others, whose doctrinal position is clearly non-Trinitarian, have not been included in the English Church Census.

The **Pentecostal Churches** comprise two main groups, the Assemblies of God in Great Britain and the Elim Pentecostal Church, which in 1989 together accounted for 88% of Pentecostal churchgoers. There are substantial smaller groups, however, such as the Apostolic Church, and two holiness groups, the Emmanuel

Holiness Church, and the Church of the Nazarene. Details of these groups are given below.

Table 11: Components of Pentecostal churches 1979-1989

Denomination	Adult churchgoers 1979*	1985	1989	Percentage change 1979-89	1989 as percentage of adult population
				%	%
Assemblies of God	51,700	44,700	47,100	−9	0.12
Elim Pentecostal Church	26,600	29,700	36,700	+38	0.10
Church of the Nazarene	3,700	4,000	4,100	+11	
The Apostolic Church	3,500	3,900	4,600	+31	
Emmanuel Holiness Church	400	400	400	0	0.03
Others	2,100	2,200	2,300	+10	
Total	88,000	84,900	95,200	+8	0.25

* Estimate based on membership figures

The Elim Pentecostal Church grew rapidly during the 1980s, as did the smaller Apostolic Church. The Church of the Nazarene and the Other Pentecostal Churches also increased considerably, especially the latter.

The Assemblies of God (AOG) declined overall, although it grew in the four years 1985-1989. This was probably caused by the defections from its association to the Independent House Church Movement, with AOG Churches declaring themselves by other names, often 'So-and-So Christian Fellowship'.

The Independent Churches

The Independent Churches are a heterogeneous group, though with sufficient in common to be described as Independent. Included are the:

- House Church Movement
- Christian Brethren both open and closed (the latter are sometimes referred to as Plymouth Brethren No 4)
- Fellowship of Independent Evangelical Churches (FIEC)
- Union of Evangelical Churches (UEC)

- Congregational Federation Churches (initially made up of those who did not combine to form the United Reformed Church in 1972)
- Evangelical Fellowship of Congregational Churches (EFCC)
- Majority of the Churches of Christ
- New Apostolic Churches
- Liberal Catholic Church
- Residential schools and colleges with a church or chapel open for public worship — there were 308 of these
- Other independent churches, such as the Independent Old Catholic Apostolic Church
- Many truly individual churches, strictly non-denominational, but fashioned after the House Church Movement.

This is the group which collectively has exploded with growth in the fourteen years 1975-1989. It is not static. Its performance against all other Free Churches is shown below.

Table 12: Changes in adult churchgoing of the Independent churches and the rest of the Free Churches 1975-1989

Church	1975	C	1979	C	1985	C	1989
		%		%		%	
Independent Churches	167,000	+23	206,000	+25	257,500	+14	292,800
All Other Free Churches	1,042,000	−0	1,041,000	−7	972,200	−2	956,200
Total Free Churches	1,209,000	+3	1,247,000	−1	1,229,700	+2	1,249,000

C = Percentage change

The Independent Churches grew between 1975 and 1989 as against the decline in all the other Free Churches. The Independent churchgoers represented 14% of all Free Church attenders in 1975, but 23% in 1989. This change in the Independent Churches was by no means uniform across them, as Table 13 makes clear (no 1975 breakdown is available).

The relatively poor overall response to the Census from the Independent sector (in comparison to say the Anglican response of 75%) was caused by non-return of forms from the residential schools (some of whom understandably did not regard themselves

Table 13: Proportions of adult churchgoers by denomination within Independent churches 1975-1989

Denomination/Group	1979*	1985	1989	Response rate
	%	%	%	%
FIEC	20	24	22	73
Congregational Federation	4	3	3	72
EFCC	3	3	2	71
House Church Movement	22	31	37	70
UEC	1	—	—	65
Churches of Christ	2	1	1	51
Residential Schools	17	12	11	49
Christian Brethren (Open)	21	16	15	38
Christian Brethren (Closed)	3	3	3	35
All Others	7	7	6	63
Total (= 100%)	0.21m	0.26m	0.29m	58

* Estimate based on membership figures

as churches for Census purposes), the closed Christian Brethren and the Churches of Christ. We might have expected the (Open) Christian Brethren to have responded in greater numbers than they did.

The next table shows the rapidly increasing dominance of the House Church Movement in the Independent sector. From just over a fifth of adult attenders in 1979 it increased to nearly two-fifths of the total ten years later. The proportion of the Open Christian Brethren and Residential Schools declined. The Closed Brethren, the Congregational Fedaration, the Evangelical. Fellowship of Congregational Churches, and the Churches of Christ hardly changed, but maintained their 'market share'. So did the other Independent Churches.

This suggests that the House Church Movement could have attracted people with a strong desire for change in the Open Brethren Churches, the only relevant large group in the early 1980s: Table 13 shows significant declines then, but as the next table shows, the actual numbers involved are not large. The Christian Brethren surveyed their assemblies in 1988 through Graham Brown and Neil Summerton, but the results have not yet been published. This may help this movement to consider their way ahead.

The FIEC's very rapid growth in the early 1980s has not been sustained since. They have in fact set up a Committee to look into their future development and have appointed the Rev Bev Savage to lead that work.

The figures behind Table 13 are given in Table 14 below.

Table 14: Components of Independent churches 1979-1989

Denomination/Group	Adult churchgoers 1979*	1985	1989	Percentage change 1979-89	1989 as percentage of adult population
				%	%
FIEC	43,400	60,900	63,400	+46	0.14
Congregational Federation	8,700	9,000	9,400	+8 ⎤	0.04
EFCC	6,400	6,600	6,800	+6 ⎦	
House Church Movement	44,400	81,000	108,500	+144	0.30
UEC	1,400	1,000	1,000	−29 ⎤	
Churches of Christ	3,900	3,200	3,300	−15 ⎥	0.08
Residential Schools	32,300	31,300	31,000	−4 ⎦	
Christian Brethren (Open)	44,000	41,300	43,500	−1 ⎤	0.13
Christian Brethren (Closed)	7,000	7,300	7,600	+9 ⎦	
All Others	14,500	15,900	18,300	+26	0.06
Total	206,000	257,500	292,800	+42	0.75

* Estimate based on membership figures

The **House Church Movement** consists of several major streams such as New Frontiers, Pioneer, Cornerstone, Isca, Team Spirit, Harvestime, the King's Church, New Life, and Ichthus, and several smaller ones. These were not separately identified in the Census. A separate survey of the constituent parts had been undertaken in 1986 for the *UK Christian Handbook* tables.

The **Christian Brethren** are largely static in both groups, although the smaller, closed group does show some growth. Perhaps this is because in their turn they are becoming more 'open' — the fact that so many responded to the Census suggests this might be so. The Open Brethren have recently republished their address list[9] and, if regularly updated, it may help their assemblies to become better known and used.

The two **Congregational Church** groups also grew slightly over the last decade. The **Residential Schools/Colleges** figures remain virtually identical since they reflect the number and size of such boarding establishments, and are not free to grow as are other churches. The **Other Independent Churches** include a number which operate very similarly to House Churches but are not 'covered' by one of the recognised streams.

It is clear that the dynamic behind the Independent Group as a whole is the remarkable growth of the House Church Movement. One of the first books describing this movement, *Restoring the Kingdom*,[10] made it clear that it was people of prayer and vision, daring and risk who started these churches and took them forward, determined to worship the Lord in the way they felt was right. As someone once said, 'Things only get done by mono-maniacs with a mission.' The pioneers of the House Church Movement like Terry Virgo, Gerald Coates, John Noble, Tony Morton, Bryn Jones and Roger Forster, could be so described. One imagines that their motto might easily have been that of Hannibal when facing the Pyrenees on his elephants, 'I will find a way across or make one.' They were determined to make the Kingdom of God relevant, and literally tens of thousands of people in England have joined their churches.

The largest five groups in the previous table, with at least 10,000 churchgoers each, are illustrated below in graphs.

Figure 3: Adult churchgoers in the large Independent groups

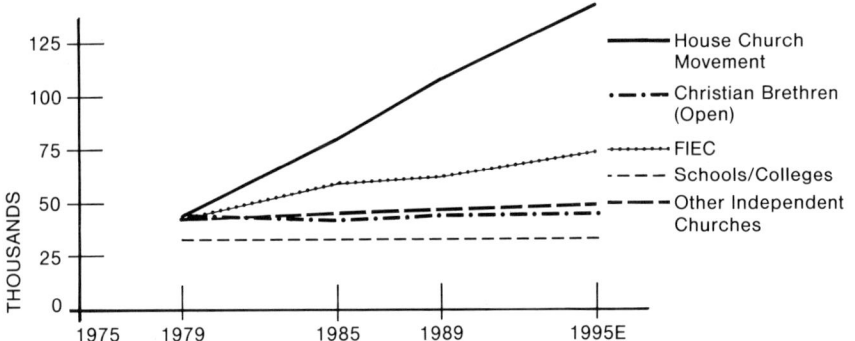

So many denominations? Like all creatures great and small, as the hymn puts it, the Lord God made them all. David Bosch perceptively linked God's six great acts with various emphases, over simplified as they may be, and in a final talk at the Lausanne II Congress in Manila, July 1989, Tom Houston helpfully retold them:

1) The incarnation, presence and continuity: the Anglicans and Roman Catholics
2) The cross, pardon and discontinuity: Lutherans and Evangelicals
3) The resurrection, and a risen life in Christ: Orthodox
4) The ascension and sovereignty of God: Presbyterians and Reformed

5) Pentecost and the power of the Spirit: Pentecostals and Charismatics
6) The advent and signs of the times: Seventh-Day and other Adventists

CONGREGATIONAL SIZE AND SERVICE FREQUENCY

Size of Congregation

Since the number of adult churchgoers and the number of churches are known it should be easy to work out the average congregation. The fact that 14% of people on average attend church twice on a Sunday means that to show true congregational averages the number of attenders must reflect the number of attendances. Table 15 shows the number of individual adults attending, and the consequential average number of different people worshipping on a Sunday. It also shows the percentage going twice, and the total attendances thus recorded, that is, total people in church with those going twice counted both times. The average Sunday congregation, that is the combined total for both services (where held) is given in the final column.

Table 15: Average adult congregations 1989

Denomination	Number of churches	Adult church-goers	Average individual adults attending	% going twice	Adult atten-dances	Average combined total Sunday congregation
				%		
Methodist	6,740	396,100	59	18	467,400	70
Baptist	2,339	199,400	85	31	261,200	112
URC	1,681	114,000	68	14	130,000	77
Independent	4,123	292,800	71	31	383,600	93
Afro-Caribbean	949	68,500	72	41	96,600	102
Pentecostal	1,002	95,200	95	48	140,900	141
Other Free	1,462	83,000	57	37	113,700	78
Total Free	18,296	1,249,000	68	28	1,593,400	87
Anglican	16,373	1,143,900	70	10	1,258,300	77
Roman Catholic	3,824	1,304,600	341	4	1,356,800	355
Orthodox	114	9,400	82	0	9,400	82
Total	38,607	3,706,900	96	14	4,217,900	109

The Roman Catholics have by far the largest average congregations. Initially they built large churches staffed by several priests, in predominantly Catholic areas, but today most new churches are smaller and staffed by a single priest. Anglicans and Free Church people, on the contrary, with their flocks more widely scattered, have always tended to build more churches, usually much smaller, and staffed them often with just one person — or increasingly today one person who looks after several churches.

The average for both Anglican and Free Church congregations is about 83 people. With some people attending twice this means 69 different faces. The comparable figure in 1979 was 71, so the decline of these churches overall has not meant greatly smaller congregations, but fewer people being accommodated in fewer churches.

The Pentecostals have the largest Free Church average congregations at 141, followed by Baptists with 112, and then the Afro-Caribbeans with 102. Independent churches average 93 partly because they have a policy of 'church planting' which means more churches with newer, smaller congregations.

Frequency of attendance

It must be remembered that these figures include those going twice. The average numbers of individuals per Sunday are shown in the second column of Table 15, and these are all slightly less than the corresponding figures for 1979, except for Independent and Pentecostal Churches. Fewer people went to church in 1989, but the half a million or so who went twice was almost certainly a smaller number than in 1979. Does so many going twice mean that churchgoers form a clique to escape the world so that their going reinforces those relationships? This is how an outsider might look at it. An insider would say that the importance of worship and meeting together regularly is enjoined in Scripture, and many Free Churches especially expect committed people to attend twice on Sunday.

The average 14% of those going to church twice in England in 1989 compares with 25% in Wales in 1982 and 13% in Scotland in 1984. Of church attenders in England going only once on a Sunday in 1989, 61% went in the morning only, and the remaining 25% went in the evening.

THE OVERALL RESULTS

Figure 4: Number of times people go to church

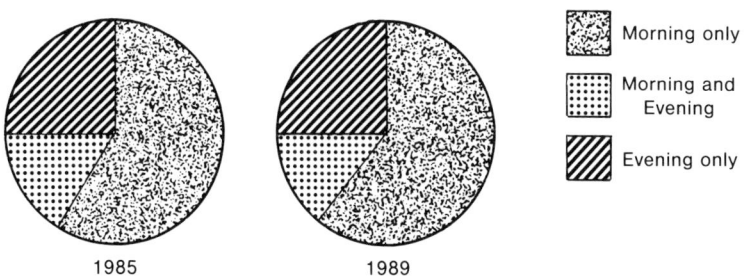

1985   1989

- Morning only
- Morning and Evening
- Evening only

Between 1985 and 1989 the percentage going to church in the morning remained at 75% (as it was in 1979) but the percentage going twice declined from an estimated 20% in 1979 to 16% in 1985 and 14% in 1989, with the percentage going just in the evening constant at 25% as shown in Figure 4. This means that in the last four years over 70,000 people across the country became 'oncers' rather than 'twicers' going to church only in the morning whereas before they went morning and evening. Sometimes this will be because the church no longer has an evening service. Much more often it will be because people are getting older and more frail and less easily able to go twice. And, of course, some will go less frequently because they have other priorities.

Table 16 shows how the 1989 figures vary across the country.

Table 16: Morning and evening churchgoers by region 1989

	North	Yorks/Humberside	North West	East Midlands	West Midlands
	%	%	%	%	%
Morning only	62	60	65	58	62
Morning and Evening (twicers)	12	15	10	16	12
Evening only	26	25	25	26	26

	East Anglia	South East (North)	South East (Greater London)	South East (South)	South West	All England
	%	%	%	%	%	%
Morning only	62	61	61	61	61	61
Morning and Evening (twicers)	15	15	13	14	16	14
Evening only	23	24	26	25	23	25

These figures are remarkably uniform. The lowest percentage of people going twice is in the North West reflecting the large Catholic presence there (only 4% of Catholics go twice) with Greater Manchester at 9%. Staffordshire also had 9% twicers but Inner London Northwest is the lowest in the country at 8%. South Yorkshire is the highest with 21%. These individual county figures, reflected in the regional values, come from *Prospects for the Nineties*.

Attendance in the evening only is highest in Inner London Southeast at 33%, possibly reflecting the Ichthus celebrations. After that it is Shropshire with 30% and Cleveland and Outer London Northeast at 29%. The lowest figure for evening only attendances are Devon at 19%, Norfolk at 20% and Cornwall at 21% on the mainland. On the Isle of Man it is 20% and on the Isle of Wight it is down to 11%.

Those going only in the morning reflect these figures. Thus South Yorkshire and Inner London Southeast have the lowest percentage across the country at 52%, with Staffordshire highest at 69% on the mainland followed by Greater Manchester with 68%. The Isle of Wight sees 72% of their people going only in the morning.

Morning and Evening Services

Half the churches have two services, morning and afternoon or evening, three-eighths morning only and the remaining eighth evening only. The actual percentages were respectively 51%, 38% and 11%. 80% of Baptist Churches had two services, as did 84% of Afro-Caribbeans, and 87% of Pentecostal, but only 44% of Anglicans. Many Roman Catholic Churches have more than two services (up to six masses in some churches) but these were not counted individually, only when they were held. A number of Anglican and Free Churches also have more than one morning service; for the purpose of the next table these were taken together; but the total of the congregations is used in discussing church attendance. Examples of the different percentages are given.

Many churches in separate towns (seven in eight) have two services, and very few (just 1%) a service only in the evening. Rural churches have more morning services only than two services a day (42% against 39%). The Broad and Low Church also have more morning than twice a day (51% against 34%), but churches Catholic in churchmanship have many more Sundays with at least two services (71%) and relatively few with services only in the morning (17%).

Table 17: Morning and evening services by denomination, environment and churchmanship 1989

	Denomination			Environment			
	Free Church	Anglican	Roman Catholic	Urban	Separate town	Rural: comm/ dorm	Rural: other
	%	%	%	%	%	%	%
Morning only	26	49	39	26	12	33	42
Morning and Evening	60	44	57	69	87	60	39
Evening only	14	7	4	5	1	7	19

	Churchmanship				Total	
	Total Evangelical	Low Church	Broad/ Liberal	«Catholic»	1985	1989
	%	%	%	%	%	%
Morning only	38	51	35	17	31	38
Morning and Evening	55	34	51	71	56	51
Evening only	7	15	14	12	13	11

Figure 5: Times when churches hold their services

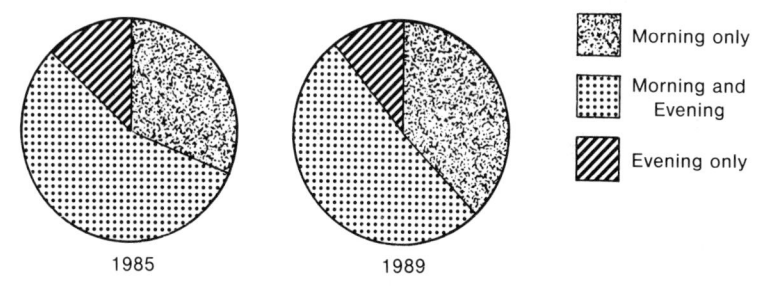

1985   1989

- Morning only
- Morning and Evening
- Evening only

One church in twenty, or nearly 2,000 churches in England, changed in the four years 1985-1989 from having two services on a Sunday to just one — 1,200 to a morning only service, and the remainder to evening service only. That is a measure of decline. The change is illustrated in Figure 5.

CHILD ATTENDANCE

The Census looked at both child and adult attendance, with children defined in this context as those aged 14 or under.

Along with 3.7 million adults, 1.2 million children were in church in October 1989, one child for every three adults. The proportion was slightly higher in 1975, but against the fall in numbers since then shown in the next table (a decline of 18% across the fourteen years) must be noted the 13% drop in the child population. Whilst the proportion of children attending church has fallen faster than the child population, the percentage attending church has remained at 14% when rounded to the nearest whole number: more exactly 14.0% of the child population attended church in 1975, 14.0% in 1979, 14.2% in 1985 and 13.7% in 1989.

Table 18: Changes in churchgoing by adults and children 1979-1989

	1975	C	1979	C	1985	C	1989
Children	1,483,000	% −5	1,416,000	% −10	1,280,900	% −5	1,221,500
Adults	4,093,000	−2	4,025,000	−7	3,755,000	−1	3,706,900
Total	5,576,000	−3	5,441,000	−8	5,035,900	−2	4,928,400

C = Percentage change

The number of children has also been dropping faster in percentage terms since 1975 than the number of adults. We have dropped 386,000 adults in the last fourteen years and 216,000 children — two children for every three adults.

The comparative figures of child attenders are given in the next table.

Table 19: Proportions of child churchgoers by major groups 1975-1989

Church	1975	1979	1985	1989
	%	%	%	%
Free Church	38	37	38	38
Anglican	30	29	29	28
Roman Catholic	32	34	33	34
Total (= 100%)	1.5m	1.4m	1.3m	1.2m

These proportions are changing little. The Free Churches are effectively constant, the Anglicans slightly declining, and the Roman Catholics growing slowly.

Figure 6 shows that the Free Church proportion of all the children attending church is slightly greater than for adults, and there

Figure 6: Adult and child churchgoers 1989

CHILD ATTENDERS   ADULT ATTENDERS

- Free Church
- Anglican
- Roman Catholic

are slightly more Anglican adults proportionately than children. The actual numbers are given in Table 20 and graphed in Figures 7 and 8.

Table 20: Changes in child churchgoing by denomination 1975-1989

Denomination	1975	C	1979	C	1985	C	1989
		%		%		%	
Methodist	208,000	−16	174,000	−21	138,100	−16	116,200
Baptist	92,000	−5	87,000	−10	78,200	−9	71,500
URC	55,000	−7	51,000	−16	42,700	−17	35,300
Independent	93,000	0	93,000	+28	118,600	+12	132,700
Afro-Caribbean	39,000	+5	41,000	−7	38,200	−7	35,600
Pentecostal	30,000	+10	33,000	+7	35,400	+6	37,400
Other Free	44,000	−2	43,000	−19	34,900	−12	30,600
Total Free	561,000	−7	522,000	−7	486,100	−6	459,300
Anglican	445,000	−7	415,000	−11	367,300	−5	348,000
Roman Catholic	474,000	0	476,000	−11	424,700	−3	411,300
Orthodox	3,000	0	3,000	−7	2,800	+4	2,900
Total	1,483,000	−5	1,416,000	−10	1,280,900	−5	1,221,500

C = Percentage change

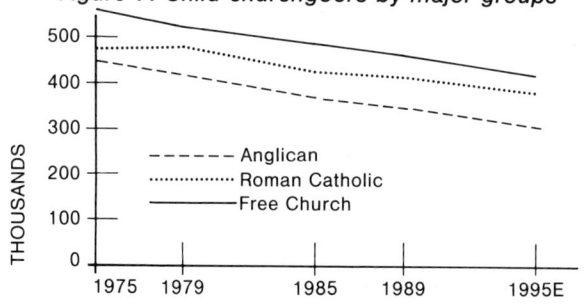

Figure 7: Child churchgoers by major groups

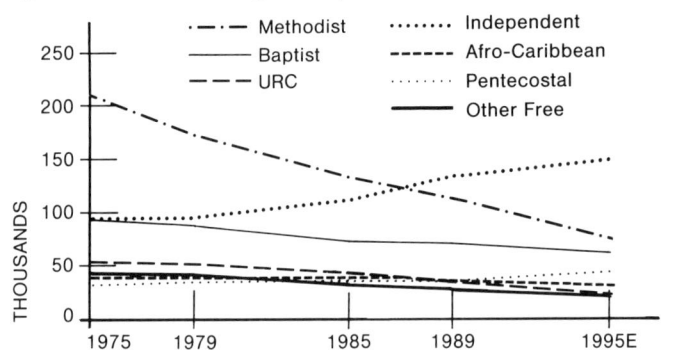

Figure 8: Child churchgoers by Free Church denominations

The graphs make clear the gravity of the situation with children. Between 1985 and 1989 adult attenders increased for Baptists, Independents, Afro-Caribbeans, Pentecostals and Other Free Churches, whereas child attenders increased only for Independents and Pentecostals. Why should this be? In the Welsh and Scottish Censuses of 1982 and 1984 respectively, child attenders increased more or less in line with adult growth. Not in England in 1989!

Why are the number of Baptist, Afro-Caribbean and Seventh-Day Adventist (the key component in the Other Free Churches category) child attenders not increasing like their adults? What makes churches attract men and women but not boys and girls? An insufficient emphasis on the family? Inadequate facilities for children? A lack of challenge? An unfriendly atmosphere? Too few friends? What should these denominations do to change what is happening to their youngsters?

CHURCH MEMBERSHIP

The Census asked for membership data only to compare results with national information available from other sources. Each denomination defines membership in its own way, whereas attendance has a universal definition which is very simple — was the seat occupied or not? But membership is a more diffuse label, vaguer and not comparable between different churches.

The 3.7 million adult churchgoers in 1989 came, in the main, from 7.2 million church members, twice as many. That number has not dropped as fast as the adult figures, however, as the following table shows.

Table 21: Changes in total adult churchgoing and church membership 1975-1989

	1975	C	1979	C	1985	C	1989
		%		%		%	
Adult churchgoers	4,093,000	−2	4,025,000	−7	3,755,700	−1	3,706,900
Church members	7,447,600	−1	7,381,600	−4	7,057,300	+1	7,162,400

C = Percentage change

The number of members actually increased slightly between 1985 and 1989, due to the Roman Catholic population increasing, itself a function of the national population increase and the immigrants from Catholic countries who formed part of it. Even so, the rate of decline in membership is less than in church-going, suggesting that although people may stop going to church or at least go less frequently, they do not give up their links with the church. Belief may continue but church-going may not. It might also be a function of an increasingly ageing church-going population who can no longer attend but still wish to be kept on the roll and visited.

The proportions of church members in the four main groups appear below, based on the definitions used in the Census, and on the total UK Church community, as given in the 1989/90 Edition of the *UK Christian Handbook*.

Table 22: Proportions of church members by major groups 1975-1989

	By Census definitions				By total church community			
Church	1975	1979	1985	1989	1975	1980	1985	1990E
	%	%	%	%	%	%	%	%
Free Church	17	17	16	16	13	13	13	13
Anglican	27	26	24	22	73	73	72	72
Roman Catholic	53	54	57	59	13	13	14	14
Orthodox	3	3	3	3	1	1	1	1
Total (= 100%)	7.4m	7.4m	7.1m	7.2m	39.8m	38.4m	37.4m	37.2m

It is important to note that the definitions being used are different and so the table could therefore be misleading. The Free Churches keep membership rolls in various ways. Baptists normally expect members to be baptised as believers, Pentecostals for them to speak in tongues. The Anglican figures used in the Census — because they were readily available — are those for the Electoral Roll, not strictly membership at all since anyone over 16 and living in a parish for at least six months can apply.

The Roman Catholic figures are for those christened or otherwise admitted to the church through their first Communion. which is why their numbers are much larger by the Census definition (on the left hand side of Table 22). They have no equivalent of the Anglican Electoral Roll or Free Church membership.

People baptised as infants form part of the Anglican community but these figures were not requested in the Census; and central estimates of this total are no longer made. The right hand side of Table 22 reflects such community figures, and the Free Church community figures published in the *UK Christian Handbook*. The basic Catholic and Orthodox numbers are the same in both parts of Table 22.

Both sides of the table show the Free Church proportion of church members virtually static, and the Orthodox's small percentage remaining the same throughout the fourteen years. However, the Anglican proportion is declining, matched by a Roman Catholic increase, rather faster on Census definitions than on total community figures.

Membership detail by individual denomination is not repeated here as it is already published in the *UK Christian Handbook*[11] for 1970, 1975, 1980, 1983, 1985, and 1987 as well as forward estimates for 1990 and 2000.

Membership and attendance

How far are membership and attendance really linked? The Methodist report, *The Missionary Shape of the Congregation,* suggested that attendance is often improved when the ministry of the church relates to people's needs, especially at major life events. 'A growing sense among members of the need to care for each other' is also a reason why members may begin worshipping more regularly, as is the quality of worship itself. Likewise, the report added, the quality and style of leadership is important. It was also vital that a church's programme should include periods specially devoted to evangelism.

One important comparison between membership and attendance must not be overlooked, and appears in the following table.

Table 23: Church members and adult churchgoers compared by denomination

	1989 Church members	1989 Church-goers	1989 Difference	Difference as % of church-goers	Difference 1985	Difference 1979	Difference 1975
				%	%	%	%
Methodist	422,200	396,100	26,100	+7	+4	+6	+13
Baptist	170,600	199,400	−28,800	−14	−15	−20	−13
URC	119,900	114,000	5,900	+5	+5	+19	+28
Independent	222,100	292,800	−70,700	−24	−23	−18	−18
Afro-Caribbean	68,200	68,500	−300	−1	−3	−5	−15
Pentecostal	68,000	95,200	−27,200	−29	−29	−24	−19
Other Free	103,200	83,000	20,200	+24	+25	+35	+17
Total Free	1,174,200	1,249,000	−74,800	−6	−6	−1	+4
Anglican	1,559,000	1,143,900	415,100	+36	+42	+51	+54
Roman Catholic	4,197,100	1,304,600	2,892,500	+222	+200	+166	+153
Orthodox	232,100	9,400	222,700	+2,369	+2,519	+6,800	+6,633
Total	7,162,400	3,706,900	3,455,500	+93	+88	+83	+82

Attendance *exceeds* membership in Baptist, Independent, Afro-Caribbean and Pentecostal Churches, four of the main growth groups (though Other Free Churches also grew 1985-1989). Is there some connection in terms of freedom or informality or welcome?

It is also interesting that the *size* of the percentage difference reflects the *rate* of growth: the higher the negative percentage the faster the growth. The 1975 Afro-Caribbean difference figure of −15% preceded a growth in the number of attenders of 20%, but the 1979 figure of −5% compares to a growth rate of only 2%, and the 1985 figure of −3% to a growth of 1%. The opposite generally holds as well — the higher the positive figure in the last four columns, usually the greater the rate of decline. The figures must be taken line by line; comparing one line against another is not relevant in this context. The absolute size of the percentage differences, gives a kind of 'nominality' ratio, with the Orthodox having by far the most nominals (members who do not attend) proportionately.

In this context, folk religion is important. The church might retreat but the needs of society have not.

COMPARISONS

Population Comparisons

Adult church membership in the four years 1985-1989 increased 1%. While the adult population of England increased 2%, so church membership did not keep up. Adult attenders declined 1% between 1985 and 1989, a 3% gap with the population. Child attenders declined 5% in the same four years, against a child population decline of only 1%, so the church is 4% worse off. In all three years there is a noticeable gap, and it is widest for the children.

Church membership was 15% of the English population in 1989. On the same basis it was also 15% in 1979 and 14% in 1985.

Adult churchgoers were 11% of the adult population in 1979 and 10% in 1989; child attenders were 14% of the child population in both 1979 and 1989.

Comparisons with Opinion Polls

Strictly comparable longer term estimates are not available, and sample surveys, such as the Gallup or MORI polls, are less accurate and have also been gathered on a different basis. Opinion polls are like a barometer showing you as others see you, and are therefore valuable. The weakness of the historical part of the English Church Census was that in most cases it was completed by the minister of the church whose memory and/or record keeping and/or estimating could leave something to be desired, though in checks on items that could be checked — membership, for example — the stated figures proved close to the actual figures. Poll data is obtained by asking individuals if they go to church, and the actual format of the question will vary from one study to another. Additionally, as others have found,[12] 'There can be an acquiescence bias where respondents tend, regardless of content, to agree rather than disagree . . . there can also be a social desirability bias where respondents tend to provide the answer that they feel they ought to give or the one that will present them in a more favourable light.'

Over a period of years, Gallup found that one in seven (14%) said they had gone to church the previous Sunday in 1957, but that this dropped to 12% in 1958, and 10% in 1963.[13] On this basis the latest figures show a remarkable constancy in the church-going proportion in the country.

International comparisons

Comparable figures for regular church attendance in other countries are difficult to obtain. A figure of 40% is quoted for the United States,[14] and an equivalent figure for France is 13% of adults,[15] of whom 12.4% are Roman Catholics.

Active church membership is calculated differently in the *UK Christian Handbook (UKCH)*, as it uses Catholic mass attendance not Catholic population. Definitions of active church membership on the same basis as in the *UKCH*, are available for various European countries, as are figures for the church community (all in a country who would identify, however loosely, with the church). These are given in the next table.

Table 24: International church activity by percentage of adult population 1990

	Church attendance	Active church members	Church community*
	%	%	%
Finland[16]	3	28	93
Denmark[17]	4	23	94
Norway[18]	5	32	95
UK[19]	10	14	65
French-Swiss[20]	13	23	84
France[21]	13	21	85
Spain[22]	14	24	69
Austria[23]	22	35	90
Australia[24]	27	N/a	57
US[25]	40	N/a	70
South Africa[26]	N/a	31	80

*Percentage of total population

'Christian' England? With only two-thirds of the population claiming some allegiance to the church, however faint, 14% active members, and 10% regularly attending, the claim to call England Christian looks thin. The UK community figure is much lower than the figures of other Western European countries, but as the Chinese proverb says, 'The journey of a thousand miles begins with the single step.' If more English people are to become Christian, what is the first step to be taken?

Chapter 2: Summary

- 10% of the English adult population were attending church on October 15th 1989, 3.7 million people.
- The percentage had declined by 1% since 1979.
- 14% of English children, 1.2 million, were in church in 1989. This is the same percentage as in 1979, but still represents a decline of 216,000 church children in the decade.
- These percentages compare with the decrease in the child population in England of 4% between 1979 and 1989, and the adult population increasing 4%.
- The adult decline was especially steep in the United Reformed Church (a change of −18% between 1979 and 1989), Roman Catholic (−14%), Methodist (−11%), and Anglican (−9%).
- There was growth in the Independent (+42%), Orthodox (+34%), Pentecostal (8%), and Afro-Caribbean (+4%) Churches.
- The Independent growth was especially due to a 144% increase in the numbers attending House Churches and to a 46% increase in those belonging to the Fellowship of Independent Evangelical Churches.
- 14% of the adults who attended church in 1989 did so twice each Sunday.
- 51% of churches held both morning and evening services in 1989; in 1985 it was 56%.
- Church membership in England declined 3% between 1979 and 1989.
- Baptist, Independent, Afro-Caribbean and Pentecostal Churches had more church attenders than members in 1989.

3. WHERE DO PEOPLE GO TO CHURCH?

The English Church Census reported 38,607 churches or congregations for the 48 million people in England. That's one church or congregation for every 1,200 people. Other comparisons for 1989 may be helpful. There was:

    1 church for every 1,200 people in England
    1 pub for every 1,300 people[1]
    1 Post Office for every 2,200 people[2]
    1 Woolworth's for every 61,000 people[3]
    1 W H Smith shop for every 113,000 people[3]

The English Church has many premises, much potential therefore for outreach. There are almost as many pubs as churches — but do the churches reach as many? There is one churchgoer for every 10 adults in England, and one child in every 7 goes to church.

In terms of space, there were in 1989 for every square kilometre or 250 acres in England

    0.3 churches
    37 churchgoers
    370 people

The maps at the end of the book show the overall strength of the Christian church in Britain. Map 47 shows the number of adult churchgoers by county, and Map 48 the number of church members.

Greater London for the purposes of the Census was divided into eight groups of Boroughs, four inner and four outer, one each Northeast, Northwest, Southeast and Southwest. Although each area is not strictly a county, it is treated as such for simplicity and comparison with other areas.

CHURCHES AND CHURCHGOING BY REGION

Before looking at the spread of churchgoers, it is worth seeing the number of churches in different parts of the country. The Census data has been analysed in ten regional groups and the number of churches in each region is given in the following table:

Table 25: Churches and population per region 1989

	Churches	Adult Population	Child Population	Total population per church
North	2,550	2,494.100	576,900	1,200
Yorks/Humberside	3,827	3,984,600	928,200	1,300
North West	4,039	5,188,500	1,239,300	1,600
East Midlands	3,911	3,221,900	748,300	1,000
West Midlands	3,868	4,206,400	1,000,200	1,300
East Anglia	2,769	1,650,000	383,700	700
South East (North)	3,943	4,037,000	962,600	1,300
South East (Greater London)	3,549	5,510,000	1,225,000	1,900
South East (South)	4,297	4,722,400	1,022,400	1,300
South West	5,854	3,817,900	815,900	800
Total	38,607	38,832,800	8,902,500	1,200

The 1,200 people in England for every church compare with an unknown average physical seating capacity of a church but it would not be anything approaching 1,200 people and is probably nearer 200 or 300 seats — it was 302 in the 1851 Census. If therefore there was a revival and everyone in the country wanted to attend church our churches would be full, probably four or six times over.

The figures in the final column of Table 25 are broken down by county in the following map. Outer Greater London has the largest numbers of people per church (2,300), followed by the West Midlands with Birmingham (2,100). The urban areas have the fewest churches proportionately; the rural areas have most, with Cornwall the lowest ratio (500), followed by Cumbria, North Yorkshire, the Isle of Man, Lincolnshire, Norfolk and Somerset (all 600).

WHERE DO PEOPLE GO TO CHURCH? 63

Figure 9: Population per church

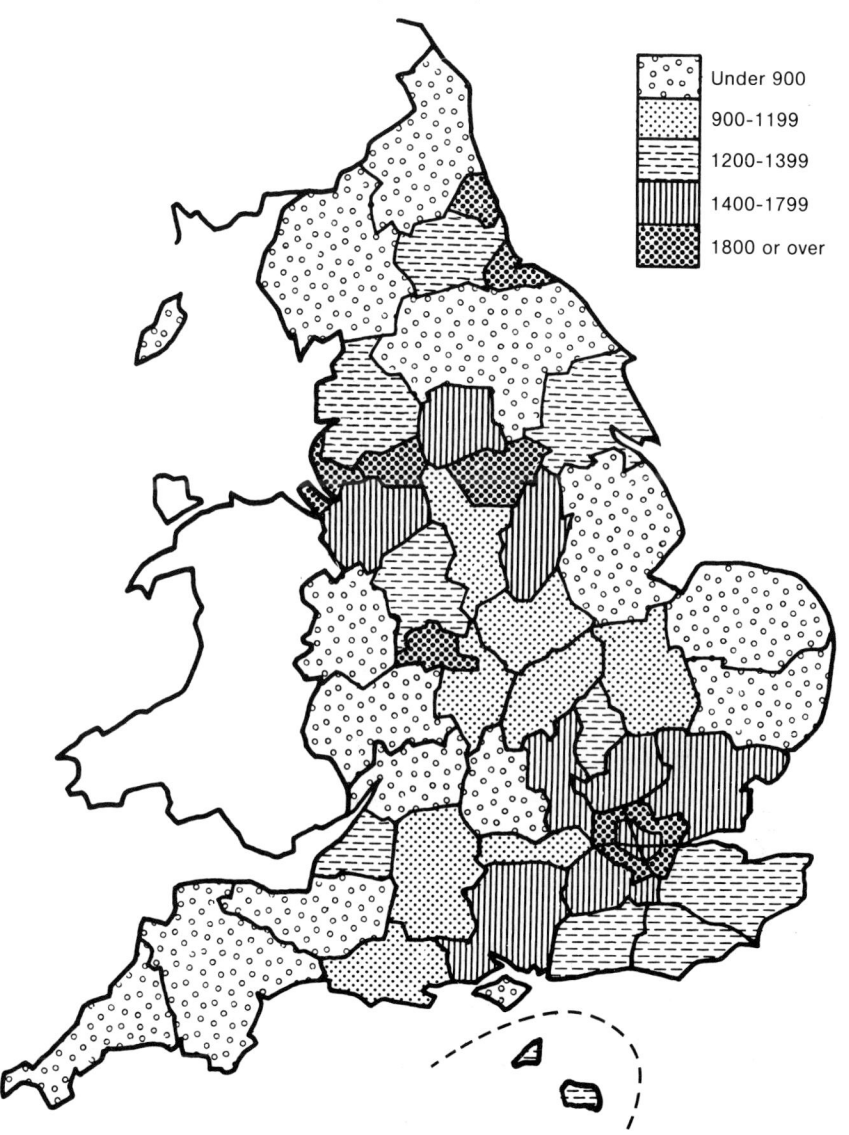

∘∘∘	Under 900
⣿	900-1199
≡	1200-1399
‖‖‖	1400-1799
▓	1800 or over

How have the numbers of churches changed over the past ten years? These are enumerated below.

Table 26: Churches/Congregations by region 1979 and 1989

	Churches 1979	Churches 1989	Difference Number	Difference Percentage
				%
North	2,638	2,550	−88	−3
Yorks/Humberside	3,896	3,827	−69	−2
North West	4,206	4,039	−167	−4
East Midlands	4,072	3,911	−161	−4
West Midlands	4,054	3,868	−186	−5
East Anglia	2,887	2,769	−118	−4
South East (North)	3,790	3,943	+153	+4
South East (Greater London)	3,350	3,549	+199	+6
South East (South)	4,305	4,297	−8	0
South West	5,866	5,854	−12	0
Total	39,064	38,607	−457	−1

Table 26 shows that the number of churches dropped 1% (against a population *increase* of 1%). This loss was greatest proportionately in the North West, the Midlands and East Anglia, with South East (North) and Greater London gaining in numbers of churches. This shows, somewhat superficially, the neediest areas of the country for church buildings and congregations.

How have the church numbers changed by denomination? Table 27 gives details.

Table 27: Churches/Congregations by denomination 1979 and 1989

	Churches 1979	Churches 1989	Difference Number	Difference Percentage
				%
Methodist	7,636	6,740	−896	−12
Baptist	2,211	2,339	+128	+6
URC	1,829	1,681	−148	−8
Independent	3,430	4,123	+693	+20
Afro-Caribbean	822	949	+127	+15
Pentecostal	950	1,002	+52	+5
Other Free	1,456	1,462	+6	0
Total Free	18,334	18,296	−38	0
Anglican	16,960	16,373	−587	−4
Roman Catholic	3,673	3,824	+151	+4
Orthodox	97	114	+17	+18
Total	39,064	38,607	−457	−1

This shows a decline in the number of Methodist and URC churches especially, followed by the Anglicans; rapid growth in the Independent, Afro-Caribbean and Orthodox sectors, and more modest growth amongst the Baptists, Pentecostals and Roman Catholics.

Areas of strength

Map 47 shows, not unexpectedly, that the urban areas have the highest number of churchgoers. This includes commuter areas, such as Essex, Hampshire, Hertfordshire, Kent, and Surrey. Devon has the ninth highest total of churchgoers in England; it is a large county with only 14 churchgoers per square kilometre, but it has 1,403 churches, the second highest in England, and only just behind Greater Manchester which has 1,444.

Conversely, the more distant rural parts of England, including the Isle of Man and Channel Islands, have the fewest churchgoers. Apart from the three islands (Isle of Man, Isle of Wight and the Channel Island group), Inner London Northeast (Islington, Hackney and Tower Hamlets) has the second smallest number of churchgoers per county on the mainland — 28,600 with Northumberland just one thousand fewer. Inner London Southwest (Lambeth, Wandsworth) has only 32,500. Not perhaps darkest England, but perhaps darkest London?

Church membership strength will be expected to correspond to churchgoing strength, so Map 48 is not a surprise. The high numbers of church members in some counties — for instance Greater Manchester, Merseyside and the West Midlands — simply follows the strength of the Roman Catholic Church which has many more members than attenders.

Suffolk has more churchgoers than its neighbours in the East Anglian Region (Norfolk and Cambridgeshire) but fewer members. Inner Northeast London may be relatively devoid of churchgoers but it has plenty of members; this reflects the strength of the Orthodox Church there — one-fifth of their entire English membership is in this area.

Non-attenders

Overall numbers are important but for practical meaning they need to be broken down by proportionate strength: what percentage of the population in each county actually go to church?

Where is the most 'heathen' part of England where fewest go? This is shown in Maps 1 and 2 for 1979 and 1989 respectively. In 1979 93% did not go to church in Humberside and South Yorkshire. By 1989, 94% did not go to church in South Yorkshire, and 93% in Humberside, Leicestershire and Inner London Northeast.

In 1979 the strongest churchgoing counties were the Roman Catholic strongholds in the North West Region, and parts of the South West (Cornwall, Dorset and Somerset), Gloucestershire, Lincolnshire and East Sussex. By 1989 the only counties where 13% or more still went to church (and 87% or less therefore did not) were Cumbria and the Catholic strongholds of Lancashire and Merseyside.

The changes between 1979 and 1989 occurred as follows, with counties where the numbers *not* going to church:

Increased by 5%: East Sussex

Increased by 3%: Buckinghamshire, Gloucestershire, Lancashire, Norfolk, Northamptonshire, Suffolk, Warwickshire and the Isle of Man.

Increased by 2%: Avon, Bedfordshire, Berkshire, Cheshire, Cornwall, Cumbria, Dorset, Essex, Hereford and Worcester, Isle of Wight, Kent, Leicestershire, Lincolnshire, Merseyside, Oxfordshire, Somerset and Wiltshire.

Increased by 1%: Cleveland, Durham, Greater Manchester, Hertfordshire, Northumberland, Nottinghamshire, Shropshire, South Yorkshire, Surrey, Tyne and Wear, West Midlands, West Yorkshire and the Channel Islands.

Remained the same: Cambridgeshire, Derbyshire, Devon, Greater London (Inner), Greater London (Outer), Hampshire, Humberside, North Yorkshire, Staffordshire, and West Sussex.

Why was the drop in church-going so great in East Sussex? One of the regions of the country from where emigration has been heaviest in the past few years is the Outer South East (which includes East Sussex). Figures from the Area Health Authority show an increase in deaths between 1987 and 1988. East Sussex has the highest percentage of elderly churchgoers over 65 years of age in the country, 29% of the total, and well above the overall average for churchgoers of 19%.

A similar reason will probably explain the severe drop in churchgoers in the South West. There are a high proportion of churchgoers of 65 or over in Cornwall (26%), Devon (27%), Dorset (27%), Norfolk (27%), Somerset (27%) and the Isle of Wight (29%). Factors other than age are undoubtedly sometimes relevant, such as community custom down the years. The 1851 Religious Census in Devon, for example, showed that almost half the population were in church that March,[4] and perhaps many elderly people today continue to go to church partly because of this tradition in their families.

Altogether four counties in five lost churchgoers in the 1980s, enough to increase the percentage not going to church by at least 1%. One in five, ten counties in all, stayed the same. The cumulative effect of all the church evangelism, church planting, and major campaigns did not increase church-going percentage in any county by even 1%, though they may well have prevented it falling further than it did.

DENOMINATIONAL STRENGTHS

The maps at the end of the book portray the strength of a particular denomination in different parts of the country, proportionate to the population. This is essential because, of course, more people go to church where there are more people: in the cities. So the number of churchgoers has been taken as a percentage of the population in that county, and these percentages are plotted. Knowing where particular groups are strongest and weakest is valuable for those wishing to take advantage of existing strengths as a basis for outreach.

The **Methodists** (Map 3) are strong in the North of England and down the East Coast from Cleveland (though not in Cleveland) to the Wash. They are also very strong on the Islands — Isle of Man, Isle of Wight and the Channel Islands — and in the South West. One person in 22 in Cornwall not just *is* Methodist but regularly goes to a Methodist Chapel. At 4.5% of the population, there are almost as many Methodists in Cornwall as all other churchgoers put together. One person in 33 on the Isle of Man goes to a Methodist Church, as does one person in 40 in North Yorkshire. These are considerable proportions.

On the other hand the Methodists are weak in the South East of England. The combined South East Region has 37% of the population but only 19% of Methodist churchgoers. Should they move their headquarters?

The **Baptists** (Map 5), unlike the Methodists, are strong in the South East and East Anglia. These two regions contain 41% of the population and 55% of Baptist churchgoers. The strongest counties are Bedfordshire and Suffolk where just over 1% of the population is a Baptist Church attender. This strength reflects the continuation of the influence of the chapels started by Cromwell three centuries ago.

They are also strong in the Outer Southeast and Southwest 'Bible Belt' of London, and along the South Coast generally, especially in Devon, but hardly at all in Cornwall. Conversely they are weak in the North.

In the area south of the line from the Wash to the Severn, along the northern boundaries of Cambridgeshire, Northamptonshire, Oxfordshire and Gloucestershire are 70% of Baptists churchgoers. Perhaps they should be called Southern Baptists! Only 39% of the Methodists are in the same area.

The strength of the **United Reformed Church** (Map 7) reflects its component churches before it was formed in 1972. It is strong in the North, especially Northumberland where nearly 1% of the population is a URC churchgoer, showing its former links with the Presbyterian Churches north of the Border. It is also strong in East Anglia and Essex from the many Congregational Chapels that were founded there, again many dating back two or three centuries. The same is true for their churches in the South West, especially Devon and Dorset.

They are weak at some of the extremities (Cornwall and the Channel Islands) and the centre, especially Inner London.

The **Independent Churches** (Map 9) are very strong in the South East of England. The streams of the House Church Movement are reflected in the counties with most churchgoers: New Frontiers in West Sussex, Pioneer in Surrey, and Ichthus in Inner London Southeast. One person in 50 in this last area goes to an Independent Church — almost invariably one of the Ichthus fellowships. Almost the same proportion (1.9% of the population) goes to an Independent Church in West Sussex. Harvestime (or Covenant Ministries) in West Yorkshire and Team Spirit in Essex do not register such an extensive impact in their immediate neighbourhood as the others.

The Christian Brethren are particularly strong in both East

Anglia and the South West. This is mostly the influence of their origins: George Müller's great orphanage work was based in Bristol. They were also originally called the Plymouth Brethren, and their numbers in Devon have always been considerable. Today 1.8% of the Devon population goes to an Independent Church, which includes the Brethren.

The Independent Churches collectively are weak in the North of the country, in both rural and urban parts. South of the line joining the Wash to the Severn lie 52% of the population, but 69% of Independent churchgoers. There is also a remarkable lack of Independents in Inner London Northeast.

The **Afro-Caribbean Churches** (Map 11) are mainly located in the central part of the country. They major on the urban areas, especially Inner London. Black people going to these churches represent 2.9% of the population in Inner London Southeast, 1.6% in Inner Northeast and 1.3% in Inner Southwest. 44% of all their church attenders are concentrated in Inner London.

The **Pentecostal Churches** (Map 13) are stronger in the North of England and the West Midlands than the South. A particularly strong group exists in South Yorkshire, Derbyshire, Nottinghamshire, and the West Midlands. They are strong too in Devon, but they are strongest in Inner London Northeast where they form as churchgoers almost 1% of the population.

They are weak in East Sussex and the Islands, and in the middle-south of the country: Northamptonshire, Oxfordshire, Berkshire and Wiltshire contain 5% of the adult population but only 1.3% of Pentecostal churchgoers. 55% of Pentecostal churchgoers are North of the Wash–Severn line against 48% of the adult population.

The **Other Free Churches** (Map 15) reflect the strengths of the various churches which form this group. They are strongest in East Anglia (0.7% of the Suffolk population) through the Religious Society of Friends, which also accounts for their strength in Gloucestershire.

The urban strength seen in London, Avon and West Yorkshire reflects the Seventh-Day Adventists who are particularly concentrated in their black churches in inner city areas.

The Salvation Army have many centres in major towns which helps explain the heterogeneity of Map 15. But why are these churches collectively so weak in Oxfordshire (when very strong in Cambridgeshire)?

Taken together, the various Free Churches have a variety of strengths and weaknesses. Some such as the Methodists and Pentecostals are especially strong in the North, whereas others, such as the Baptists and Independents are strong in the South. Some are concentrated in the urban areas, while others are strong in rural areas. Map 17 shows all the Free Churches combined together, for easier comparison with the Anglicans and Roman Catholics.

The Free Churches collectively are strongest in the South West, much of East Anglia, Cumbria, North Yorkshire, West Sussex, the Isle of Man and Inner London Southeast. The highest percentages of the total adult population attending Free Churches are:

Inner London Southeast	6.4%
Devon	5.7%
Cornwall	5.5%
Suffolk	5.1%
Isle of Man	4.7%

The weakest Free Church areas are Cleveland, Merseyside and then Tyne and Wear, South Yorkshire, Staffordshire and Outer London Northwest but these are only just the weakest areas. In other words the strengths and weaknesses of the various Free Churches largely even out with each other (there is very little variation in Map 17). It is where they combine their strengths that their impact is greatest and these are given above.

Anglican Churches (Map 19) shows that the Church of England is strong in the rural countryside where it has thousands of village churches and weak in the urban areas. In five of the seven English Metropolitan Counties, the Church of England attracts less than 2% of the population in their churches (except for Inner London Northwest). In the other two it musters between 2 and 3%. The Church Urban Fund gives help to struggling Anglican inner city churches where the need is obviously great. Perhaps it should have been started in 1936, not 1986.

On the other hand, in the North of England, the East Coast and towards the South West (but not as far as Devon and Cornwall) it sees over 4.5% of the population in church every Sunday. In the top three counties the percentage is over 5% — Somerset with 5.8%, Gloucestershire with 5.4% and Cumbria with 5.2%.

Comparing the Free Church and Anglican maps shows an overlap of ten counties where they are jointly strong, plus the Isle of

Man, but 22 where they are jointly weak, plus the Channel Islands, leaving 21 where one is weak and the other is strong. In the Northern urban areas they are significantly weakest in tandem. Often the big conglomerations have proved hard for these churches.

The **Roman Catholic Church** (Map 21) is clearly very strong in the North West and North East of England. One person in 11 in Merseyside goes to Mass each Sunday — the highest county population proportion for any church in England. One person in 16 likewise attends in Lancashire and Inner London Northwest, followed by one person in 17 in Cleveland, one person in 18 in the Channel Islands, and one person in 19 in Cheshire and Outer London Southeast. These are very considerable concentrations of Roman Catholics.

The Catholics are very strong in urban areas but very weak in rural areas with major parts of the country with relatively little significant presence at all. They are lowest in Somerset and Gloucestershire where only 1% of the population attends mass each Sunday. Outside the immediate environs of Greater London and Surrey they are not strong in the Home Counties, along the South Coast, or the heart of England outside Warwickshire and West Midlands (with Birmingham). In South Yorkshire all three major churches in England, Free, Anglican and Catholic, are collectively weak — church attendance there is the lowest (merely 6% of the adult population) in the whole of England.

The **Orthodox Church** is often strong where other churches are weak. There is no Map showing their distribution by county as they are too few for such to be meaningful. Although their churchgoing collectively is only 0.25% of the total in England, they are present in reasonable numbers for them in South Yorkshire and Outer London Northwest. They are also relatively strong in Inner London Northeast (where all the others are weaker). 55% of their total attendance is in Greater London.

The figures underlying these maps, summarised for convenience into regions, are given below. Those wanting full county information should consult *Prospects for the Nineties* or the appropriate regional volume.

Table 28: Adult churchgoers

	Methodist	Baptist	URC	Independent	Afro-Caribbean	Pentecostal	Other Free
	%	%	%	%	%	%	%
North	13	2	3	4	—	2	2
Yorks/Humberside	20	3	3	4	1	3	3
North West	11	2	3	5	$1/2$	2	1
East Midlands	15	7	3	6	$1/2$	4	3
West Midlands	11	5	2	6	2	3	1
East Anglia	8	8	4	11	0	1	5
South East (North)	8	9	4	10	1	2	3
South East (Greater London)	4	6	3	10	8	3	3
South East (South)	7	8	3	13	0	2	2
South West	15	7	3	11	$1/2$	2	2
NORTH[1]	13	3	3	5	1	3	2
SOUTH	9	7	3	11	3	3	2
Overall	11	5	3	8	2	3	2

[1] Defined as the top five Regions, all north of a line joining the Wash and the Severn, except

This table shows the clear divergence between North and South. In the North there are more Methodists and Roman Catholics; URC, Pentecostals and Other Free churchgoers are equally balanced and in the South there are more Baptists, Independents, Afro-Caribbeans and Anglicans.

APPLICATION

Assessing Strengths and Weaknesses

Note the process adopted in this chapter, and consider using it in your own situation. Are you responsible for a church? A diocese? A Christian or secular organisation? Do you have a responsibility as part of a church or department at work? What are the basic demands made on you at work or by your peers?

● *Assess the strengths that you have.* Your responsibilities may not be countrywide, but you can still think geographically. Where do your people (churchgoers, Sunday School supporters, customers etc) come from?

● *Obtain relevant external information.* The population Censuses of 1981 and 1991 yield much valuable data, in small geographical areas, on demographic, employment, housing, education, transport,

by denomination and region 1989

Total Free	Anglican	Roman Catholic	Total (= 100%)	% of total	Adult population
%	%	%		%	%
28	28	44	248,700	7	7
37	29	34	336,800	9	10
24	23	53	607,000	16	13
38	38	24	255,300	7	8
30	30	40	410,200	11	11
37	40	23	177,500	5	4
37	36	27	339,900	9	11
37	18	45	502,500	13	12
35	40	25	429,100	12	14
41	41	18	399,900	11	10
30	28	42	1,819,900	49	49
38	34	28	1,887,000	51	51
34	31	35	3,706,900	100	=38.8m

Northamptonshire in the East Midlands Region which is included with the South

health and other major variables. Most Central Reference Libraries will have the main publications, and hours spent perusing these can be a valuable investment.

● *Obtain the addresses of your people* if you do not already have them. If you are considering a local area, plot their addresses on a large map and join those addresses with your church or meeting place in a straight line. You may get a result which resembles Figure 10 on page 74 (taken from an actual example in Aberdeen[5]).

If you are able to do this nationally, construct maps similar to those mentioned in this chapter and given at the end of the book.

● *Look at where your people are strong.* Ask — and answer — the questions:
 — Why are they strong in those areas?
 — How can you build on those strengths to extend your influence further?

● *Look at where your people are weak.*
 — Why are they weak in those areas?
 — What steps can you take to help change that position?
 — What is the thinking, the social, physical, spiritual, economic position of those in these areas which needs to be altered, in-

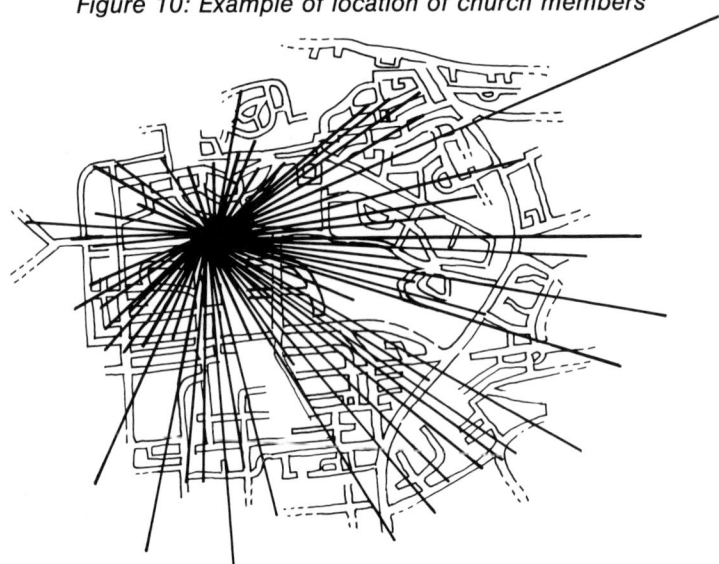

Figure 10: Example of location of church members

fluenced, challenged, helped, supported, encouraged by you to win them over?

Jesus said, 'Those who have ears to hear, let them hear'. Perhaps this should be extended to: 'Those who have eyes to see, let them see'. What do *you* see? This was the question God asked Ezekiel, Amos, Jeremiah, Zechariah and other prophets. In the introduction to one of his plays, George Bernard Shaw wrote, 'Some see things as they are and ask why. I see things that never were, and ask why not?' Precisely so! That is the stuff of which visions are made.

'Christian' England? Well, why not? As more people choose the Christian path, so will our country reflect the joy, morality and integrity of its guiding principles.

This chapter has looked at the denominations on a national level. Let us apply the above to one specific group in a detailed case study.

Afro-Caribbean Churches

In his excellent book, *Ethnic London*,[6] Ian McAuley introduces us to the eight main ethnic neighbourhoods in London. He identifies the key central locations of these communities, which are indicated on the following map (some have more than one).

WHERE DO PEOPLE GO TO CHURCH?

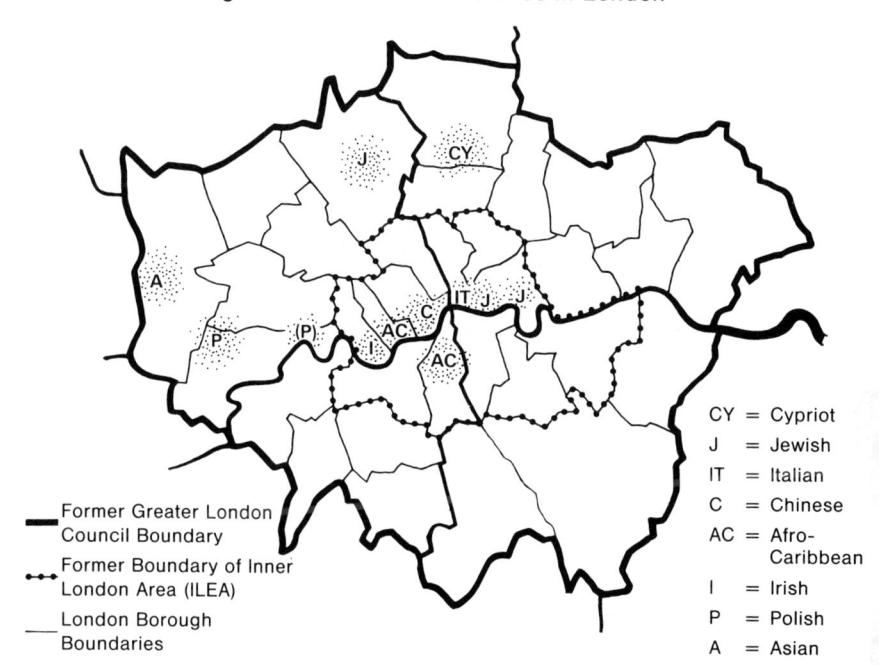

Figure 11: Ethnic Communities in London

CY = Cypriot
J = Jewish
IT = Italian
C = Chinese
AC = Afro-Caribbean
I = Irish
P = Polish
A = Asian

— Former Greater London Council Boundary
••• Former Boundary of Inner London Area (ILEA)
— London Borough Boundaries

Only one of these has any extensive church-going activity — the Afro-Caribbeans. Their relative locational strength is shown in Figure 11, but let us ask what are their strengths and weaknesses?[7]

Their *strengths* include:
- High degree of commitment to their churches. When people find themselves living in a different country this is not unusual.
- Attractive worship culturally relevant to those who come.
- Unity, initially through rejection by white Christians in the mid-1950s, and that unity is still recognised.
- Two associations, the Afro-Caribbean Evangelical Alliance, which has concern for the group as a whole. This springs from a combined churchmanship: 91% are evangelical. The other is the Afro-West Indian United Council of Churches.
- Similarity in age-structure. 60% are of working age (20-64 in this context) and only 6% are over 65 years of age.
- Similarity in residential areas and lifestyles.

Their *weaknesses* include:

- Problems in continuing their past growth. Tighter immigration laws have prevented so many new faces appearing and not all churches have a specific strategy for dynamic outreach.
- Many West Indians are leaving to retire and go back to the West Indies. The English churches lose their commitment, their wisdom and their history as a consequence.
- Not owning their own premises. Some are forced to close down because they could not find anywhere to worship.
- Many congregations using different venues on different Sundays. This affects their church attendance.
- Tendency of black people in England to be in the poorer parts of society, and often with menial jobs. Many of these jobs require working unsocial hours inhibiting church attendance. Many church members hold two jobs or do night duties.
- Low incomes of attenders and therefore churches. As a further consequence of their employment, finances in their churches are often low and full-time ministers can't be afforded. Ministers therefore work to support themselves — giving less time to church development, which means that most churches have to have several ministers to cope with the workload, and this brings problems of communication, delegation and team building.
- Fragmentation. Black-led churches often guard their independence jealously. Very often new congregations are formed from an existing one and the new one will not have any links with the old one. This is the basic reason for the 164 different groups identified through the Census. Such independence can also lead to disagreement, confrontation and separation. This does not always lead to Christian support, brotherhood, and forgiving understanding.
- Acceptance in white-led churches. Many black people are joining these instead to save travel time, money and inconvenience.

There are more weaknesses than strengths, which is not unusual. From such a list answers can now be developed about how future work should be guided, the types of strategic planning to be adopted and the development of a vision for where the Afro-Caribbean churches will be in the year 2000. They may well decline if no action is taken in the next year or two, even though an extrapolation of their figures suggests some small growth. What might such strategy be? By way of example, this might include:

1) Encouraging church leaders across the different groups to meet, holding such meetings in inner city areas in the evenings, to retain what is left of their cultural identity and to formulate a vision for their combined churches for a year ahead.
2) Providing quality training for these church leaders, cheaply so they can afford to come, again in the evenings in inner city locations, to help with team and vision building skills, delegation and communication needs.
3) If culturally appropriate, trying to find permanent places of worship, which they can own to establish identity and rapport, perhaps in association with white churches wanting to link with inner city areas. Such centres could then focus on evangelism in their immediate neighbourhoods.

Chapter 3: Summary

- There is one church for every 1,200 people in England.
- There are proportionately fewer churches in urban areas than rural areas.
- The number of churches fell 1% between 1979 and 1989.
- South Yorkshire has the smallest percentage (6%) of adult churchgoers of any county.
- East Sussex's church-going population changed more than any other county between 1979 and 1989.
- Cumbria and Merseyside, with 14%, have the highest percentage of adults in church.
- Methodists are strongest in the North and South West. Baptists are strongest in the South East.
- The United Reformed Church is strongest in the North, East Anglia and the South West.
- Independent Churches are strongest in the South East and along the South Coast.
- Pentecostals are strongest in the North and West Midlands.
- Roman Catholic and Afro-Caribbean Churches are strongest in urban areas.
- Anglicans are strongest in rural counties.

4: CHURCHGOERS BY AGE AND GENDER

This chapter looks at two specific characteristics of churchgoers that were examined by the English Church Census — gender and age. Since the youngest age group includes children, we also examine here what the results had to say about Sunday School. Most churches (97%) supplied information on age. One Lancashire church minister wrote that it was 'impossible to complete attendance. We are about 50% female, 30% male and 20% the rest'!

GENDER

The population of England is 49% male and 51% female. More boys than girls are born (105 boys to every 100 girls[1]), but women live longer than men and thus more than compensate in the population overall. The ratio has varied historically, but not since the Second World War.

In 1979 the proportion of male churchgoers was 45%. In 1989 in England it had dropped to 42%, nearer to the 1982 Welsh figure of 38% and the 1984 Scottish figure of 37%. A 3% drop is a lot — a loss of 360,000 men in the decade, against a drop of only 150,000 women. So, two-thirds of the change in church-going in the last decade reflects a fall-off by males. Almost one-third (100,000) of these died,[2] leaving a net loss of 260,000 men. Some, like the evangelist Jim Smith[3] for example, are especially concerned about this. In the same period 150,000 church-going women died, but the loss of women in the church is not solely due to these deaths. Those who have become invalided, lost their faith, and so on were replaced in equal numbers by others. These are net figures, and must be tempered by over six million children being born in Britain in this decade. If a quarter of them had come to church that would represent a gain of 640,000 boys and 610,000 girls for those in England.

Gender and geography

In which parts of the country were men least represented? Table 29 looks at the regional variations of male attendance in the church. All England 1979 figures of 45% of men in church meant 55% of churchgoers were women, a percentage which had grown to 58% by 1989, an increase of 3%. Decline in men and growth in women are two sides of the same coin; we focus here on decline.

Table 29: Proportion of male churchgoers by region

	North	Yorks/Humberside	North West	East Midlands	West Midlands
	%	%	%	%	%
1979	44	44	45	45	46
1989	40	40	41	42	41
Difference	−4	−4	−4	−3	−5

	East Anglia	South East (North)	South East (Greater) London	South East (South)	South West	All England
	%	%	%	%	%	%
1979	45	46	43	45	44	45
1989	41	43	42	42	41	42
Difference	−4	−3	−1	−3	−3	−3

The North of England has tended to lose more male churchgoers than average, and the West Midlands most of all. The Southeast (especially Greater London) and the South West have lost fewer. The counties most affected are Staffordshire (−8%), Cheshire (−6%), Hereford and Worcester (−6%), Northumberland (−6%), South Yorkshire (−6%) and Tyne and Wear (−6%) and the Channel Islands (−8%). The counties affected least are West Sussex where they stayed the same, Berkshire (−1%), Greater London (−1%) and Northamptonshire (−1%).

It may be helpful to get an overview of the changes by age-groups, and these are given in Table 30, along with population percentages for 1989, which are illustrated immediately after.

CHURCHGOERS BY AGE AND GENDER

Table 30: Age and gender of churchgoers 1979 and 1989 compared with general population 1989

	Churchgoers in 1979			Churchgoers in 1989			Population 1989		
Age group	Men	Women	Total	Men	Women	Total	Men	Women	Total
	%	%	%	%	%	%	%	%	%
Under 15	13	13	26	12	13	25	10	9	19
15-19	4	5	9	3	4	7	4	4	8
20-29	5	6	11	4	6	10	8	8	16
30-44	7	9	16	7	10	17	10	10	20
45-64	9	11	20	9	13	22	11	11	22
65 & over	7	11	18	7	12	19	6	9	15
All ages	45	55	100	42	58	100	49	51	100

Figure 12: Total 1989 Churchgoers contrasted

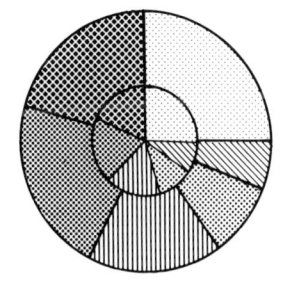

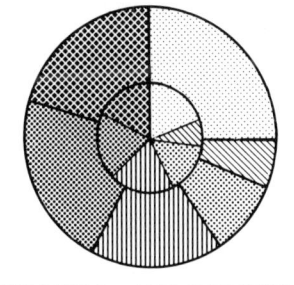

OUTER CIRCLE – 1989 CHURCHGOERS OUTER CIRCLE – 1989 CHURCHGOERS
INNER CIRCLE – 1979 CHURCHGOERS INNER CIRCLE – 1989 POPULATION

Under 15 ▨ 15-19 ▨ 20-29 ▥ 30-44 ▨ 45-64 ▨ 65 and over

The main features which emerge from this table and diagram are:

● A small percentage fall in children going to church between 1979 and 1989. Children formed 21% of the population in 1979, and the proportion going to church was higher. In 1989 this is still the case, with the population proportion dropping two points to 19%, but the child attendance only one percentage point to 25%.
● More boys than girls stopping going to church.
● A decline in churchgoers between 1979 and 1989, especially among 15-19 and 20-29 males.
● The proportion of churchgoers in their twenties being considerably less than the population proportion. This is the missing age-group.

- A greater percentage of women aged 30-44 attending church in 1989 than 1979, but men still well short of their relative population strength.
- A relatively high percentage increase in churchgoing in those aged 45 and over in the 1980s. The 3% increase is equal to the decrease in those aged 15-29. The church has aged in the 1980s.
- The percentage of 45-64 year olds being the same as population proportion, but with fewer men and more women.
- The considerably greater percentage of those 65 or over than in the population proportion, with a likelihood of many deaths in the 1990s.
- The 65 and over age group being the only one with more men in church than their population proportion.
- Over two-fifths of churchgoers in October 1989 being over 45 and two-fifths under 30.

These stark percentages are brought into sharp relief by the actual numbers involved. How old are the men and women who are thus lost to regular churchgoing? Table 31 gives details, which are illustrated in Figure 13.

Table 31: Net change in churchgoers 1979-1989 by age and gender

	Under 15	15-19	20-29	30-44	45-64	65 & over	All ages
Men	−124,000	−64,000	−52,000	−56,000	−29,000	−35,000	−360,000
Women	−70,000	−91,000	−43,000	−19,000	+43,000	+27,000	−153,000
Total	−194,000	−155,000	−95,000	−75,000	+14,000	−8,000	−513,000

In 1979, 1,416,000 children and 4,025,000 adults went to church each week, a total of 5,441,000 or 11.6% of the entire population. By 1989, these numbers fell to 1,221,500 children and 3,706,900 adults, or a total of 4,928,400 or 10.3% of the entire population. This is a drop of 512,600 people in the ten years — over half a million people in England stopped going to church each week, a loss of 51,000 a year or 1,000 every week. These are serious losses.

Table 31 shows the age make-up of this decline. Two-fifths were among children under 15, reflecting the drop in the birth-rate in the early 1980s. Thus part of this drop (perhaps a fifth) is because new churchgoing children were not born to replace those moving into the next age group. Church people as well as others marry later, start their family later and have smaller families. Probably, also, not so many church people as unchurched people have abortions. Of the 194,000 drop under 15, note that almost two-thirds are boys.

There was also a massive drop-out among the older teens. There were 150,000 fewer teenagers in church in 1989 than in 1979. This may be because there were fewer people of that age, or because teenagers became disenchanted and left. This number represents three people in every ten in the shortfall in churchgoing in the 1980s. Almost two of these were young women — the young men by and large left when younger.

Twenty percent of the churchgoing loss in the 1980s was among those in their twenties, and thus 87% of the total drop in church attendance in these ten years is accounted for by all those under 30. How many did we fail to win? How many did we fail to keep? These numbers are not known since the table shows only net figures. But it is clearly crucial to make major efforts to win this generation. One person in seven of the overall decline was aged 30-44, the age when many people have families. The children's decline is greater than this decline, but even so some of the children's drop must reflect parents no longer going to church. We are losing families as well.

There was a net inflow of women over 45 into the church during the 1980s, against a continuing but smaller outflow of men, much because of death. The previous table of changes in churchgoing numbers hides an important fact. Of the 100,000 men who died a substantial number will have been over 65, so the fact that the churches lost 'only' 35,000 men over 65 actually hides an increase of men in this age group because it is offset by an even larger number of deaths.

The negative 35,000 for men over 65 reflects a greater loss in fact. If there were say 50,000 men newly attending in the 1980s then 85,000 men in the same period were lost. Unfortunately the Census can give no information on that 50,000 — or even if it was 50,000 or 5,000. All it yields is the net difference between 1979 and 1989, but that information is enough to guide strategic thinking. Of course, we must be concerned about older people, but the decline in older people who do come to church is mostly due to natural demographic change.

The table covers ten years, so many of those in a particular age group would have been in the previous one in 1979. So the 43,000 women aged 45-64 who 'joined' the church in the ten year period might simply have been those aged 35-54 in 1979. Almost certainly however the 43,000 will include some who freshly joined the church in this age-band, and an equivalent number will have left. These are all *net* figures.

Figure 13: Net change in churchgoing numbers 1979-1989 by age and gender

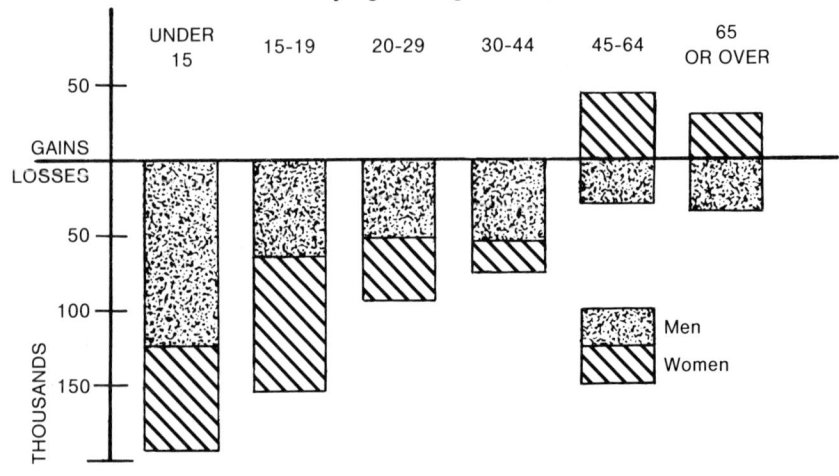

It is worth comparing the figures for changes in churchgoing numbers with the net change in population over the same period.

Table 32: Net change in population numbers 1979-1989 by age and gender

	Under 15	15-19	20-29	30-44	45-64	65 & over	All ages
Men	−198,000	−435,000	+504,000	+464,000	+34,000	+260,000	+629,000
Women	−206,000	−426,000	+448,000	+497,000	−92,000	+226,000	+447,000
Total	−404,000	−861,000	+952,000	+961,000	−58,000	+486,000	+1,076,000

Comparing Tables 31 and 32 suggests:

● The drop in the numbers of boys and girls in church generally follows the population fall, except that the churches have lost fewer girls than boys.

- The decline in the teenager group is less marked in the church than in the population as a whole. There are many fewer teenagers around, so it is not surprising there are fewer in churches.
- It is the twenties and thirties age groups that the churches seem to be missing out most. In the population these groups are in the ascendancy but not in the church.
- The church gained people in the 45-64 age group whereas the population declined. This is especially so among women, where the church's work is very strong.
- Older people are increasing in the population but men in particular are not joining the church significantly.

Gender and denomination

How did the percentages of those going to church vary by denomination? Table 33 gives the figures.

Table 33: Proportion of male churchgoers by denomination 1979 and 1989

	Methodist	Baptist	URC	Independent	Afro-Caribbean	Pentecostal	Other Free
	%	%	%	%	%	%	%
1979	40	43	43	47	41	46	44
1989	37	40	37	49	41	44	41
Difference	−3	−3	−6	+2	0	−2	−3

	Total Free	Anglican	Roman Catholic	Orthodox	All Denominations
	%	%	%	%	%
1979	43	45	46	45	45
1989	41	39	45	44	42
Difference	−2	−6	−1	−1	−3

The Independent Churches gained men; the Afro-Caribbeans remained at the same percentage. The URC and the Anglican Churches lost most as a percentage and the Roman Catholic and Orthodox least, but percentages can be misleading in this context, because they need to be interpreted against the relative strengths of each denomination.

The actual net losses by denomination in the next table include both adults and children.

*Table 34: Net change in churchgoers 1979-1989
by denomination and gender*

	Metho-dist	Baptist	URC	Inde-pendent	Afro-Carib-bean	Pente-costal	Other Free
Men	−59,000	−16,000	−27,000	+68,000	−1,000	+3,000	−16,000
Women	−50,000	−3,000	−14,000	+59,000	−2,000	+9,000	−12,000
Total	−109,000	−19,000	−41,000	+127,000	−3,000	+12,000	−28,000

	Total Free	Anglican	Roman Catholic	Orthodox	Total
Men	−48,000	−170,000	−143,000	+1,000	−360,000
Women	−13,000	−9,000	−132,000	+1,000	−153,000
Total	−61,000	−179,000	−275,000	+2,000	−513,000

This summary table shows that the main decline in women was in the Roman Catholic Church, which lost almost as many women as men. This was not the experience of any other church except the Methodists. In particular, the Anglicans suffered a massive decline in men against a very small decline in women, explained more in the next table. Only the Independents, Pentecostals and Orthodox gained people, and in all cases both men and women increased.

GENDER, DENOMINATION AND AGE GROUP

Tables 35 and 36 categorize men and women in Table 34 by age group, and figures are here given to the nearest hundred rather than thousand for those wanting more exact detail.

Tables 35 and 36 are also misleading in that some of the numbers are small, suggesting relatively little movement. In fact, there was a lot of movement. If the estimated 100,000 male churchgoers over 65 who died is correct there must have been at least 64,800 men who joined in that age group, to give a net drop of −35,200. Male churchgoers who stopped coming to church for loss of faith, health, transport must be added to the 100,000 who died and to the 64,800 who replaced them.

Nevertheless these two tables, interpreted correctly, are of considerable importance. Some of the drastic loss of children is simply because there were no younger children already in the church to replace them as they got older. There were generally fewer births in the population. The loss also partly reflects fewer children being born to churchgoers. The loss is considerable and will show itself through the life of the church as the 'missing generation' gets older (since about two-thirds of the children of churchgoing parents end up as regular churchgoers themselves).[4] So this loss is serious, especially as the norms and values concerning fertility in different denominations only gradually changes.[5]

The loss of children going to church was especially notable for Methodists and Anglicans. Could this reflect a decline of choirs in these churches? The Afro-Caribbeans and URC suffered a greater decline in boys than girls — why should this be? Leslie Francis, who has undertaken many studies of young people, in a study of Gloucestershire primary schools[6] found boys much less likely to be going to church than girls. How do we change this? Could it be because many Sunday School and primary school teachers are women, and boys find few suitable role models?

The Independent Churches were able to see a good number of teenage boys (and girls to a lesser extent) coming to their churches. They were the *only* churches with an increase in this vital age-group. Does this reflect the type of worship which is often led by groups of musicians, many of whom are teenagers?

Both the Anglicans and the Catholics suffered a large net drop in teenagers. Could this be because this increasingly mobile group went to other churches? The institutional loss became the Free Church gain? The Baptists, URC and Afro-Caribbeans lost more teenage girls than boys. Teenagers often say that they are 'bored'[7] with the normal, expected and regular. Could the freer worship in the Independent Churches be more attractive? Even if it was, the numbers still indicate an overall net high loss, a feature experienced in Australian church life also.[8]

Roman Catholic men in their twenties fell considerably in the 1980s, and a smaller drop in women. This has serious implications for their future ministry. Could it be that men in this age group want responsibility and accountability speedily and are not attracted to a system which allows people to remain assistant priests for perhaps twenty years? Perhaps this drop partly comes about from moves in search for employment. A study based on Falkirk[9] showed that Catholic people moved frequently and often did not join their new local Catholic Church. If true to any large extent, some kind of formal follow-up to a transfer system would seem useful. It could also be that such younger people simply find the church not relevant

Table 35: Net male churchgoers change 1979-1989 by denomination and age

MEN	Metho-dist	Baptist	URC	Inde-pendent	Afro-Carib-bean	Pente-costal	Other Free
Under 15	−41,500	−7,600	−12,100	+20,500	−4,800	+300	−5,300
15-19	−2,100	−600	−800	+26,300	−100	−900	−2,900
20-29	+3,000	−1,000	−2,700	+8,800	+1,900	+500	−2,000
30-44	−5,300	−1,400	−3,900	+10,000	−200	+2,000	−2,300
45-64	−8,500	−1,400	−5,100	+7,300	+900	+600	−1,600
65 or over	−4,400	−4,300	−1,900	−5,200	+1,100	+100	−1,400
Total	−58,800	−16,300	−26,500	+67,700	−1,200	+2,600	−15,500

	Total Free	Anglican	Roman Catholic	Orthodox	Total
Under 15	−50,500	−41,200	−32,300	−300	−124,300
15-19	+18,900	−37,900	−45,200	−100	−64,300
20-29	+8,500	−26,400	−34,000	+300	−51,600
30-44	−1,100	−22,700	−32,100	+200	−55,700
45-64	−7,800	−31,100	+9,400	+600	−28,900
65 or over	−16,000	−10,900	−8,500	+200	−35,200
Total	−48,000	−170,200	−142,700	+900	−360,000

to them, as a detailed study in the Archdiocese of Glasgow found.[10]

The Independent Churches in the 1990s gained both men and women in their twenties, as did the Afro-Caribbeans, the Pentecostals, the Methodists and the Orthodox. Baptists gained women in this group, but not men. The parity of numbers of male and female churchgoers in the Independent, Methodist, and Pentecostal Churches suggests that these are young families coming to church. What draws them? These are the 'baby boomers' — children born at the time of rapid increase in births during the late 1950s and early 1960s, are now grown up, with children of their own. Some research[11] has suggested that these people return to churches after years away because they want to give their children a religious education and value system.

This is also true of the next age-group, 30-44, where again Independent Churches saw a substantial net gain in both sexes. The Baptists gained women, but not men (perhaps women coming without their husbands, single women, or divorced women appreciating

Table 36: Net female churchgoers change 1979-1989 by denomination and age

WOMEN	Methodist	Baptist	URC	Independent	Afro-Caribbean	Pentecostal	Other Free
Under 15	−16,300	−7,900	−3,600	+19,200	−600	+4,100	−7,100
15-19	−3,200	−3,700	−2,700	+14,800	−3,300	−800	−2,000
20-29	+2,000	+1,900	−1,600	+7,600	+5,000	+600	−3,300
30-44	−7,500	+3,600	−3,200	+15,500	−2,400	+3,300	−2,700
45-64	−28,300	+200	−300	+6,100	−300	+2,000	−800
65 or over	3,4400	+3,100	−2,800	−4,400	−100	−200	+4,000
Total	−49,900	−2,800	−14,200	+58,800	−1,700	+9,000	−11,900
Grand total*	**−108,700**	**−19,100**	**−40,700**	**+126,500**	**−2,900**	**+11,600**	**−27,400**

	Total Free	Anglican	Roman Catholic	Orthodox	Total
Under 15	−12,200	−25,800	−32,400	+200	−70,200
15-19	−900	−39,600	−49,700	−200	−90,400
20-29	+12,200	−30,900	−24,800	+600	−42,900
30-44	+6,600	−7,500	−18,100	+200	−18,800
45-64	+21,400	+77,100	−13,300	+400	+42,800
65 or over	+3,000	+17,800	+5,900	+200	+26,900
Total	−12,700	−8,900	−132,400	+1,400	−152,600
Grand total*	**−60,700**	**−179,100**	**−275,100**	**+2,300**	**−512,600**

* of men and women

the Baptists' warm welcome). The Pentecostals and Orthodox also gained in this age-group. Significantly the Anglicans did not, and, like the Catholics, *lost* men heavily in this age-group though retained the loyalty of women of this age. Could this again be a reflection of the responsibilities given in leadership? Many Independent churches give great freedom to men and women of this age — activity and responsibility often generate commitment. One of the key attributes that men (and women?) desire, according to a Mintel Survey, was to be 'loyal and trustworthy'.[12] How do you know men are trustworthy? By giving them responsibility and seeing how they get on with it. Have the Independents tapped a key trait of men today?

Anglicans not only did not attract men in this age-group, they saw a loss of women as well. Could this suggest that Family Services have lost their appeal? These typically monthly events do not seem to have gained or held the parents of today.

Methodists and Roman Catholics both suffered a net decline in numbers of women of 45-64, perhaps because more of them were 55-64 ten years ago and have moved into the 65+ age group. The Independent Churches gained in this group, both men and women, and so did the Orthodox and Pentecostals. The Catholics and Afro-Caribbeans gained men but lost women and the Baptists gained a few women but lost men. The Anglicans gained an astonishing number of women in this age group — perhaps because the many women of 35-44 ten years ago previously stayed on, or perhaps because of the increasing importance of highly active organisations like Mothers' Union, which have a clear vision of how they wish to help women in this age group especially. The loyalty of women to the church is evidenced by figures like these.

In the oldest age group there were striking gains of women among Methodist, Baptist, Other Free Churches, Anglican and Roman Catholic Churches. This almost certainly reflects their strength in the previous age-band ten years before. The Orthodox gained men at this age also and the Afro-Caribbeans and Pentecostals experienced increasing numbers of men but small losses of women. The URC and Independent Churches did not gain, however — the emphasis of their ministry is for younger people, and, for Independents, suggests a concern since this was the only age group in which there was no increase.

The Baptists also should be worried by Tables 35 and 36. They show an increase in the numbers of women aged 20 upwards but without a corresponding increase in men. Is it fair to ask if the Baptists are becoming a denomination only for women?

Age group and denomination

It may help by way of summary to show graphically the proportion of broad denominational groupings by age groups. This relates to current strength not change. What proportion of boys and girls under 15 in church today are Anglican, for example? This is illustrated in Figure 14.

This diagram reflects the smallest groups in Anglicanism — the teens and twenties — and the dominance of the Roman Catholics in

CHURCHGOERS BY AGE AND GENDER

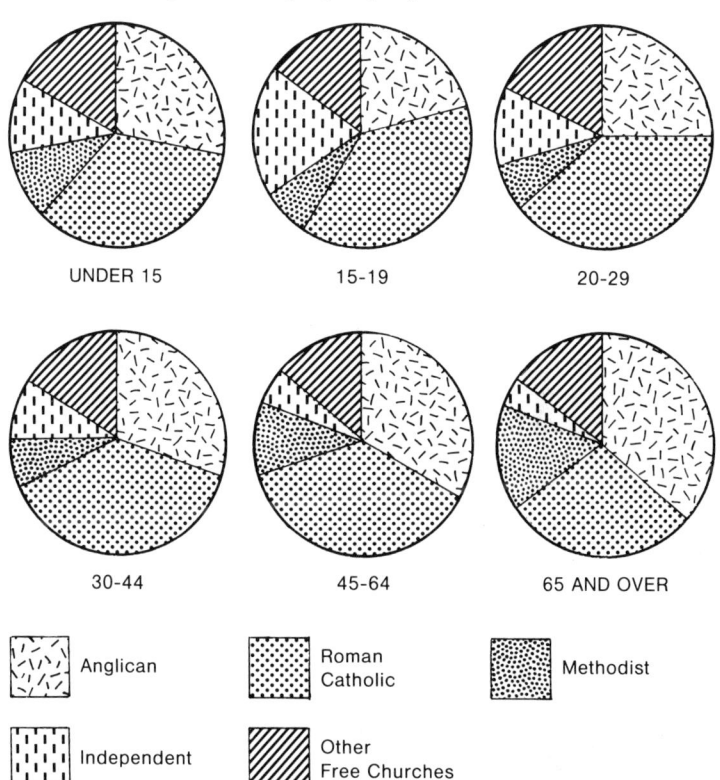

Figure 14: Age group by denomination

UNDER 15   15-19   20-29

30-44   45-64   65 AND OVER

Anglican

Roman Catholic

Methodist

Independent

Other Free Churches

these age groups and the next two — 30-64. It shows the drop-off in Methodist children and their increasing numbers with increasing age. It demonstrates the importance of the Independent Churches especially with teenagers, and that the impact of the other Free Churches together is much the same collectively across all age groups. These results are similar to the Australians.[13]

Reginald Bibby, author of *Fragmented Gods,* a major book on Canadian church life, recently wrote, 'As things stand, there will be an ongoing decline in church attendance during the 1990s. The reason is simple: people who attend as adults are primarily people who attend as children. Active churchgoers seldom come out of nowhere; they are homegrown. And the proportion of children being exposed to religious instruction outside the school day has dropped from three in four in 1945 to less than one in four at present.'[14] The English statistics are different but their direction and consequences are not.

Figure 14 looks at the denominational breakdown of each age group. It is also worth looking at the age groups in each denomination, and these are given in Figure 15.

Figure 15: Churchgoers by age group and denomination

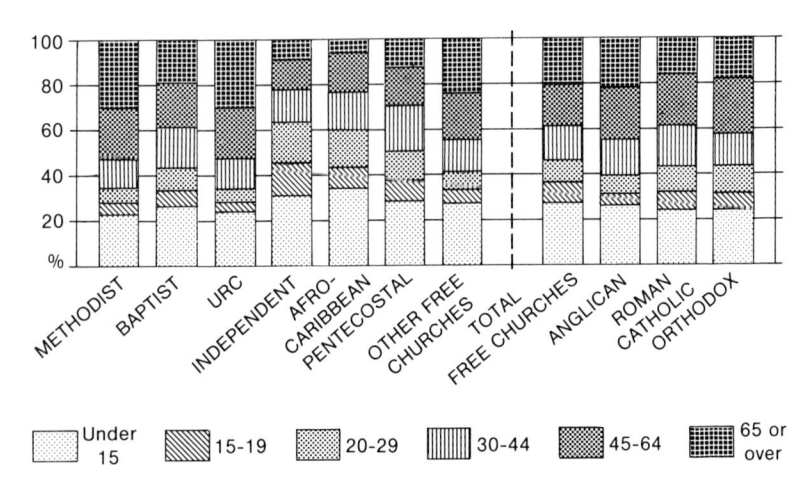

[Bar chart showing percentages by denomination: METHODIST, BAPTIST, URC, INDEPENDENT, AFRO-CARIBBEAN, PENTECOSTAL, OTHER FREE CHURCHES, TOTAL FREE CHURCHES, ANGLICAN, ROMAN CATHOLIC, ORTHODOX. Legend: Under 15, 15-19, 20-29, 30-44, 45-64, 65 or over]

Free Churches have proportionately more children than Anglican or Catholics, and the Anglicans and the Methodists the smallest percentage of teenagers. The Orthodox have the highest percentage of those aged 45-64. The Independents and Afro-Caribbeans score high with children, but both are very low with the over 65s. The latter is similar to the Australian scene (as measured by their Pentecostals), but their Catholics have fewer young people and more elderly, and their Anglicans have many more elderly but more in their thirties.[15]

SPECIAL GROUPS

The importance of mothers

A Jewish proverb states that 'God could not be everywhere, so He made mothers', and a Spanish proverb enforces their worth, 'An ounce of mother is worth a pound of clergy'.[16] One of the most successful attractions for them is a Mum and Toddlers' Group, Mothers' Club, Mothers' Union, or whatever it might be called. Such a gathering is often a:[17]

- Place to make and meet new friends and share experiences, worries, concerns and joys
- Way of offering mutual support to new mothers
- Link to other church groups — keep fit, flower arranging, etc
- Counterforce to postpartum blues
- Part of a larger programme for parents of young children
- Successful entry point for new members
- Feeder channel to Sunday School classes
- 'Arts and crafts' circle
- Way of facilitating the incorporation of new adult members

If your church doesn't have an effective group of this kind why not start one? If your ministry or work is not church related is there one key part of your 'market' on which you can place special emphasis?

The value of families

Despite the rise of single parent families — some 17% of all households in England and Wales — most children still grow up in a usual family of two adults, their mother and father. We must not neglect the Dads either! While their work is traditionally difficult — there are so many competing priorities — many churches have found that reaching families as a unit can be more successful in winning men than concentrating on the men alone.

One church modified its premises extensively and found that its new look generated an image of warmth and welcome, and, partly as a consequence, found that families started to attend as never before. Let us not neglect the strategy of reaching couples and families as an entity.

The 'Baby Boomers'

The new generation of young people have different values, standards and interests from their parents. The generation of people in their twenties in 1990 were born in the 1960s of whom there were many. An important report by the American researcher, Dr James Engel,[18] suggests that Christian baby boomers are the key to accelerated evangelism in the next decade. He identifies seven major characteristics:

● *Baby boomers are a generation with different values.* They have an entrepreneurial spirit and a desire for immediate gratification. There is much greater tolerance for diversity and acceptance of formerly taboo lifestyles. Institutional distrust is commonplace. Their greatest priorities are for economic well-being and a comfortable family life. Yet, there is also a willingness to contribute both time and money to worthy causes.

● *Christian baby boomers share many of these values but show some differences.* They are serious about their faith and are less materialistic. If anything, they are even more open to investing time, effort, and money in causes they believe to be significant.

● *Local Christian causes and initiatives are of far greater interest to them than spreading the gospel overseas.* Only 10% (in Engel's research) voiced strong interest in overseas missions, and 50% were not at all interested.

● *Those who are interested in world outreach much prefer to support holistic causes and training of nationals as opposed to sending expatriates.* Only 10-15% (in Engel's research) voiced a strong interest in the more traditional expatriate-oriented strategy.

● *Boomers who have visited a Christian organisation or site overseas, volunteered their time in other ways, or have made a financial contribution are significantly more interested in overseas causes.* This is also true of those who have played a role in someone's conversion in the past year.

● *Boomers are active financial contributors to local churches and Christian causes.* They prefer to support individuals as opposed to organisations. Also they want to support individuals and causes while, at the same time, contributing to the church missions budget.

● *They have little interest in becoming a career missionary* at this point in time. Much greater interest is expressed in short-term service.

George Barna believes that baby boomers 'will be the first generation in the twentieth century to break the pattern in which people increasingly embrace the church as they age'.[19] They look like maintaining their indifference to church, and if true, the consequences for churches' finance, leadership and attendance are enormous.

Baby boomers have little institutional loyalty. Many 'believe that no institution deserves their total loyalty'.[20] So they are likely to leave for another denomination if there is a successful church near where they live. They 'choose which church to attend on the basis of which one will address their most keenly-felt needs'.[21] The church is seen *as a place which provides a service, rather than providing an outlet or opportunity to allow one to serve others.* People therefore choose the best service, in the same way that they choose the most suitable car or furniture. As the Bishop of Southwark, Rt Rev Ronnie Bowlby, recently said, 'We have moved from where Christianity is culture to where Christianity is choice'. This reinforces a significant age factor. For those aged about 45 and over the culture of Christianity is relevant, for those under 45 the choice factor is much more important.

Non-churchgoers and the population

If 10% of the population goes to church, then 90% do not. How does this vary by age group? The next table gives this information, illustrated on page 96.

Table 37: Percentage of churchgoers and non-churchgoers in the population by age 1989

	Churchgoers 1989			Non-churchgoers 1989			Non-churchgoers 1979
	Men	Women	Total	Men	Women	Total	Total
	%	%	%	%	%	%	%
Under 15	13	15	14	87	85	86	86
15-19	8	10	9	92	90	91	88
20-29	5	8	6	95	92	94	91
30-44	7	10	9	93	90	91	91
45-64	8	12	10	92	88	90	90
65 & over	12	14	13	88	86	87	87
Overall	9	12	10	91	88	90	89

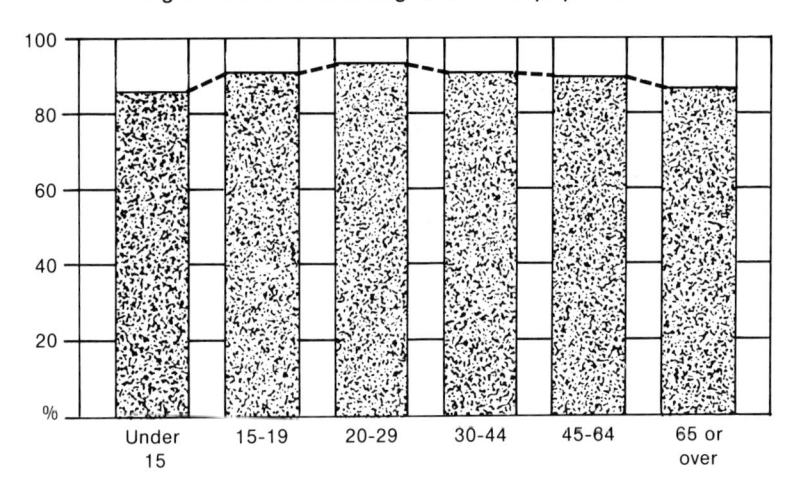

Figure 16: Non-churchgoers in the population

The highest percentage of non-churchgoers in 1989, as it was in 1979, is those in their twenties. Only 6% of this age went to church in 1989, against the 9% who went in 1979. The proportion of children outside the church remains the same, at 86%, as does the proportion of those over 65 — 87% in both 1979 and 1989. The number of people in England not going to church is over 35 million adults and 8 million children — 43 million people.

The proportion of the elderly going to church in 1989 may be the same as in 1979, but it still leaves over six million people over 65 outside the church. David Newton suggests 'the over sixties is probably the most neglected mission field in Britain today despite many congregations being strong in this age group'.[22] Many elderly people are desperately lonely. One church in South East London recently started a coffee morning for older people, which was received with great enthusiasm, and has now developed into a luncheon club. Many older unchurched people come each week. These and other similar initiatives seem a fruitful avenue for exploration.

AGE GROUPS

The time when we were born is important. The various generation groups in our churches have had different experiences, and church life needs somehow to relate to each of these. Some of the significant social patterns are reflected in the following table:[23]

Table 38: Social experience by age or birth

Born	Age in 1990	Common Social Experience
1900-1920	90-70	First World War
1920-1935	70-55	Inter-war Depression
1935-1950	55-40	European tension; Second World War; Cold War
1950-1963	40-27	Post-war affluence; Baby boom
1963-1970	27-20	Counter Culture
1970-1990	20-0	Post-industrialism; high unemployment; technological advance; communication revolution

Rapid social change has been a feature of this century. It is sometimes helpful to relate the age groups in our church to the experience they have had. One Baptist minister discovered that some of his elderly women members had, some sixty years ago, one Saturday placed their weekly pay packet on the plot of ground where the church now stood, as an initial gift for the starting of the church. He used this example of faith to challenge the teenagers in his congregation.

Afro-Caribbeans by age

The age group breakdowns of the Afro-Caribbeans are markedly different from that of the general population and of the churchgoing community. The most recent Government figures, 1988, estimate 495,000 West Indians of all generations in Great Britain, and a further 112,000 Africans.[24] The Government figures relate to Great Britain, and how many live in England is not known. On the basis of the number of church members[25] 99.8% will do so. This means a combined relevant population, including children, of 607,000. Of these 17% or one in six were in church in October 1989 — much higher than the norm!

The age breakdown of this 17% compared with the general population is given in Figure 17. The population in each age group is based on the Labour Force Survey results.[26]

Figure 17: Afro-Caribbean churchgoers and the population

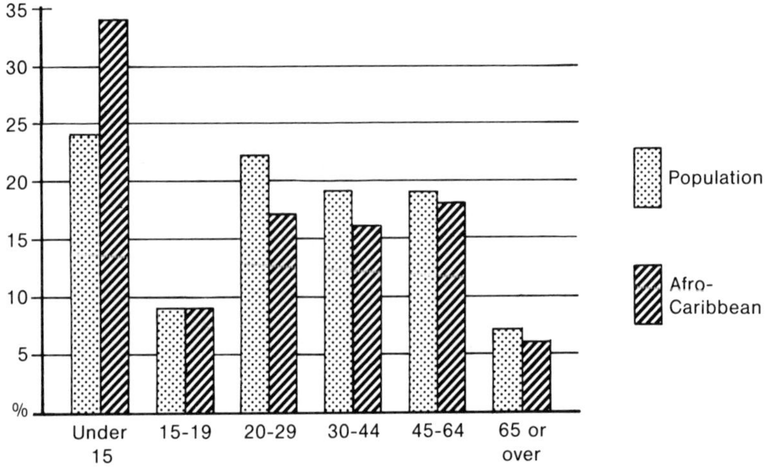

The diagram shows they have a specially large number of children attending their churches (about 34% of the relevant proportion of the population) and a proportion equal to the entire population in their teens. What is the attraction for so many? A Government survey, *Young People in the 80s,*[27] said that the chief reason for this age group going to church was to meet their peers (33%), followed by the opportunity to serve/participate (25%), and doing something useful/helpful (19%). Could this example aid other churches?

Figure 17 also shows that for the older age groups the proportion in church is less than the general population, especially those in their twenties. They are almost entirely children of the immigrants who came in the 1960s. Has contemporary British culture made their church roots less strong? But even if it has, the numbers going reflect 13% of the black population in their twenties, a much higher proportion than for whites (6% in Table 37). How can other churches best learn from them how to retain and attract (Tables 35 and 36) people in their twenties, of both sexes? Why are they more successful?

Age group by churchmanship

The various proportions of churchgoers by age group and churchmanship (Low church, Liberal, Evangelical, Broad and so on) are given in Figure 18.

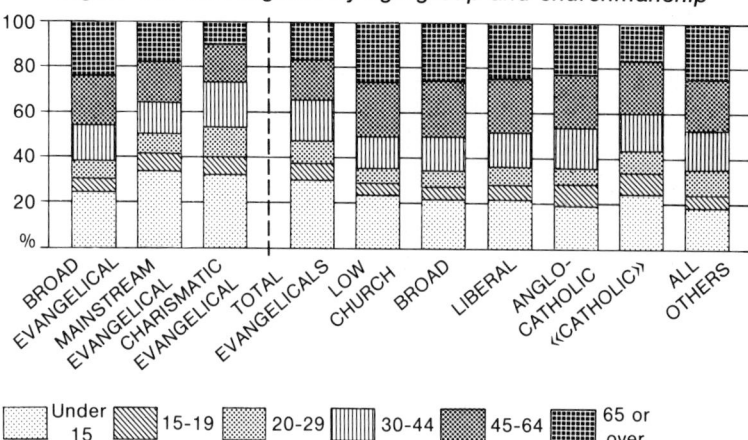

Figure 18: Churchgoers by age group and churchmanship

The Charismatic Evangelicals have the smallest proportion of elderly churchgoers (10%), followed next by those of «Catholic»* persuasion (used in a churchmanship not denominational sense) (17%). On the other hand the Mainstream and Charismatic Evangelicals have the highest percentage of children (33% and 32% respectively) but the Anglo-Catholics and Others the lowest (19% and 18% respectively). The Anglo-Catholics and «Catholics» have the highest proportion (9%) of teenagers, but the Charismatics come in again with 13% of those in their twenties, where the Low and Broad Church is weakest (7%). The Broad group has the highest proportion of those aged 45-64 (25%).

---

*The reason for using these special brackets is given on page 156.

Age group by region

Thus far we have considered the various age groups nationally. How much do they vary across the country? Table 39 gives details.

Table 39: Churchgoers by age and region

	Under 15	15-19	20-29	30-44	45-64	65 or over	Total (= 100%)	Average age in years
	%	%	%	%	%	%		
North	23	7	10	15	24	21	324,500	41
Yorks/Humberside	25	7	9	16	22	21	446,800	40
North West	26	7	9	16	23	19	818,300	39
East Midlands	26	7	8	16	22	21	346,000	40
West Midlands	24	7	9	16	23	21	536,500	40
East Anglia	25	7	8	16	22	22	235,500	40
South East (North)	27	8	10	18	20	17	464,600	37
South East (Greater London)	24	7	12	20	21	16	661,400	38
South East (South)	25	8	8	18	21	20	570,500	39
South West	24	8	8	15	22	23	524,300	41
NORTH[1]	25	7	9	16	23	20	2,421,200	40
SOUTH	25	8	10	18	21	19	2,507,200	39
Overall	25	7	10	17	22	19	4,928,400	39

[1] See Table 28 for definition

Churchgoers are slightly older in the North than the South (43% against 40% of over 45s) and conversely slightly younger in the South than in the North, but as the average figures indicate there is nothing much between them. There is however no population variation in age between North and South — in both 37% are over 45.

SUNDAY SCHOOL

We should be encouraged that 14% of the population of children under 15 attended church in 1989, a percentage unchanged since 1979, despite reducing numbers. How many of those attended Sunday School? The proportions of children going to Sunday School have been dropping ever since their peak in the 1880s of 19% of the *entire* population.[28] The Catholics and Orthodox do not have Sunday School in the same way as the Free Churches and Anglicans, so no figures are given for them. In 1989 64% of the children attending Anglican churches were in Sunday School, and 82% of the Free Churches, just 7% of the child population in

England. These had dropped from 71% and 87% respectively in the four years since 1985 when they represented 8% of the child population.

The variation of these figures across the country are given below. Sunday School details were not requested in 1979 so no comparisons are possible. Sunday School children may have spent some of their time in the full church service.

Table 40: Sunday School attendance by region 1989

	North	Yorks/ Humberside	North West	East Midlands	West Midlands
	%	%	%	%	%
Percentage of churchgoing children					
All Free Churches	84	81	84	83	84
Anglican	61	59	70	64	62
Total as percentage of child population					
1989	6	6	6	7	6
1985	6	7	7	8	7

	East Anglia	South East (North)	South East (Greater London)	South East (South)	South West	All England
	%	%	%	%	%	%
Percentage of churchgoing children						
All Free Churches	76	84	79	83	83	82
Anglican	61	64	67	65	62	64
Total as percentage of child population						
1989	8	7	5	8	9	7
1985	9	8	6	9	11	8

As a percentage of children going to church, the numbers attending Sunday School is remarkably consistent around the country. There are rather fewer in Free Churches in East Anglia and rather more in Anglican churches in the North West. The percentage they represent of the population has likewise uniformly dropped, but, apart from Greater London, Sunday School scholars represent a percentage point more of the child population in the South than the North.

The change in adult and child church attendance from 1979 to 1989 is as follows by denomination:

Table 41: Child and adult churchgoers

Denomination	1989 child church-goers	Percentage child Change 1979-89	Percentage in Sunday School	1989 adult church-goers	Percentage adult Change 1979-89
		%	%		%
Methodist	116,200	−33	86	396,100	−11
Baptist	71,500	−18	87	199,400	−2
URC	35,300	−31	81	114,000	−18
Independent	132,700	+43	78	292,800	+42
Afro-Caribbean	35,600	−13	77	68,500	+4
Pentecostal	37,400	+13	78	95,200	+8
Other Free	30,600	−29	84	83,000	−15
Total Free	459,300	−12	82	1,249,000	0
Anglican	348,000	−16	64	1,143,900	−9
Roman Catholic	411,300	−14	N/a	1,304,600	−14
Orthodox	2,900	−3	N/a	9,400	+34
Total	1,221,500	−14	N/a	3,706,900	−8

This table shows that in the two denominations where child attendance is increasing (Independents and Pentecostals), adult attendance is also on the rise. Where child attendance is decreasing, adult attendance is also falling, except for the Afro-Caribbeans and Orthodox which have adult increases but child decreases. These are related it would seem; though which is the chicken and which the egg? Do increasing numbers of children in a church cause their parents to be involved or, as seems more logical, do increasing numbers of adults automatically mean more children?

The two denominations with growing numbers of children have the *lowest* percentage in Sunday School among the Free Churches, with the Afro-Caribbeans one point lower. A similar result emerged from both the Welsh Census and the Scottish Census. Children's churchgoing seems to increase if children are not in Sunday School. Does this reflect the need, as Lord Young of Darlington, Director of the Institute of Community Studies commented, to 'bring social ageing and biological ageing more into line'?[29] Do children need to be regularly in the 'adult' church itself?

Monica Hill, Secretary of the British Church Growth Association, recently argued[30] that while Sunday Schools may have been replaced by Junior Church, Junior Church still suffers from the disadvantage that unchurched children will rarely come. The opportunity to touch, even marginally, those non-churchgoers who sent their children to Sunday School on a Sunday has gone and has not been replaced. The attractions of travel, sport, television and much else have replaced Sunday School. But if we are to reach our children — and many parents appreciate the value of religious education — we need to form new bridges.

APPLICATION

Our children

'The Picture's not all Black' is the heading of a chapter in a report by 'Tricia Blombery[31] where she tells the story of her 17-year-old son coming home from school and enthusiastically asking questions about the number of Christians in Australia. Why did he want to know? 'I was talking to Peter at lunch-time,' he said. 'There's a lot of you out there, isn't there?' Peter had challenged. Her son exclaimed, 'I wanted to tell him how many!'

'Our children are our greater riches,' said a delegate from China at an international conference.[32] 'Children are no longer the rebels of society. They are happy, well-informed people who are highly active and enjoying their leisure pursuits and social life to the full,' enthused Felicity Randolph of Young Direction, a specialist youth market research agency.[33]

That might be true for some. It clearly isn't true for all. 'I wanted to be loved. I wanted someone to care for me, and a place to stay'[34] would be echoed by many, and not just by a 17-year-old called Sybil. If our young people are tomorrow's church today, our greatest riches, then we need to put our resources to work in this greatest of harvest fields.

The map in Figure 19 highlights the drop in the percentage of child churchgoers between 1979 to 1989. The country's national figure was −1%, down from 26% of churchgoers in 1979 to 25% in 1989. Greater London and Tyne and Wear are the two urban areas which have decreased most, but the North (not far north) and the South East generally in 1989 saw a higher percentage of churchgoers as children than in 1979.

In the 1980s the churches in England have seen their children and teenagers diminish by over a third of a million. If that rate of decline continues for the next ten years we must seriously question the

104   'CHRISTIAN' ENGLAND

Figure 19: Change in percentage of child churchgoers 1979-1989

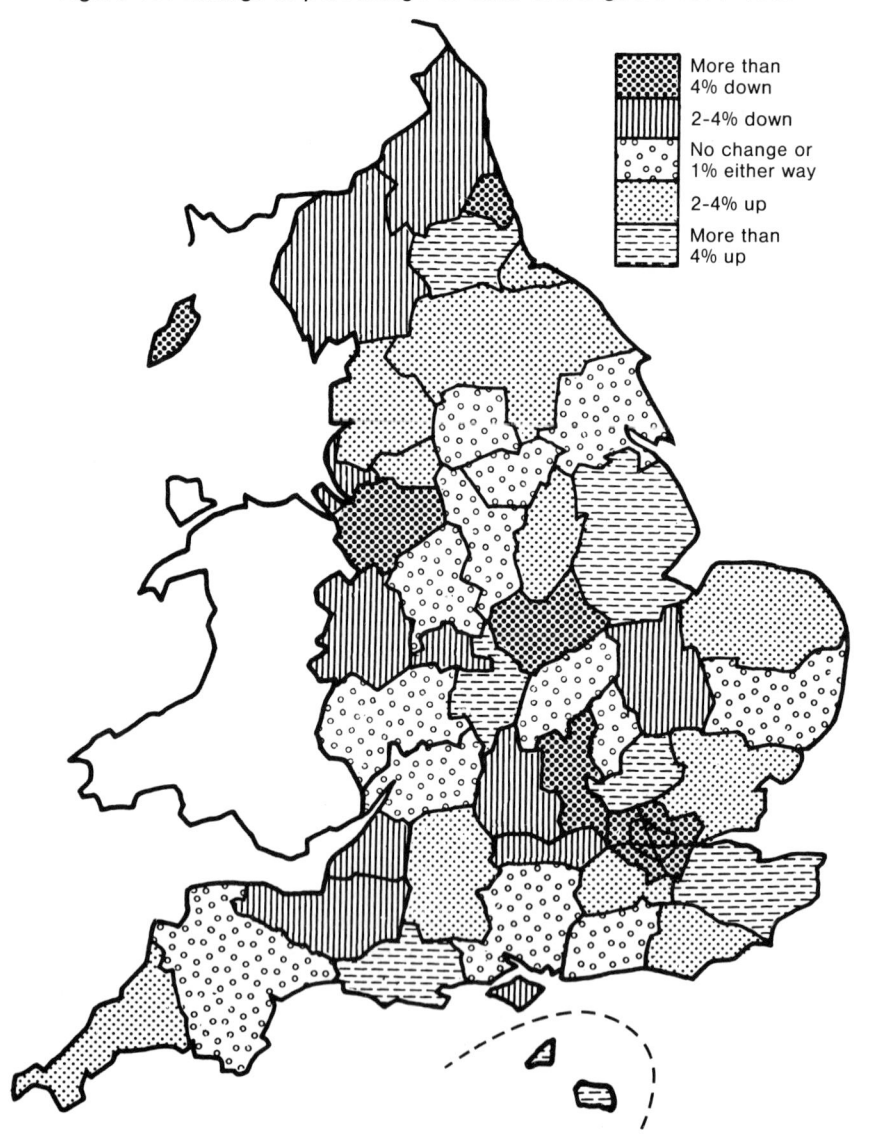

survival of the church in the decades ahead. The critical mass to generate momentum and growth will have diminished. The churches need to follow the Regular Army in their MARILYN Project (*M*anning *A*nd *R*ecruitment *I*n the *L*ean *Y*ears of the *N*ineties).[35]

'Now is the day of salvation' we often quote. Yes, and now is the day for action, vision, commitment and concern. Children might be tomorrow's church but they are today's church too.

The Church of England's report on children[36] is not just for Synod to debate. It affects us all. We face a very serious situation. Ask:

- What children and teenagers are you in touch with now?
- How many could you be in touch with?
- What actions have to be taken to reach them?
- What resources do you need?
- What action will you take today to begin to develop those resources?

As the famous Salvation Army poster campaign said, 'For God's sake care' — and care today.

Chapter 4: Summary

- The proportion of men in church was 42% in 1989 against a population figure of 49%.
- The male proportion has fallen from 45% in 1979.
- The church has seen a drop of 513,000 people between 1979 and 1989, equivalent to losing 1,000 people every week.
- Two-fifths of this drop are children under 15, partly because of the low birth rate in the early 1980s.
- 30% of the drop was among older teenagers.
- Women over 45 years in church increased between 1979 and 1989.
- Only the Independents, Pentecostals and Orthodox gained people, both men and women.
- The new generation has different values, standards and interests from their parents'.
- 82% of Free Church children and 64% of Anglican children were in Sunday School in 1989.

5. WHICH SOIL IS THE BEST?

Unlike the 1979 Census, the 1989 Census asked those completing the form to indicate in which one of eight types of area, or environment, their church or congregation was situated. The choices were:

- City Centre (which often means a church attracting people in from further afield).
- Inner City (the areas around the heart of our major cities where the middle class tend not to live).
- Council Estate.
- Suburban/Urban Fringe (again mostly near our major cities).
- Separate Towns (including seaside resorts and new towns).
- Other built-up areas (not covered by any other classification, and often mixed urban rural).
- Rural Area: Commuter or dormitory areas.
- Rural Area: other types.

This is not an exhaustive classification nor the one used by Local or Central Government. It is possible today, through the linkages between population census and areal information, to assign one of thirty or forty environment types by analysis of address via the postcode. This possibility was not pursued partly because it is expensive, and partly because some ministers' homes (the addresses we mainly had) are not close to their churches, and are sometimes in a different type of area. Asking the minister to code on the basis of a brief description clearly has disadvantages in possible lack of consistency (two ministers working in the same area might code their church differently), lack of clarity (is a commuter village a separate town or not?), and lack of conformity (data external to the Census cannot be readily reconciled with the Census information). Much thought and discussion went into the matter, and those answering the two pilot projects seemed happy enough with the above choices. So, for better or for worse, we kept them as given.

OVERALL RESULTS

The results are given in the next table. The different categories show the variation in each environment. For example, in column two, whilst 7% of churches or congregations are in inner city areas, 9% of all children go to church in these areas, 10% of all churchgoing adults, and 12% of all church members. Thus the population of people associated with inner city churches is higher than might be thought just by looking at the percentage of church buildings or congregations there. The complete reverse is the case in the two rural categories.

Table 42: Churches/congregations, child and adult churchgoers, and church members by environment 1989

	City centre	Inner city	Council estate	Sub-urban/urban fringe	Separate town	Other built-up area	Rural: comm/dorm	Rural: other	Total (= 100%)
Churches	% 4	% 7	% 6	% 22	% 12	% 4	% 16	% 29	38,607
Child churchgoers	4	9	8	36	15	5	13	10	1,221,500
Adult churchgoers	5	10	8	34	16	5	11	11	3,706,900
Members	5	12	9	36	16	4	10	8	7,162,400

Three churches in ten (29%) are in the remoter rural non-commuter areas, and just over a fifth (22%) are in the suburban and urban areas around our cities, together over half of all churches.

People mostly did not cluster in the same proportions as the churches. Over a third of all adult churchgoers (34%) and marginally more children and members were in the suburban/urban fringe. A further sixth (16%) were in separate towns, the two areas accounting for half the churchgoers between them. The major differences between church and adult churchgoer numbers were in these two categories, plus the commuter and remoter rural areas well provided for in churches but not in people.

Differences between the three types of people (children, adult churchgoers and members) in Table 42 were slight. There were rather more church members than church children in the inner city, and rather more children than members in the two rural areas. Because of the similarity, after the next two tables we concentrate only on the adult attenders. These are compared with churches from Table 42 and are illustrated in Figure 20.

Figure 20: Churches and adult churchgoers by environment

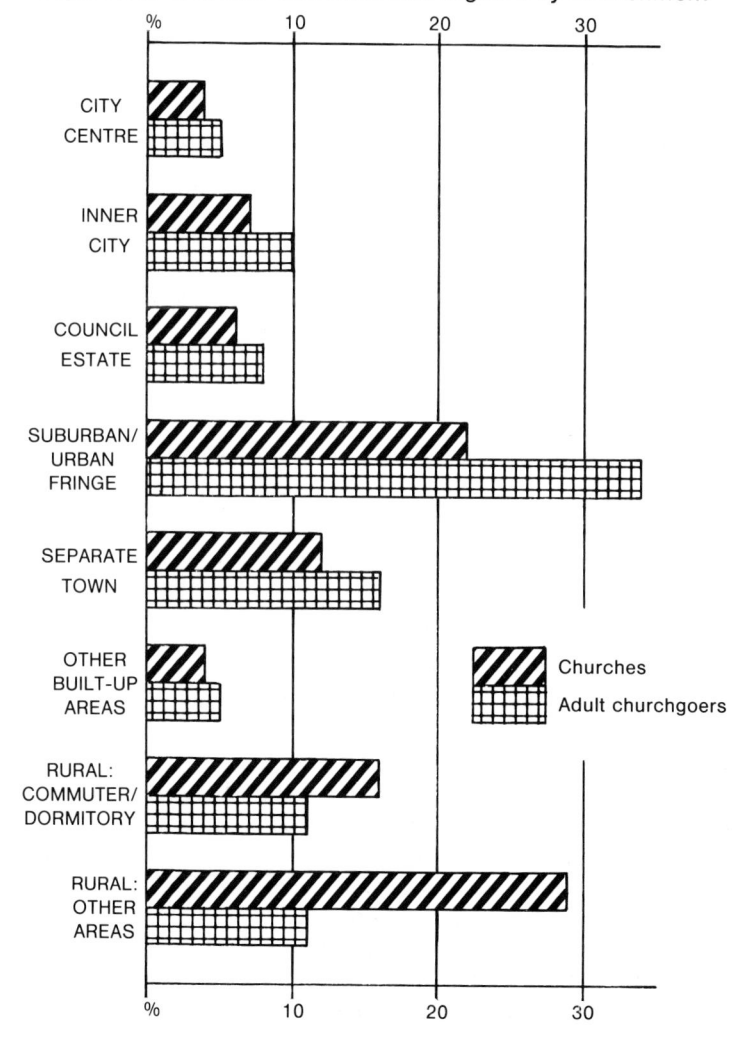

The effect of these variations may be seen in the average numbers associated with each environment type, as follows.

Table 43: Child and adult churchgoers and church members per church by environment 1989

	City centre	Inner city	Council estate	Sub-urban/ urban fringe	Sepa-rate town	Other built-up area	Rural: comm/ dorm	Rural: other	Overall
Child churchgoers	32	41	42	52	40	40	26	11	32
Adult churchgoers	120	137	128	148	128	120	66	36	96
Members	232	318	278	304	247	186	116	51	186

For many Free Church or Anglican readers these figures will look exceptionally high while for many Roman Catholic readers they will look low. These are average figures across all the denominations and with the average Catholic Church attendance at 340 but Free Church and Anglican at 68 and 70 respectively, the average becomes a bit of a no-man's land. We shall look at the differences by denomination shortly. Meanwhile note the effect of so many rural and very small churches. These figures are all tiny, making the others seem large by comparison.

It is the suburbs which have the largest churches (on all three counts, except membership where the inner city figure is slightly higher). Children are roughly one third of adults except in the city centre (only a quarter) indicating the student numbers in many of these congregations (that is, single people mostly without children). Membership is roughly double the number of attenders, but is larger in the inner city and council estate areas (people wish to be associated with their local church but are not always willing or able to go). Membership is smaller proportionately in other built-up areas and the rural areas.

Information on people was collected for 1985 and 1989 so it is possible to say where these figures are growing. The figures in the following table represent the percentage change from 1985 to 1989. In the city centre 200,300 adults were attending church in 1989, where in 1985 there had been 211,600. 200,300 is 5% less than

Table 44: Change in child and adult churchgoers and church members by environment 1985-1989

	City centre	Inner city	Council estate	Sub-urban/ urban fringe	Separate town	Other built-up area	Rural: comm/ dorm	Rural: other	Overall
	%	%	%	%	%	%	%	%	%
Child churchgoers	−7	0	−3	−5	−5	+1	−5	−8	−8
Adult churchgoers	−5	−3	−1	−2	+2	−1	−1	−1	−1
Members	−1	0	+1	+3	+3	+4	0	−3	+1

211,600, which is what the −5% at the beginning of the adult attenders line represents. The actual numbers appear in *Prospects for the Nineties.*[1]

The only environment in which child attendance is growing is the other built-up areas. The numbers are level pegging in the inner city. The numbers are especially declining in the two extremes — the city centre and the remoter rural areas. In both cases children will need transport and so have to be accompanied.

Adult attenders are growing in the separate towns, which the Independent Churches (especially the House Church Movement) have frequently targeted for starting new churches. The growth here reflects the success of that activity. Adult numbers are dropping in the city centres and inner city areas, partly because it is more convenient to go to a local church than to spend time and money travelling.

Membership is declining only in two areas — city centre and remoter rural areas. Commitment here is scarce, and has worrying implications for those with churches in this type of area. Membership is especially growing in the suburban/urban fringe, separate towns, and other built-up areas.

ENVIRONMENT BY DENOMINATION

How were the various denominations represented in the different environments? Table 45 gives the percentage of churches in each type of area. If a denomination's adult attendance was significantly growing or declining in 1989 a plus (+) or minus (−) sign respectively follows the percentage figure.

Table 45: Churches/congregations by environment and denomination 1989

	City centre	Inner city	Council estate	Sub-urban/ urban fringe	Separate town	Other built-up area	Rural: comm/ dorm	Rural: other	Total (= 100%)
	%	%	%	%	%	%	%	%	
Methodist	2	5	5	21	11	5	13	38	6,740
Baptist	3+	8	6+	29	16	5+	14	19	2,339
URC	3+	7	4+	33	20	5+	12	16−	1,681
Independent	4+	8−	8	30+	18	6	11	15	4,123
Afro-Caribbean	7	50−	14+	14+	7−	6	1+	1+	949
Pentecostal	3−	13+	13	25	25	7+	6	8+	1,002
Other Free	3	10	9	29	24+	5−	7−	13+	1,462
Total Free	3+	8−	6+	26	15	5+	12	25	18,296
Anglican	6−	6	5	18	7−	3+	20	35	16,373
Roman Catholic	4−	10	13	27	18+	4−	11	13	3,824
Orthodox	9−	20	3	29	18+	6	12	3	114
Total	4	7	6	22	12	4	16	29	38,607

Anglicans and Methodists especially have a large number of rural churches — more than a third of all Anglican Churches are in the remoter rural areas, as are an even higher percentage of Methodists. Both denominations have more than half their churches in all types of rural area (51% Methodists, 55% Anglicans).

At the same time the Anglicans have a relatively high proportion of city centre churches, as do the Orthodox and Afro-Caribbeans. Half the Afro-Caribbean Churches are in the inner city, the Orthodox have 20%, the Pentecostal 13%, and Roman Catholics and Other Free Churches 10%. The Catholics, Afro-Caribbeans and Pentecostals are strong on council estates.

The Anglicans are weaker in the suburban areas. Earlier we saw that they are also weak in the urban counties. It is in suburban areas rather than the city centres where they have relatively few churches (but still nearly 3,000).

Independent Churches are strongest numerically in the suburbs followed by the Baptists and Other Free Churches. The URC, Pentecostal and Other Free Churches have the highest percentages of churches in separate towns.

WHICH SOIL IS THE BEST? 113

These figures are shown the other way round in the illustration below, that is, how many of what type are in each environment? The size of the circle represents the proportionate number in that category.

Figure 21: Major churches in each environment

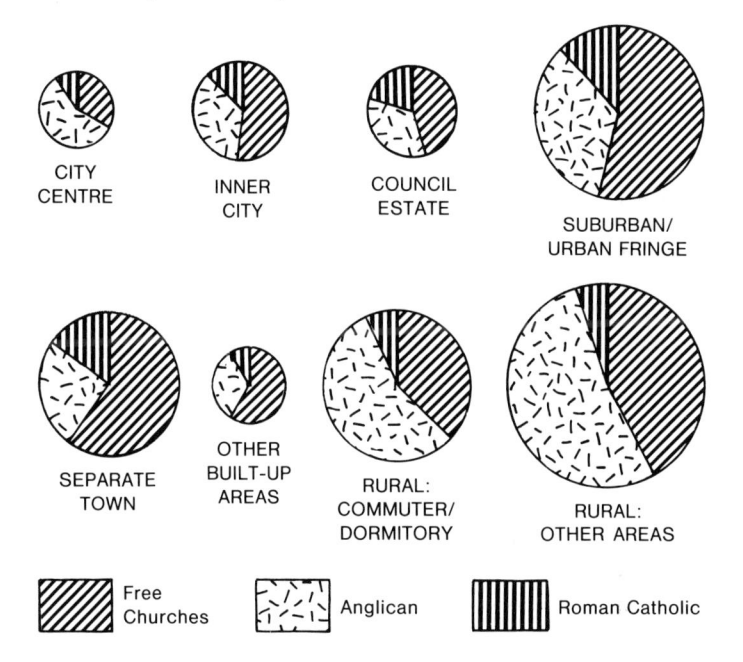

CITY CENTRE

INNER CITY

COUNCIL ESTATE

SUBURBAN/ URBAN FRINGE

SEPARATE TOWN

OTHER BUILT-UP AREAS

RURAL: COMMUTER/ DORMITORY

RURAL: OTHER AREAS

Free Churches   Anglican   Roman Catholic

The Free Churches dominate in the inner city (because of the Afro-Caribbeans and Pentecostals), the suburban/urban fringe (because of the Independents, the Baptists and Other Free Churches), separate towns, and other built-up areas. The Anglicans dominate in the city centre and the two rural areas. The Roman Catholics are strongest proportionately on council estates.

How does the number of the adult churchgoers vary in these environments? Table 46 gives these figures:

The Free Churches have lower than average attendances on council estates and in the rural areas, and much higher numbers in the city centres and elsewhere. The Anglicans have their largest

Table 46: Adult churchgoers per church by major groups and by environment 1989

	City centre	Inner city	Council estate	Sub-urban/ urban fringe	Separate town	Other built-up area	Rural: comm/ dorm	Rural: other	Overall
Free Church	102	92	60	89	92	76	54	28	68
Anglican	90	84	71	118	117	91	60	34	70
Roman Catholic	359	395	350	478	294	349	205	179	341
Orthodox	88	158	29	79	68	29	29	58	82
Overall	120	137	128	148	128	120	66	36	96

congregations in the suburbs/urban fringes and the separate towns. The Roman Catholics are also most plentiful in the suburbs, but draw good numbers in the inner city areas too. This is where they are particularly strong, as are the Orthodox.

Table 47: Churches/congregations by environment and churchmanship 1989

	City centre	Inner city	Council estate	Sub-urban/ urban fringe	Separate town	Other built-up area	Rural: comm/ dorm	Rural: other	Total (= 100%)
	%	%	%	%	%	%	%	%	
Broad Evangelical	4	5	5	23	13	4	16	30	4,190
Mainstream Evangelical	5	9	9	27	15	5	11	19	4,344
Charismatic Evangelical	4	12	10	28	18	6	12	10	5,107
Total Evangelical	4	9	8	26	15	5	13	20	13,641
Low Church	3	4	4	15	6	4	18	46	4,441
Broad	3	2	3	15	8	3	21	45	6,056
Liberal	4	6	5	27	12	4	19	23	5,258
Anglo-Catholic	5	10	7	21	9	4	18	26	2,050
«Catholic»	4	7	9	23	14	4	16	23	6,205
All Others	3	8	5	16	8	3	19	38	956
Total	4	7	6	22	12	4	16	29	38,607

ENVIRONMENT BY CHURCHMANSHIP

The term 'Churchmanship' is explained in the chapter on belief. But it is more logical to examine the variations of churchmanship here. Table 47 on page 114 gives details and helps to highlight the particular strengths of each.

The variations by churchmanship in strength in the different environments are much less significant than by denomination. The Low church and Broad groups are weak in the suburbs but strong in the remoter rural areas. The Anglo-Catholics and Charismatic Evangelicals are specially strong in the inner city compared with others. The evangelicals as a whole are relatively strong in the separate towns and weaker in the remoter rural areas. Liberals are strongest in the suburbs, the «Catholics» on the council estates. The four environments with most variations are illustrated below, with the circle size reflecting churchgoing numbers in each environment.

Figure 22: Churchmanship in major environments

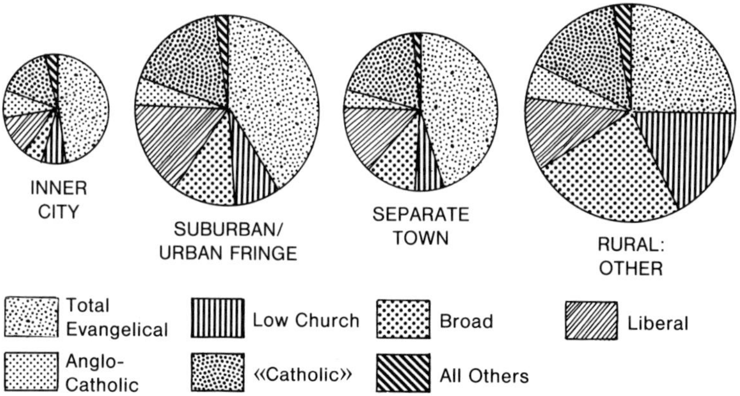

Evangelicals are poorly represented in rural areas, but Broad churches and Low churches are very prominent in the remoter rural parts.

DIFFERENT ENVIRONMENTS

There is increasing concern for the environment, partly stimulated by the New Age Movement. Christians need to rethink their theology and ecology. When Paul writes that all creation is groaning in bondage to decay what implications does that have for the way we live now? That theology should include perspectives on rural concerns.

The Rural Church

Are our rural areas dying? Some think so. Many farmers are leaving the outlying areas, and fewer sheep dot the hills and valleys. 'A way of life that has bridged generations is under threat,' concluded one newspaper report.[2] 'The local school has closed, the post office has gone, and the two village shops went out of business,' said a farmer's wife of Keld in the Yorkshire Dales. What drives people away? Partly it is hardship. Partly it is alternative ways of earning a living — grouse shooting is more lucrative than sheep farming. Partly it is the attraction of the city and few children in these areas wish to follow their parents.

There is *much implicit religion* in the rural areas. The key question is how to use that latent interest and fan the fire into a glowing hearth attractive to all? That is the crucial challenge for the rural church.

The location of the church building is not always ideal. The mark of the Black Death in rural life seven centuries ago still survives. For instance, in Oakley, North Suffolk, the church today is in the middle of cornfields. The village did surround it once, but when the plague came and killed so many, the survivors rebuilt the village a mile away. The church was not affected so they left it where it was. Oakley is typical of many hundreds of others.

There is also the extraordinarily high *expectation of the minister.* People expect them to visit, to be available for counsel, to take regular services, to participate in all the local activities. So the question becomes one of priority; what are the most vital things the minister should do this year? this month? *today?*

Multiple churches are common. Many villages share a minister. In East Anglia the average is four.[3] In Gloucestershire ministers have formed a special 'club' called the 'Four plus', open to those clergy looking after at least four churches.

What hope then for the rural church? People may question whether they should still be kept open. The answer must be 'yes', because they offer the chance of *building a committed community*. The proportion of people in a village who come to church is often high, even if the actual numbers are small because the population is low.

Some ideas for growth

● *Each church with a service each week.* Rt Rev Peter Nott, Bishop of Norwich, in his strategy for his Diocese,[4] would like to see each village church with a Sunday service at the same time every week, led where necessary by trained lay people. Regularity of worship can lead to commitment and vision.

● *Communities need a catalyst.* This might well be the local minister, but not always. It could be a local Christian family keen to share their faith and take the initiative. The rural areas have people, but they do not always have leadership and verve. Start something and others will gather around. But that person needs to be a local person, preferably living in the community itself.

● *Different thinking may help.* In the little village of Blackstone, Essex, where Martin Sellix is vicar, a new service has been started. It only lasts for an hour, is recognisably Anglican but non-traditional and uses new songs, an overhead projector, and is, above all designed to be relevant. After four years, it now attracts a larger congregation at 11.00 am than the traditional Matins at 9.30 am.

● Barry Osborne, of Rural Sunrise, stresses *the importance of change management,*[5] and offers consultancy and training which will help. That may mean using unlikely people, working in alternative modes (lay not clergy), and, above all, being contemporary.

Urban advance

Much has been written on urban evangelism and its needs. The *Faith in the City* report highlighted the plight of many inner city areas. Christian urbanologists like Ray Bakke[6] and Harvie Conn have given much wisdom for ministry. Colin Marchant's excellent book *Signs in the City*[7] contains two moving poems which sum up city life and Christian aspiration. The first is by Jane Galbraith, living in a 'hard-to-let' old flat in Camberwell, South London, and the first three verses are:

> Lord of our city, we bring you its pain,
> The muggings, the dole queues, the lifts bust again.
> The fear of each stranger and nowhere to play,
> The waiting for buses at the start of the day.
>
> The Lord of the homeless we bring you their cry.
> The waiting on promises — pie in the sky —
> The red tape and questions and sent on their way,
> The sense of frustration at the noon of the day.
>
> Lord of all races, all colours of skin,
> Please make us fight racism, help us begin
> To see how our prejudice colours the way
> We treat friends and neighbours at the end of the day.

The second, written by Kathryn Hansford from Plaistow, East London, includes the lines:

> What reality can I present
> In this world of pretence?
> I can offer only myself
> And the Jesus who is within me —
> No outward miracle will change the city
> But the inward miracle
> Which God can work in a man's heart.
> For this miracle the heart
> Of the city yearns
> For it is the heart which is corrupt.

The city is all about the people who live there. Marjorie Idle's[8] description of the work in Limehouse, where her husband was Vicar for many years, underlines their potential.

Faith in the City identified three key ways of looking at Urban Priority Areas: via poverty which is at the root of powerlessness; via the increasing inequality in our society; and via polarisation which separates suburban from inner city and privileged from deprived.[9] The difference in the ratio of clergy to population between (Anglican) urban area dioceses and others is illustrated in the following diagram.[10]

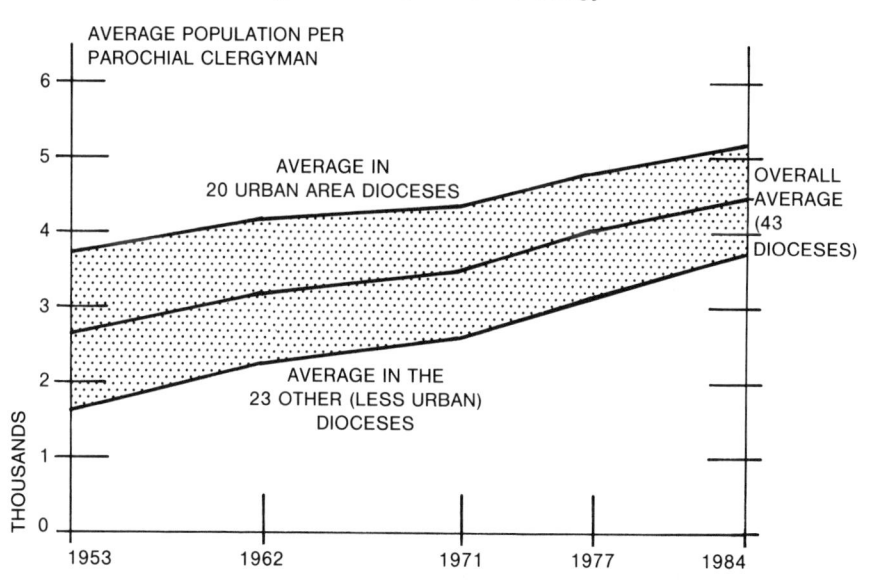

Figure 23: Population to Clergy

Clergy training for such areas 'has not been simply inappropriate, but in many ways has positively unfitted them for the inner urban ministry to which they find themselves committed'.[11] No wonder burnout or clergy exhaustion is so much greater in these areas than elsewhere, especially among the younger, particularly young married, clergy. These are the areas where migration loss is high,[12] but where commitment by church members (financially and in other ways) is also high.[13]

Is there any hope? Yes! Colin Marchant highlights the following:[14]

- Continuing, and strategically placed, strength of Roman Catholicism.
- Lively, strongly rooted fellowship despite retrenchment in many Free and Anglican Churches.
- New congregations constantly emerging.
- Attitude changes within churches as team ministries operate.
- Indigenous commitment with young couples wanting to stay.
- Appreciation of different theologies.
- Wider concern as national groups realise the need.

Rt Rev David Sheppard, Bishop of Liverpool, whose books on the city[15,16] have made much impact, would agree with these. Ultimately he focuses on people and their interaction with each other. 'The kingdom of right relationships challenges people to believe that they can bring about changes in community and in industry. Then people can be people, families can be families, neighbours can be neighbours and workers can be workers. We must hold on to the dream that it is possible for a place to be built as a city, and to know in the thick of its life right relationship between men and with God.'[17]

Likewise Greg Smith, and others in the Evangelical Coalition for Urban Ministry, say that 'some of the distinctives of inner city churches are likely to be a high level of commitment as opposed to spectator religion on Sundays, a preferential option for the poor expressed in down to earth social and political involvement, strong supportive communities with plural charismatic leadership, and lively and flexible worship adapted to local cultural forms'.[18]

Separate Towns

There are perhaps two thousand towns in England with a population of under 10,000 people.[19] Many of these will have at least one Free Church as well as at least one Anglican Church. Sometimes these churches become protective because few new members join and they want to keep the ones they have already got. A minister comes, continues, and then goes. It takes commitment to stay in a tough place. 'I've done everything I know how to in my district,' said one minister, 'and nothing has come of it. Maybe I should leave the ministry.' Guilt doesn't just de-motivate — it destroys. So what do you do? The Seventh-Day Adventist author of the article who listened to that minister suggested:[20]

- Making a long-term plan and sticking to it.
- Taking time for yourself (which includes relaxation and time off).
- Making something happen, and then enjoying your success.
- Widening your field of mission.
- Finding some close friends to whom you can reveal yourself as a real person needing others. Non-church acquaintances are not just objects for evangelism.
- Matching the needs to your strengths; one person cannot do everything.
- Remembering you are in your church/situation because the Lord wants you there.

ENVIRONMENT BY REGION

If we now return to the Census analysis in the light of these brief descriptions of hopes and needs in these areas, what are the overall strengths or weaknesses by region? We would naturally expect the proportions of churches in different environments to vary by region, and the actual details are given in Table 48.

There are proportionately more city centre churches in East Anglia (which includes Cambridge) than elsewhere. Inner city churches are especially numerous in the West Midlands (with Birmingham) and Greater London. One church in ten in the North of England is on a council estate, but only one in thirty in the South. There are half as many more churches in the suburbs in the North as in the South (5,100 against 3,300), which is perhaps surprising. On the other hand churches in separate towns and seaside resorts are stronger in the South.

The West Midlands and Greater London are two regions dominated by their urban life; there are naturally hardly any rural churches in either. Elsewhere, however, on average almost one church in two is a rural church. They are more numerous in the South than the North (56% against 32%) partly because of their high dominance in East Anglia (67%) and the South West (58%).

The proportion of churches or congregations in a particular county does not necessarily match the proportion of church people

Table 48: Churches/congregations by environment and region 1989

	City centre	Inner city	Council estate	Sub-urban/ urban fringe	Sepa-rate town	Other built-up area	Rural: comm/ dorm	Rural: other	Total (= 100%)
	%	%	%	%	%	%	%	%	
North	2	7	10	18	14	5	10	34	2,550
Yorks/ Humberside	3	7	8	25	10	4	15	28	3,827
North West	4	9	10	35	11	7	12	12	4,039
East Midlands	4	4	7	15	12	3	18	37	3,911
West Midlands	3	21	14	44	4	10	3	1	3,868
East Anglia	8	1	3	9	10	2	19	48	2,769
South East (North)	4	1	5	19	16	4	30	21	3,943
South East (Gt London)	5	35	8	47	1	3	1	0	3,549
South East (South)	5	2	5	20	18	5	22	23	4,297
South West	5	4	3	14	13	3	13	45	5,854
NORTH[1]	3	10	10	29	10	6	11	21	17,602
SOUTH	5	4	3	16	14	2	20	36	21,005
Overall	4	7	6	22	12	4	16	29	38,607

[1] See Table 28 for definition

there. Four maps at the back of the book show the variations in strength of those going to church in an urban setting (defined in Map 43 as the total of those going to city centre, inner city, council estate and suburban/urban fringe churches); in a rural setting (defined in Map 44 as the total of the two rural environments used), and how these strengths are changing (Maps 45 and 46). Did the number of churchgoers in these environments grow over the four years 1985-1989, decline or remain static?

Urban churchgoers (Map 43) are significant proportions of all churchgoers (between half and just over three-quarters) not only in metropolitan counties such as Tyne and Wear, Cleveland, South Yorkshire and West Yorkshire, but also Leicestershire, Nottinghamshire, Staffordshire in the Midlands, Gloucestershire and Avon (which includes the cities of Bristol and Bath) towards the South and West, and Berkshire and Hampshire in the South. Many of these counties include important cathedral cities or large towns, no longer truly separate as the suburban fringe has extended and grown.

Understandably, there are fewer urban churchgoers in rural areas, but by comparison of Maps 43 and 44, which show the relative strength of urban and rural churchgoing, will demonstrate how many counties today are significant mixtures of both. This means that outreach or products geared to urban environments might have greater relevance and use than the immediate type of area for which they are planned.

The number of urban churchgoers is growing in only a few places. In the eight counties in Map 45 where numbers increased by at least 5% between 1985 and 1989, six are normally thought of as rural counties, and have fewer than half their adults in church on a Sunday in an urban setting. The two truly urban areas where numbers are significantly growing are Inner London — Northeast and Southeast. That growth is almost entirely due to two groups — the Independent and Afro-Caribbean Churches. It is the House Church Movement within the Independent sector that is dominant in the Southeast, through the activities of the Ichthus Fellowship which has closely identified with the social needs of the area. The numbers of urban churchgoers are declining sharply in the South West, South Midlands and outer South East North (except Oxfordshire) and in the Northern counties of Durham, Tyne and Wear, and North and West Yorkshire. This means they are declining where they are sometimes strong. In some counties could this suggest a switch of allegiance by churchgoers since mobility today is so easy, and parking in the town or city is often difficult?

Rural churchgoers (Map 44) are in a majority in only three counties — Cornwall, Lincolnshire and Somerset. They also constitute 53% of churchgoers on the Isle of Man and 62% in the Channel Islands. But they have large numbers in East Anglia, Buckinghamshire, West Sussex, Oxfordshire and Wiltshire in the South East, Hereford and Worcester, and Shropshire in West and North Yorkshire and Northumberland in the North.

Numbers of rural churchgoers are growing (Map 46) in three truly rural counties (Buckinghamshire, Lincolnshire, West Sussex) and the Isle of Man where they are strong. In all three counties the fastest growing groups are the Independent Churches and Pentecostals. It is the same phenomenon giving the increased numbers, with the House Churches again the dominant force in the Independent sector. The Anglicans have also seen growth in Buckinghamshire and Lincolnshire.

Numbers of rural churchgoers are also growing in four other counties (Cambridgeshire, Devon, Durham, Humberside) where there is a mixture of urban and rural environments, but other denominations are involved here as well. In Durham, the Baptists, URC and Other Free Churches have all achieved some growth, as have the Independents and Pentecostals. In Humberside the Baptists and Catholics saw some growth over the four years 1985-1989. In Cambridgeshire the Baptists, URC, Afro-Caribbeans, Anglicans and Catholics have also grown. In Devon it is additionally just the URC.

Rural churches are declining in areas where they are also strong (as well as where they are weak). Hereford and Worcester, Norfolk, Northumberland, Suffolk and Wiltshire are attracting fewer rural churchgoers. In Norfolk and Northumberland urban numbers are increasing: could the reverse be happening — rural people be travelling into the towns and cities to go to church?

APPLICATION

So what? Some action points

What are we to make of all this maze of detail? Can we find our way out?

● Ask yourself what kind of environment your church is in, and are your supporters, your students, the people among whom you minister mostly in the same environment?

● Are your people homogeneous, or are they mixed, as so many groups are?

● What are the relative proportions in the different areas? Roughly what percentage are in city centres, inner city areas, council estates, suburban/urban fringes, separate towns, other built-up areas, commuter dormitory rural areas, or remoter rural areas? The percentages are meant to add up to 100%. Which are your dominant groups?

● How are the numbers in each environment, and especially your dominant groups changing?

- Compare your results with those outlined in this chapter, or with more detailed figures in *Prospects for the Nineties* or its associated regional volumes.

- If your people are growing in number and from the information given here you know other Christian groups are too, can you get together with those with like experience? What can you learn together? How best can you build on your strengths and go further? How can you share your development best with others who need your help because their experience is different?

- If your members are declining, to whom can you turn to find help with experience the reverse of yours? When can you visit them to learn from them? Is it worth organising a seminar or workshop to learn together with others? Be willing to cross boundaries. You don't just need to go to those of your own churchmanship or denomination.

- Remember action is imperative! That great missionary statesman John Mott, said, 'The end of the planning is the beginning of doing.' Dietrich Bonhoeffer wrote, 'The response of disciples is an act of obedience, not a confession of faith in Jesus'.[21]

Chapter 5: Summary

- Almost a third of the churches in England are in the remoter rural areas, and a quarter in the suburban/urban fringe areas.
- However, only one person in nine goes to church in the remoter rural areas and a third attend in the suburbs.
- Adult attendance is increasing in separate towns.
- Adult attendance is decreasing fastest in the city centres and inner city areas.
- Churches are growing in counties of high population density.
- Resource needs in both the urban and rural areas are high.

6. GROWTH, DECLINE AND STATICNESS

What encourages churches to grow? 'Faith,' said Alan Howe, Vicar of St Mary's, Camberley, Surrey. 'That is our business and it has struck a rich vein of support here.' Canon Harry Wilson, Vicar of St Peter's, in nearby Yately said, 'providing a spiritual need in a material age.' Church people brought their friends to the church and 'they stayed on because we are promoting the family unit'.[1] Families, faith and friends — the key components towards a Christian England?

Bill Hybels, minister of the 12,000 strong Willow Creek Church in Chicago would agree with these three elements. He majors especially on the third — friendship — in his seven steps for growth in his church. The first of these steps urges every member to be a bridge-builder, a friend to a neighbour or other non-churchgoer, perhaps belonging to some organisation to make friends with outsiders to whom they can eventually share their faith. Peter Kaldor, a key Australian researcher, defines bridge building in this way: 'Christians willing to live out and communicate their faith to those around. People who are prepared to do this in a committed way, to come alongside others from perhaps very different cultural backgrounds, to share and to learn. They will need to be risk-takers, often finding themselves in isolated territory, depending on God's Spirit for strength and guidance.'[2]

If that is what is needed, how is it working? Did churches grow in England in the last four years of the 1980s? If so, where? What constitutes church growth anyway?

For purposes of the English Church Census, church growth was defined purely numerically, as an increase in adult attendance. Other measurements of growth could have been used, such as decreasing average age, decreasing average length of membership, or expanding geographical base,[3] or a deepening sense of maturity, a greater faith, improved mid-week meeting attendance, but for simplicity, convenience and continuity with earlier studies, change in adult attendance was taken. Such results do not tell the whole story, but they do tell an important part of it and can lead to conclusions and strategies for increasing advance.

The definition was used as follows: A church with a congregation of 50 or more on a Sunday in 1989 which had grown by 20% or more over the previous four years (average 5% a year) was counted as growing. When the 1989 congregation was less than 50 a 100% increase over the four years was required (because with small congregations, one new person is a significant percentage change). Likewise a church with a drop in congregation of similar proportions over four years was defined as a declining church. All churches between these two extremes were regarded as static. The same definition was used in 1979 (except that declining churches were not counted), in 1982 for the Welsh Census and in 1984 for the Scottish Census. Ian Shaw, of Eccles College, Salford, wrote, 'It is as good a definition as any.'[4]

OVERALL GROWTH

On this basis 25% of English Churches grew between 1985 and 1989. This compares with 18% which grew in England 1975-1979, 10% in Wales 1978-1982,[5] and 26% in Scotland 1980-1984.[6] Declining churches accounted for only 8% of all English Churches (against

Figure 24: Overall change 1985-1989 in English churches

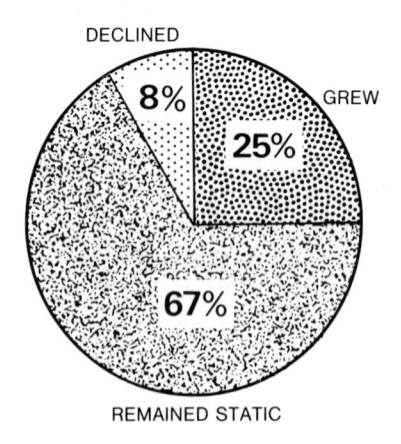

22% in Scotland earlier) and static churches therefore were the remaining 67% in England (against 52% in Scotland).

Note this is a count of *churches* not attenders, although of course the numbers are based on the number in each church. Regrettably, it does not follow that 25% of churches growing means 25% of growth in the congregations. In fact there are 25% growing churches against a net decrease of 1% in people. Imagine a hundred swimming pools, all different sizes, each fed by its own water supply, and each with its own drain. The volume of water may well increase in 25 and decline in eight, but the overall total volume of water varies little because 67 pools do not change at all. The water lost in the eight could exceed the gains in the 25. Applied to the church, this represents an overall loss due to a decline in bigger 'pools' and growth in smaller 'pools'. 11% of all Roman Catholic Churches declined and these are generally much larger churches. 28% of Anglican Churches grew but these churches are on average one-fifth the size of the average Roman Catholic Church.

The figures also mean that the overall 'volume of water' hardly changed. It suggests that many churches are not moving at all — happy and content to be as they already are, doubtless providing for their fellowship or congregation well, but not dynamically moving. A picture of a herd of cows sitting on the grass quietly chewing the cud. Do they need to be prodded and moved?

GROWTH BY REGION

My colleague, David Longley, Director of Communications at MARC Europe, emerged very excited from a session on the computer, 'Two-thirds of the churches in Tunbridge Wells are growing,' he said. Great news! The percentage of growing churches certainly varies across the country, as Figure 25 indicates.

A larger than average proportion of growing churches are to be found in the South East generally, in Outer London and Inner London Southeast, Kent and East Sussex especially, and in the West Midlands particularly. Parts of the North West (Lancashire and Cheshire), the Isle of Man, Nottinghamshire, Northamptonshire and Cambridgeshire are the other places where many experience growth. Actual figures for the regions are in Table 49.

130 'CHRISTIAN' ENGLAND

Figure 25: Percentage of growing churches 1985-1989

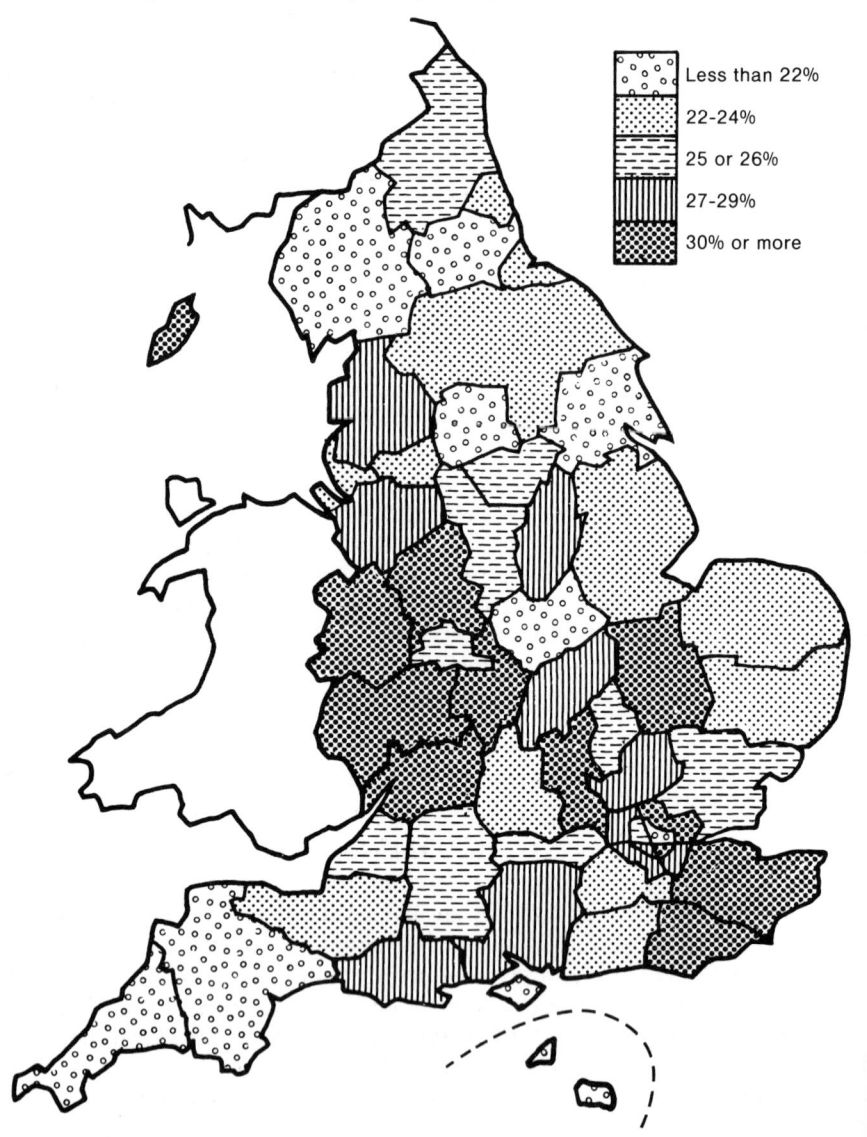

Table 49: Percentage of churches/congregations where adult churchgoers changed 1985-1989 by region

	North	Yorks/ Humberside	North West	East Midlands	West Midlands
	%	%	%	%	%
Grew	22	21	26	24	28
Remained static	70	71	64	69	64
Declined	8	8	10	7	8

	East Anglia	South East (North)	South East (Greater London)	South East (South)	South West	Overall
	%	%	%	%	%	%
Grew	26	26	29	27	25	25
Remained static	67	67	62	67	68	67
Declined	7	7	9	6	7	8

There are more declining churches in the North West (Merseyside has 12%) and Greater London. Both Inner London Northwest and Southeast have 14% of their churches declining, and Outer London Southeast have 12% declining, and Outer London Southwest have 10%. In other regions, Cleveland has 13% and Greater Manchester 12%. Overall, however, the figures by region do not differ significantly from the national percentages.

GROWTH BY DENOMINATION AND CHURCHMANSHIP

How have the proportions of growth varied by denomination and churchmanship? Tables 50 and 51 supply this information.

The Pentecostals, Baptists and Independents have most growing churches with Methodists and Other Free Churches least. The Roman Catholics and Methodists had most declining churches, and the Independent Churches least. The Methodists, Other Free Churches and Catholics had most static churches, and the Baptists and Pentecostals least.

By far the highest percentage of growing churches were Charismatic Evangelical ones, which had more than two in every five

Table 50: Percentage of churches/congregations where adult churchgoers changed 1985-1989 by denomination

	Methodist	Baptist	URC	Independent	Afro-Caribbean	Pentecostal
	%	%	%	%	%	%
Grew	16	33	21	33	29	35
Remained static	73	61	70	63	64	58
Declined	11	6	9	4	7	7

	Other Free	Total Free	Anglican	Roman Catholic	Overall
	%	%	%	%	%
Grew	18	24	28	16	25
Remained static	73	68	65	73	67
Declined	9	8	7	11	8

Table 51: Percentage of churches/congregations where adult churchgoers changed 1985-1989 by churchmanship

	Broad Evangelical	Main Evangelical	Charismatic Evangelical	Total Evangelical	Low Church
	%	%	%	%	%
Grew	24	26	41	30	20
Remained static	72	62	52	63	71
Declined	4	12	7	7	9

	Broad	Liberal	Anglo-Catholic	«Catholic»	All others	Overall
	%	%	%	%	%	%
Grew	23	24	25	21	18	25
Remained static	68	68	68	71	73	67
Declined	9	8	7	8	9	8

growing. The Low Church and Others had the least. Other groups like the Liberals, Anglo-Catholics and Broad churchgoers had 23%-25% of their churches growing; the phenomenon of growth occurred across all churchmanships.

The Mainstream Evangelicals have the highest percentage of declining churches, and the Broad Evangelicals the smallest; they consequently have respectively a smaller and larger number of static churches.

Apart from these two groups, the percentage of declining churches, 7%-9%, occurred across all groups. Broad Evangelicals, the Low church, «Catholics» (churchmanship, not denomination) and Others have the highest proportion of static churches, with the Charismatic and Mainstream Evangelicals the lowest. Tables 50 and 51 are illustrated in Figure 26 on pages 134 and 135.

GROWTH BY ENVIRONMENT

Growth and decline by denomination and churchmanship are fairly even across the different categories. Not so by environment, for which figures are given in the next table and illustrated on page 136.

Table 52: Percentage of churches/congregations where adult churchgoers changed 1985-1989 by environment

	City centre	Inner city	Council estate	Sub-urban/ urban fringe	Separate town	Other built-up area	Rural: comm/ dorm	Rural: other	Overall
	%	%	%	%	%	%	%	%	%
Grew	11	20	23	15	12	20	33	42	25
Remained static	82	77	71	83	87	76	60	39	67
Declined	7	3	6	2	1	4	7	19	8

All the urban areas, separate towns, and other built-up areas had a smaller proportion of growing churches than the average. Some were well below the average (such as city centre with just 11%, separate towns 12% and suburban/urban fringe 15%). The larger proportion of growing churches in rural areas makes the overall figure what it is. Without the rural churches, only 14% of churches in all environments would be growing.

One-third (33%) of churches in rural commuter areas were growing, and 42% in the more remote rural areas. These high figures are supported by the *More than one Church*[7] survey which showed 39% growing churches in rural East Anglia. In contrast the rural areas also had the most declining churches — 19% in the

134 'CHRISTIAN' ENGLAND

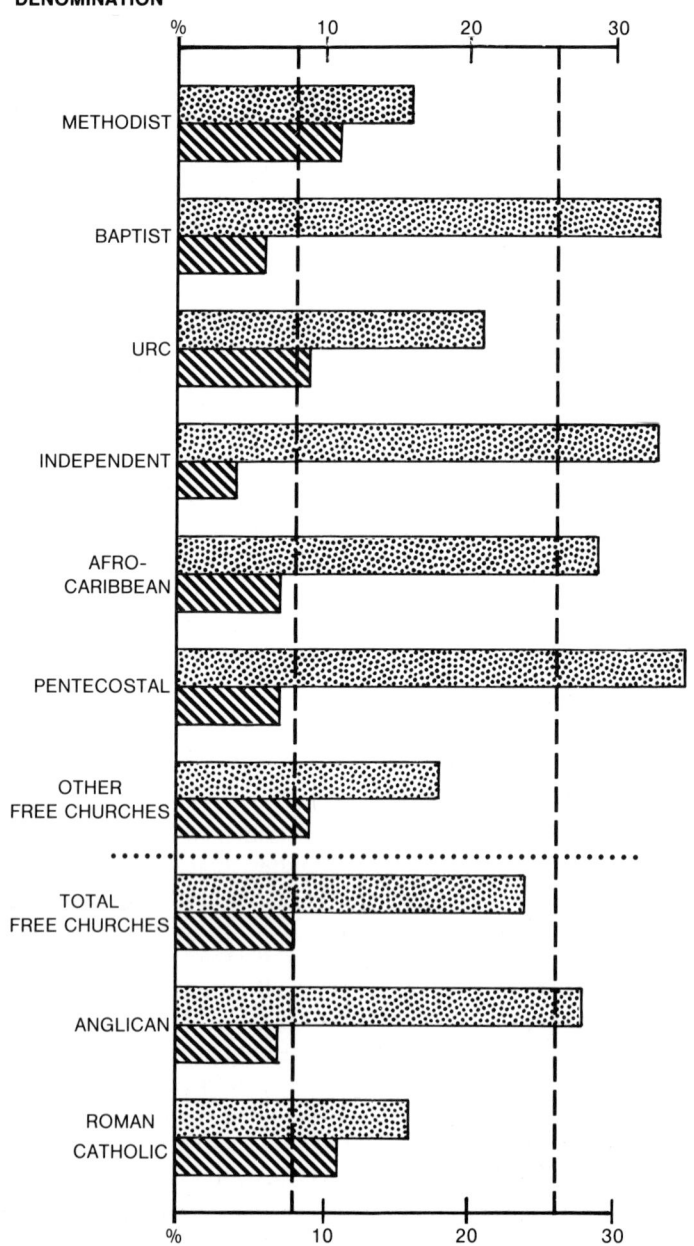

Figure 26: Growing and declining churches 1985-1989
DENOMINATION

GROWTH, DECLINE AND STATICNESS

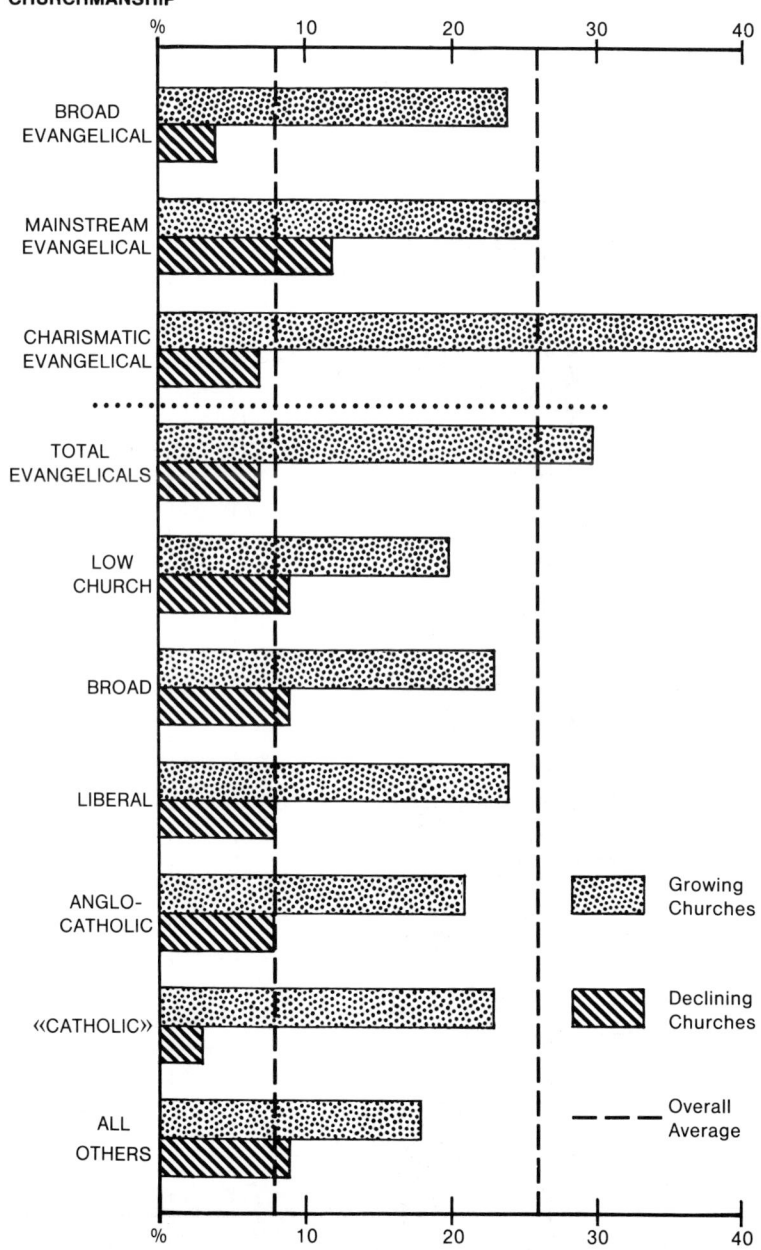

Figure 26 (Contd): Growing and declining churches 1985-1989
CHURCHMANSHIP

136 'CHRISTIAN' ENGLAND

Figure 27: Growing and declining churches 1985-1989

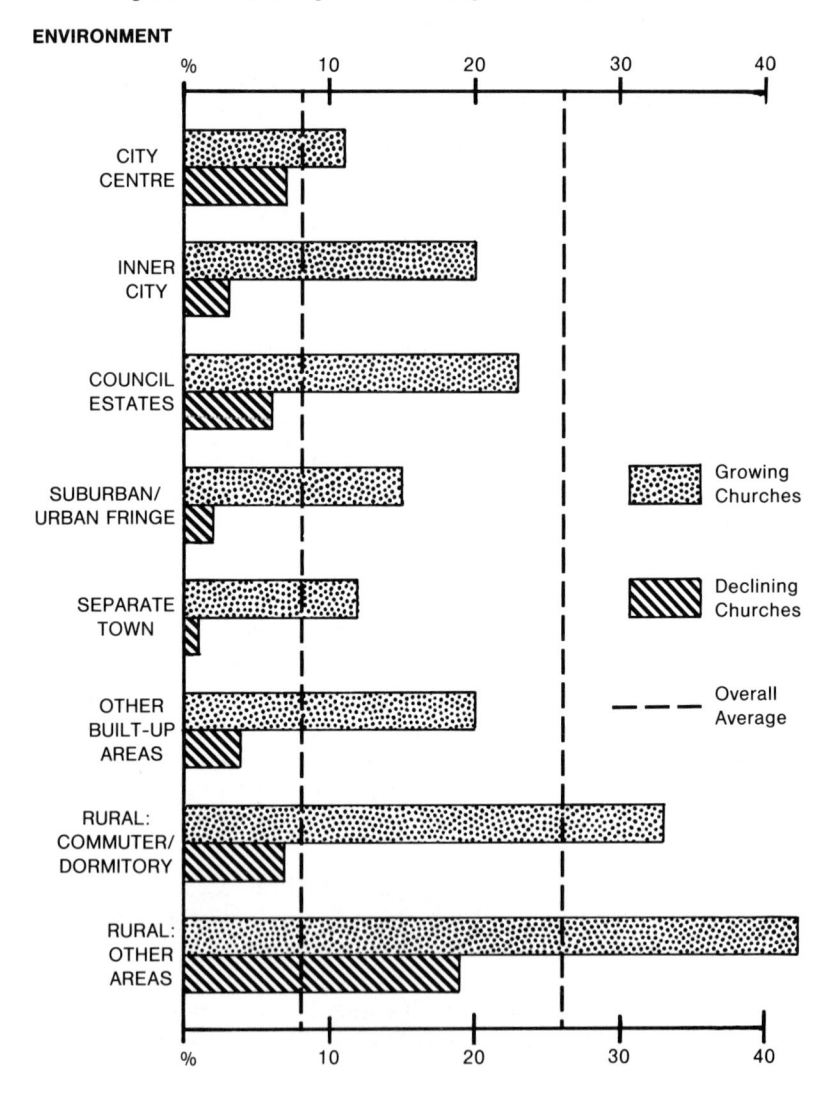

ENVIRONMENT

remoter areas. So the number of static rural churches, especially in the more distant parts, is much less — instead of the two-thirds average, the figure is only six points over one-third.

This means fewer declining churches in the urban and other non-rural environments. Only 1% of churches in separate towns declined between 1985 and 1989, 2% in the suburban and urban fringes, and only 3% in the inner city. Without the rural churches, only 3% would be declining in other environments. Of the non-rural churches an incredible 83% were therefore static.

Table 53: Percentage of churches/congregations where adult churchgoers changed 1985-1989 by rural and non-rural environments

	Non-rural churches	Rural churches	Overall
	%	%	%
Grew	14	39	25
Remained static	83	46	67
Declined	3	15	8

GROWTH BY SIZE OF CHURCH

An earlier chapter looked at the average overall congregational size of each church. We need to focus briefly here on what the Census showed about the numbers of different sizes. How many congregations are what size? The following table gives the total number of attendances, including all those for people who went more than once.

We are a nation of small congregations. But we have changed since 1979 when 48% of Anglican and Free Churches services attracted 50 or under in size (compared with 77% in Wales in 1982 and 37% in Scotland in 1984).[9]

Of all the Anglican and Free Churches, 39% or two in five, have congregations of 50 or fewer, and of these 14% are 25 or under. That means that 13,500 churches have fewer than 50 people, and 4,900 under 25. No wonder many look to larger churches for resources for developments. A further 25% have between 51 and 100, and another 28%, or just over one in four, between 100 and 200. Only 8%, or one in twelve, have above 200. Details are given in Table 54.

Table 54: Average congregation

	Percentage of congregations whose weekly				
	10 or under	11-25	26-50	51-100	101-150
	%	%	%	%	%
Free Church	2	7	25	28	20
Anglican	4	15	24	22	16
Roman Catholic	1	1	1	2	7
Orthodox	0	35	23	2	8
All Churches	3	11	22	22	16
Anglican and Free					
1989	**3**	**11**	**25**	**25**	**18**
1979	5	19	24	24	12
Roman Catholic					
1979	0	0	1	1	2

Roman Catholic Churches are, on the whole, much larger than other churches. Nearly half their churches have over 400 attending Mass on Sunday, and only 5% are less than 100 strong. This reflects their quite different church planting philosophy. They have decreased since 1979 when 60% of their churches were over 400 strong (against 39% of churches in Wales in 1982 over 300 strong and 60% in Scotland in 1984 also over 300). The previous table is illustrated in Figure 28.

Figure 28: Proportion of total churches by size 1989

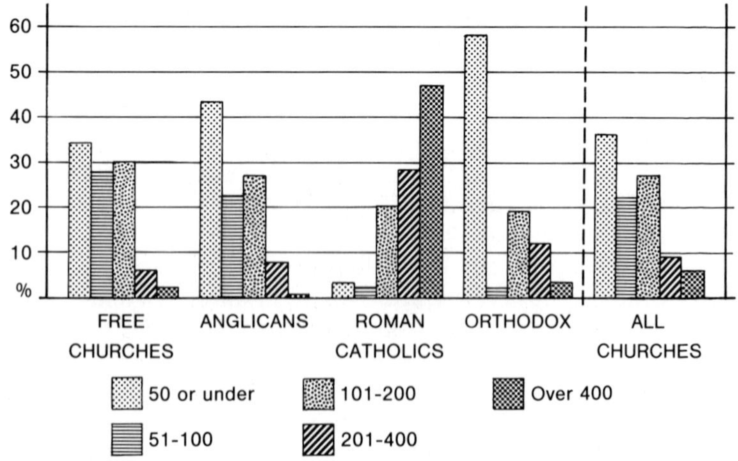

by major groups 1979 and 1989

	adult attendance in 1989 was:			Over 400	Average size[8]	Total (= 100%)
151-200	201-300	301-400				
%	%	%	%			
10	4	2	2	87	18,296
11	6	1½	½	77	16,373
13	14	14	47	355	3,824
11	12	0	3	82	114
11	6	3	6	109	38,607
10	**5**	**2**	**1**	**82**	**34,669**
8	8	2	1	71	35,294
5	13	18	60	412	3,673

How does the number of churches in a particular size group vary according to whether the church is growing or not? Proportions by size for the main church groups appear in the next three diagrams.

These diagrams show that Anglican and Free Church size have several features in common:

● Growing churches are likely to be the larger churches.
● A sizeable percentage of growing churches are the smaller churches.
● The smallest churches are very likely to be static.

Figure 29: Proportion of Free Churches 1989

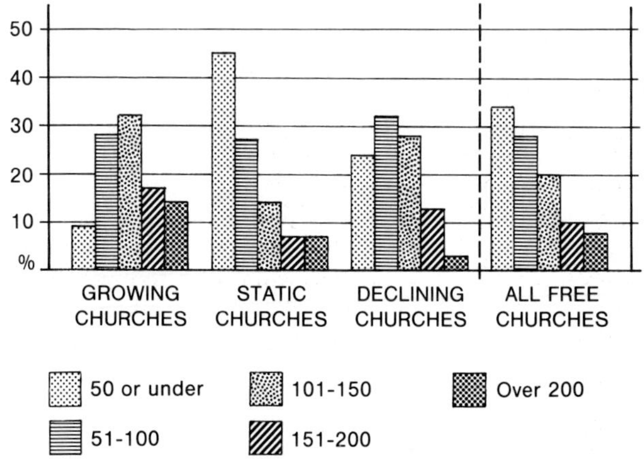

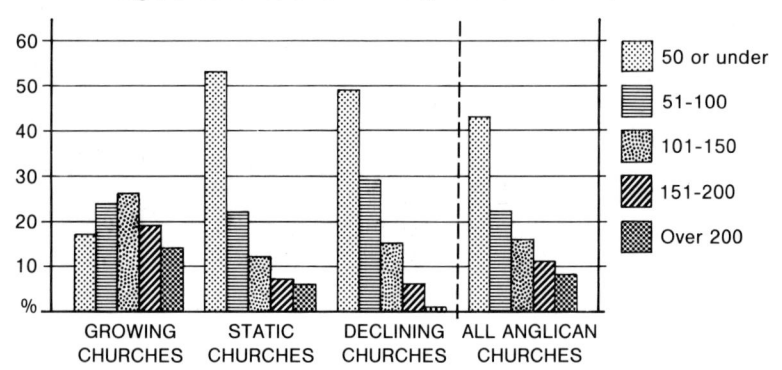

Figure 30: Proportion of Anglican churches 1989

- Static churches can be any size.
- Declining churches are often small or middle-sized churches.
- Very few of the largest churches are declining.

Many of the smaller churches are in rural areas. That so many are static reflects their constituency and situation. Older people, often fairly numerous in villages, still go to church, and they keep on going. 'Remnantitis' they might have but their churches are static. That may be good for 1989 but if the situation continues for another decade, and another 250,000 church people over 65 die in the 1990s as they did in the 1980s, we will have a grim rural situation. The time to change that is now, which is why the Archbishop's Commission on Rural Churches Report, published in *Faith in the Countryside,* September 1990, is so well timed.

Growing Roman Catholic Churches are likely to be the larger churches, though again growing churches can be any size. Static churches are often larger churches, in contrast to Free Churches and Anglicans. Declining churches are much less likely to be the largest Catholic Churches, but still could have high average Mass attendance of 301 to 500.

The English Church Census suggests that 9,700 of all churches are growing, 25% of the total. These are distributed by size and denomination as indicated in Figure 32, with circle area proportionate to number.

The Anglicans have equal proportions of growing and declining churches with congregations under 100. Nearly two-thirds of the

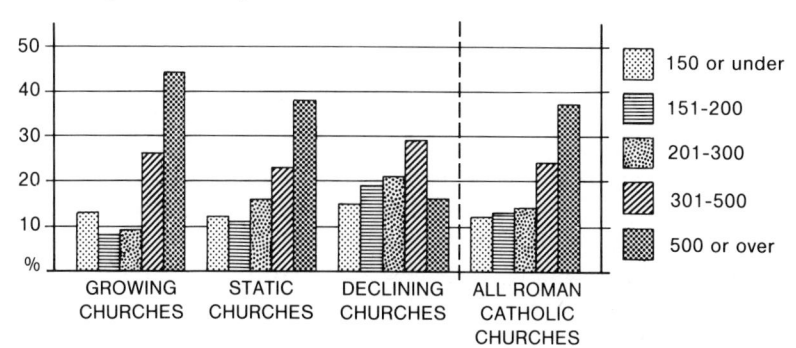

Figure 31: Proportion of Roman Catholic churches 1989

growing churches with 101-200 attenders are Anglican, but only one-third of declining churches are this size. Roman Catholic growth is small except in the larger churches, but they dominate the declining larger churches and are also significant in smaller ones. The Methodists have significant numbers of both growing and declining congregations of 100 or less, the Baptists and Independents

Figure 32: Growing and declining churches by size and denomination

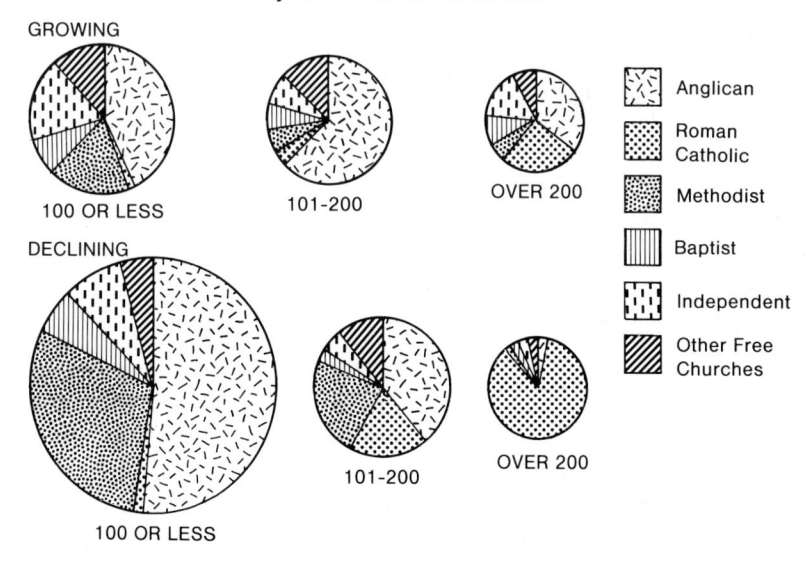

only in growing churches of this size. The Independents are important in larger growing churches, accounting for 1 in 6 of these.

GROWTH AND DECLINE BY CHURCH PEOPLE

We have looked thus far at the number of growing and declining churches. But how have the individual denominations, for example, grown by number of people? Overall the number of adults going to church in England declined 1% between 1985 to 1989, from 3,755,000 people to 3,706,900. By contrast the number of children declined 5% and the number of members increased 1%.

How this 1% adult figure varied by region, denomination, churchmanship and environment is given in the following table.

Table 55: Change in percentage of adult churchgoers 1985-1989

Region	%
North	−3
Yorks/Humberside	−3
North West	−2
East Midlands	0
West Midlands	0
East Anglia	0
South East (North)	−2
South East (Greater London)	+1
South East (South)	0
South West	−3
Overall	−1

Churchmanship	%
Broad Evangelical	−3
Mainstream Evangelical	+2
Charismatic Evangelical	+7
Total Evangelical	+3
Low Church	−4
Broad	−5
Liberal	−4
Anglo-Catholic	−5
«Catholic»	−2
All Others	+3
Overall	−1

Environment	%
City centre	−5
Inner city	−3
Council estate	−1
Suburban/urban fringe	−2
Separate towns	+2
Other built-up area	−1
Rural: commuter/dormitory	−1
Rural: other	−1
Overall	−1

Denomination	%
Methodist	−6
Baptist	+2
URC	−6
Independent	+14
Afro-Caribbean	+1
Pentecostal	+11
Other Free Churches	+2
Total Free Churches	+2
Anglican	−3
Roman Catholic	−2
Orthodox	+12
Overall	−1

Of the four categories, the one with the greatest variation of numbers from the overall figure is that for denominations with the Independents, Pentecostals and Orthodox (the last based on very few returns) all in double-figures for growing churches. The largest negatives are the Anglo-Catholics and the city centre churches. Where are the various denominations growing or declining? Maps 4, 6, 8, 10, 12, 14, 16, 18, 20 and 22 at the end of the book show this detail. Denominations whose attendance dropped at least 5% over the four years 1985 to 1989 are described as declining, whereas if they increased they are counted as growing. The rest are called static.

These maps point to widespread decline among the **Methodists** (Map 4) in both urban and rural counties, and both in the North where they are strongest and in the South. Only in the Isle of Man did adult congregations collectively increase in the period. They declined in Cornwall, their strongest county proportionately, but were static in North Yorkshire and Humberside.

The **Baptists** (Map 6) have both grown and declined. Decline was greater in the South East and parts of London especially Inner London South, and also in other cities such as in Merseyside and West Yorkshire. But growth in urban areas is reflected in the West Midlands, South Yorkshire, Tyne and Wear and Cleveland. Growth occurred in the North (where they are weak), and West Midlands (where they are also relatively weak), with far less growth and some decline where they are the strongest (Berkshire, Buckinghamshire and Cambridgeshire are the exceptions with both strength and growth).

The **United Reformed Church** (Map 8) grew only in six counties. That includes Northumberland where they are strong and Durham where they are less well represented. They are growing in Cambridgeshire and Derbyshire. Some growth in their strongest concentrations must be an encouragement and suggests that decline where they are strong (Dorset and Suffolk particularly) may be reversible. Like the Methodists, they too have enjoyed little urban growth (except Inner London Southeast).

The **Independent Churches** (Map 10) achieved widespread growth across the whole country except in the three island groups (Isle of Man, Isle of Wight and Channel Islands), East Anglia (Norfolk and Suffolk especially) and Outer London Southwest, where in all cases they were static. No decline is evident. This polyglot grouping however hides significant variations within it. The Christian Brethren, for example, do not appear to be growing significantly, and a careful paper[10] by Neil Summerton, a member of the Census Council of Reference, suggests if anything a slight decline of about 5% between 1985 and 1989. The grouping also includes the FIEC churches which grew rapidly in the 1980s and had about a 5% increase between 1985 and 1989. They are strongest in the North, Yorkshires and Humberside, Greater London, and weakest in the East Midlands and East Anglia.[11] This group also includes those Churches which have grown significantly through starting new churches. Philippine experience would bear out this combination: 'Those churches which put a priority on church planting experience greater growth'.[12]

The **Afro-Caribbean Churches** (Map 12) were mostly static, as one would expect from their overall attendance and membership being virtually the same for 1985 and 1989. Growth was mostly in the urban areas, and the North (Greater Manchester and West Yorkshire), West (Avon) and South East (especially Inner London and Southeast London). Decline in parts of London and other, mostly South East counties, is to be noted.

The **Pentecostal Churches** (Map 14) enjoyed widespread growth over much of England, especially and consistently in the major urban areas where they are strong. They declined where they are weak in the South East (East Sussex, Essex and Kent) and in the North (Cumbria, Lancashire and Northumberland) where they are stronger. They were static in the Central Midlands where they are strongest.

The **Other Free Churches** (Map 16) present such a composite mixture of growth and decline as to defy comment. They are both growing and declining in urban areas and rural areas. They are static, growing and declining where they are weak and where they are strong.

The **Free Churches** (Map 18) picture as a whole then is one of some growth (North Greater London and other parts of the South East, Cambridgeshire, Staffordshire and Warwickshire) and of patchy decline (Lincolnshire, Inner London Southwest, South Yorkshire and Wiltshire). Very largely the movements of the various Free Churches cancel each other out, giving an overwhelming picture of stability (in 69% of the counties).

The **Anglican Churches** (Map 20) experienced little growth between 1985 and 1989 except in Lincolnshire, Staffordshire and the Isle of Man (all strong areas). But in most of the other areas where they are strongest they have remained static (in contrast to 1975-1979 when they declined in many counties). This suggests a period of consolidation which may well presage growth in the decade ahead, given leadership, energy and vision. They continue to suffer urban decline (as in 1975-1979) where they are weak. The urban priorities recommended in *Faith in the City* are surely in place.

Speaking at a conference on church planting in the Anglican Church the Most Rev George Carey, then Bishop of Bath and Wells, said that the Church of England had moved (a) from maintenance to mission, (b) from one-man band to shared ministry, (c) from decline to growth, and (d) from inward-looking worship to witnessing worship.[13]

The **Roman Catholics** (Map 22) grew more between 1985 and 1989 than between 1975 and 1979. Again, as then, it has tended to be in the rural counties (though also Inner London East) where they are relatively weak, and may reflect a strategy for building new churches and communities to follow some of the internal migration patterns. It follows perhaps too 'the awakening of the Catholic Church throughout the world to a new period of evangelization'.[14] Where they are strong they mostly remained static, again unlike 1975-1979 where they frequently declined. The picture of consolidation emerges here too, though their decline in the North of England, South Midlands and South West especially give cause for concern.

The **Orthodox Churches** are too fragmentary with too few returns to justify any reliable country growth picture, though overall they grew strongly (on very small attendance figures).

WHAT MAKES CHURCHES GROW?

Where growth has occurred, what accounts for it? Many books have been written and analyses made on this subject so it is with some trepidation that another is attempted. To guide our thinking, and because of the impact the Ichthus Fellowship has made on church life in Inner London Southeast, we visited two of their services at the kind invitation of their leader, Roger Forster. This helped to put into focus the following four key areas.

Church location

The actual physical setting of a church is undoubtedly important.

● *Accessibility* by the local community was a feature of Norman churches built at village centres, and copied today by Independent Churches starting new congregations within easy walking distance of local residents.

● *Affinity* with the local community is needed, whether that be through a common social life, nationality, race or customs, or a common background or experience which will tend to bind a group together. Tom Houston felt this was especially important in the 1970s, and is still true in the 1980s.[15]

● *Acceptability* culturally is a factor identified by Peter Kaldor in his Australian analysis. Affinity helps the process of acceptance but is no substitute for it. There needs to be a receptivity between the local church and the local community.[16]

● *Size* of a church or congregation seemed important in the 1970s and, according to Lyle Schaller[17], who has authored several books and articles on this subject, is still a major factor in American church growth. Evidence in England suggests this is far less true now, however. The important Methodist report *The Missionary Shape of the Congregation*[18] found no correlation between growth and size of churches. Rt Rev Michael Turnbull, the Bishop of Rochester, in an analysis of his Diocese[19] suggests also that growth can take place irrespective of size.

Church life

The American urbanologist Ray Bakke, has visited this country many times. As a result of his visit in June 1987, he circulated a report summarising his observations then, and in it said: 'Churches are growing when they are specialist welcoming places, often for a particular sub-culture. Growing churches are relationship or celebration centred. A few are based on commitment to mission.' He points to two key reasons for growth:

● *The warmth of people's friendliness.* Some churches focus on people, and their welcome of them and support of them. Those who are lonely, unhappy and disadvantaged will often gladly be drawn into such a fellowship.

● *The experience of worship.* The actual mechanism of the worship service can clearly attract many, particularly in the Independent and Pentecostal sectors. Those churches which put an emphasis on participation and experience seem to grow. But it should be noted that the more formal worship in Anglo-Catholic Churches, for example, also appeals to some.

Both emphases are underlined by Census findings. Other aspects are important too:

● *Emphasis on evangelism.* A senior civil servant friend identified the consistent insistence on outreach as a major factor in the growth of the Ichthus Fellowship. *The Missionary Shape of the Congregation* also indicated that growing churches were those which regularly had times of evangelism, and many churches other than Methodists would testify to the same experience. Likewise starting new churches can be a strong dynamic for growth. True in many parts of the world, it is also British experience.

● *Retention of existing numbers.* As George Barna has also pointed out,[20] while acquiring new members is obviously important, retaining existing ones is equally necessary. A strategy for one without the other can be counterproductive. That people wander away from churches is undoubted. Perhaps that is why Billy Graham always includes a 'Re-dedication' response in his crusades. In Mission 89 such made up 26% of the total response.[21] A detailed survey of church attendance in Nairobi, Kenya[22] put the re-dedication of members to Christ as one of the three main reasons for growth (the other two were growth by conversion and by adding people who had left other churches). One key strategy in the Renew programme in Catholic Dioceses, such as Arundel and Brighton and Glasgow, is to make contact with lapsed Catholics.

● *Involvement with the community.* The Ichthus Fellowship own a non-alcoholic public house, the Brown Bear, and also run a pregnancy and VD clinic as part of their counselling service. Churches interact in numerous ways with local people and that bridge-building is critical for development. Social work and evangelism go hand in hand.

Church leaders

Good leadership is always essential for the well-being of any enterprise, and the church in this respect is no different. What are the characteristics of leaders which seem specially pertinent in growing churches?

● *Vision.* Leaders need to know where they are going and they need to share that with their congregations. The pastor of one fast-growing South African Church, Ray McCauley, preaches on his long-term vision for his church the first Sunday in every year. Roger Forster had been working in Sydenham for twenty years. His key ideas were crystallised 10 to 15 years ago, and he has been following them ever since. Perseverance helps!

● *Independence.* It is the Baptist, Independent, Pentecostal and Afro-Caribbean Churches in England that have especially experienced growth in the 1980s. One feature they all have in common is the autonomy of the local congregation. Such autonomy is also part of the Anglican parochial system, and 28% of Anglican Churches grew between 1985 and 1989.

● *Integration of the family.* This is suggested by the growth of many churches which have children participating in the adult services. Independent Churches, especially perhaps FIEC churches, which emphasise the importance of reaching out to family units, have also grown. With the family unit under threat today, opportunities to participate in an activity with all the family can appeal. Many families want to give their children a religious upbringing. Involvement of the family lessens formality but part of the spirit of the age is the spirit of informality.

● *Teaching programme.* George Barna[23] identifies as a key factor in successful churches, their desire to build up people in the faith presenting each person mature in Christ 'measured by nothing less than the stature of Christ himself'.[24] A strong and varied teaching ministry is vital.

● *Quality.* One pastor of a large church said 'In everything, strive for excellence'. Where this is a major criterion for ministry, churches are often successful.[25]

- *Spirituality.* 'Churches die when leaders die. Churches die from the top downwards. Show me a growing church and you have shown me visionary leadership. It is leaders who make growth. Where you have spiritual leaders, men of prayer, women of prayer, imaginative, alert, intelligent, then we have growth. We are told human death either starts in the heart or the head. That is true of church growth also,' George Carey also said at the conference on church planting.[26]

- *Principles of leadership.* Churches, and all organisations undoubtedly go through a life cycle. (This has been initially explored in the Christian context by missiologist David Burnett.[27]) It will be interesting to see how much of the energy currently in the House Church Movement passes on to the next generation of leadership. But the initiation phase is irrelevant where many churches are centuries old. Any growth in these is independent of the institution as such. It will depend on the operating philosophies and conviction of the current leadership. Quality church management helps enormously, as testified in Rochester[28] or the Caister Leadership Conference.[29]

Church values

What are the major underlying principles that operate in a church? What is its culture, its internal environment, its operating concepts? In particular, what are the values that seem to be followed by growing churches?

- *Theological vision.* The churches which grew most in the 1980s (the Independents, Afro-Caribbean and Pentecostals) are all charismatic. It is most unlikely that their theology and their growth is not related, but it needs to be remembered that the growing churches in these groups only account for one-fifth of all the churches which grew between 1985 and 1989. Half the growing churches were Anglican.

- *High expectations of members.* Members of these churches were expected to be involved in the life of the church. An air of excitement and expectancy prevailed. Attendance was not just observance but a commitment. It meant something to be involved in such churches. Spectator religion was absent.

- *Every person counting.* Whatever their background or present circumstance, each person was valued. There was an identification with each person's situation and opportunities. People were invited to share what they were doing, as an expression of what it meant to belong to a loving fellowship. Each person was important, worth praying over, worth following through. One specific application of the principle that each person counts is when young people are seen to be valued.

- *Each person allowed to be anonymous.* One special facet that emerged through contact with the Ichthus Fellowship was the realisation of letting people be anonymous; folk walked into their services and celebrations without being shown to their seats. They were able to find their own way, and absorb the atmosphere of the meeting. Many church people have never visited a night club and, if invited, would be unsure of what to wear, what to do or what to say. Many unchurched people have only visited a church for a wedding or a funeral and when visiting normally are likewise uncertain as to what to wear, do, or say. Allowing people to sit and watch, with a freedom to participate or not as they wish, gives a respect to their personhood, and allows the quality and warmth of the service to draw them in at their own pace, perhaps specially important for those suffering strains in their family life.

- *Their relevance.* Involvement with the needs of those present, be they children going up from primary to secondary school, students about to go to college, a manager looking for staff, a worker going to a country in the Middle East, an involvement with a local programme of outreach, an interview with the local radio station, a hospital service, or a friend visiting from a troubled part of the world, is a key feature of a growing church. Commitment is two-way — the leaders to the people as well as the people to the leaders. The Sunday service provides an opportunity for appraisal for the week ahead, and an exposition to help each to live as God would wish them to. Church was not just what happened on Sunday morning; worship and praise are needed at all times.

- *They do not try to do everything.* Churches are not omnipotent, and growing churches know their limitations, and focus on what they, and they alone, can do. Their priorities follow their strengths, not their weaknesses.

APPLICATION

Encouragement

It is very easy to look at some of the figures in this chapter and feel discouraged. Yet a quarter of English churches grew between 1985 and 1989. That growth is seen in all denominations. It is reflected across all churchmanships. There is no part of England where some part of the church is *not* growing. Growth is seen even among the smallest churches. Over half the churches in the country have two services every Sunday, and one churchgoer in seven (that means one adult in every 70) goes to church not once but twice on a Sunday. Many people are concerned about church growth and are devoting their thinking, their research, their commitment to it.

Many churches, such as St Thomas Crookes in Sheffield, have grown spectacularly over the 1980s. A special study of the Anglican Churches in the Diocese of Sheffield[30] showed adult attendance had grown 14% between 1982 and 1988 and this growth was reflected across large and small churches, and across all ages of ministers, and this is in the county (South Yorkshire) where the smallest percentage of people go to church.

So be encouraged. It may be difficult to get encouragement and friendship from members of your congregation. So how might we cope?

● *Stop and evaluate where you are.* 'We need to redefine our PACE — our *P*erception, our *A*ctions, the *C*hallenges we face, and how we *E*valuate our efforts and circumstances' is how one person put it.[31]

● *Do not be disheartened* if your church is small. Small churches are especially important for some people because it is easier for them to talk with the church leaders, and have access to the people who make decisions.[32]

● *Consider the best strategy.* Many churches are finding the value of small groups and one church minister responsible for a small church, David Hersh,[33] has a men's Bible Study early in the morning before work. Five men meet in the local cafe from 6.20 to 7.20 am, always ending precisely on time. Catherine Butcher looking at the impact of house groups,[34] commented 'New spiritual life has been marked by the emergence of small groups'.

● *Reflect on your calling.* 'He who calls you is faithful, and He will do it' (1 Thess 5:24). A recent issue[35] of the International Christian Chamber of Commerce newsletter noted that the churches of Sardis and Laodicea were rebuked by the angel in Revelation, and today they are both in ruins. The churches of Ephesus, Pergamum and Thyatira received both rebuke and encouragement, but today they are insignificant places. However, Smyrna and Philadelphia both received unqualified encouragement and both today are blossoming, with a third of the population of Smyrna Christian. Be encouraged! 'In the Lord, your labour is not in vain' (1 Cor 15:58).

Cartoon from Grid[36]

Chapter 6: Summary

- 25% of English churches grew between 1985 and 1989.
- 8% declined; the remaining 67% were static.
- The highest proportions of growing churches were in Greater London (29%) and the West Midlands (28%), the lowest in the North (22%) and Yorks/Humberside (21%).
- The highest proportions of growing churches occurred among the Pentecostals (35%), Baptists (33%) and Independents (33%) and the lowest among the Roman Catholics (16%) and the Methodists (16%).
- The highest proportions of growing churches occurred among the Charismatic Evangelicals (41%) and the lowest among the Low Church (20%) and All Other churchmanships (18%).
- The highest proportions of growing churches occurred among the remoter rural areas (42%), and the commuter rural areas (33%), and the lowest in separate towns (12%) and the city centres (11%).
- Rural churches also had the highest proportion of declining churches (15%).
- 8% of all Anglican and Free Churches had congregations over 200 in 1989. It was 11% in 1979.
- 75% of all Catholic Churches had congregations of over 200 in 1989, and 47% are over 400. The figures were 91% and 60% in 1979.
- Churches grow partly because of their location, their life, their leaders and their values.

7. HOW OUR BELIEFS ARE PRACTISED

One of the questions included in the 1989 Census, not asked in any previous such study in Great Britain, concerned the churchmanship of each church. A rather quaint word, not yet changed to church-peopleship, it was meant to indicate the theological belief system of each church. This is not the sense how it is defined by the *Oxford English Dictionary,* but in this respect we feel it is wrong. At least half the correspondence accompanying returned forms concerned this question, but it was not the meaning of the word that people queried.

The question of belief clearly concerns many. When Robert Towler, now the Religious Editor of Channel 4, analysed the 4,000 odd letters received by John Robinson in response to his book *Honest to God,* the majority concerned people's basic beliefs.[1] A few felt strongly that the question should not have been included in the Census at all, but overall 89% of those who replied answered it. Undoubtedly some ministers answered it in the light of their own particular persuasion rather than for their church as a whole, but the actual question asked was 'Which of these terms or which combination of them would best describe your congregation?'.

The final results of asking this question are important. They give an overview of church belief today not available before. This is comprehensive, so all are included. They give a framework of analysis quite separate from the normal denominational breakdown. Due to interest in this analysis, a detailed explanation is given describing the derivative of the terms used.

THE TERMS USED FOR ANALYSIS

One of the prime reasons for the two extensive pilot studies was this question. The first time terms such as 'Arminian', 'Ecumenical',

'Renewed' and 'Reformed' were included, but few ticked these, so these were omitted next time. One term not included was 'Broad' which many included in the 'Other, please specify' box. The second pilot added Broad and it was clear from the response this was a term to be retained. The final list was in the following order, with the response given:

Anglo-Catholic	(7%)	Charismatic	(12%)
Liberal	(15%)	Low Church	(27%)
«Catholic»	(19%)	Orthodox	(7%)
Evangelical	(41%)	Radical	(2%)
Broad	(38%)	Other, please specify	(1%)

Respondents could tick up to three. 54% ticked just one, 31% two, 15% three, and 0.2% four or more. The 'Other' was chiefly ticked by Quakers (Religious Society of Friends) and the Salvation Army.

While Evangelical and Broad were the two most popular classifications — virtually equal — the terms as such could simply not be used by themselves. Too many people had used combinations to describe themselves, and the total ticks came to 169% of the forms.

Analysed categories of churchmanship

Consequently it became essential to combine these terms suitably for analysis. Such combinations were checked by a well-known church leader. For those wanting the detail, a list in *Prospects for the Nineties* not only gives the numbers ticking every single combination, but precisely which of these combinations were put into which category. The designations adopted are as follows:

Catholic Includes the 2,367 ticking just Catholic, 610 Broad Catholic, 158 Evangelical Catholic, 138 Broad Catholic Evangelicals, 133 Orthodox and/or Radical Catholic, and 33 Charismatic Catholics, but not the 68 Evangelical Catholics who were also charismatic. **It *must* be remembered this term is *not* being used here solely to represent Roman Catholics. To avoid confusion the word Catholic when used in this sense is printed thus: «Catholic».**
Anglo-Catholic Includes all those ticking the Anglo-Catholic box, except the 320 Liberal Anglo-Catholics.
Liberals All those ticking the Liberal box and whatever other combinations were ticked, including 320 Anglo-Catholic Liberals, but

excluding 218 Broad Liberal Evangelicals, and 41 Charismatic Liberal Evangelicals.

Low Church All those ticking the Low Church box unless they also ticked Liberal (373), Anglo-Catholic (70), «Catholic» *and* a third box (Evangelical, Broad) (30), Broad *and* a third box (Evangelical, Charismatic) (321), or both Evangelical and Charismatic (219).

Broad Those ticking the Broad box, including Broad Charismatics, Orthodox Broad, and Radical Broad. It excluded Broad Evangelicals and all third combinations with that. Broad Catholics, Anglo-Catholics, and Liberals and all third combinations were included with «Catholics», Anglo-Catholics, or Liberals.

Broad Evangelical All those ticking these two boxes and any third.

Mainstream Evangelical Those ticking the Evangelical box *only,* plus 167 Orthodox Evangelicals, and 44 Radical Evangelicals.

Charismatic Evangelical All those ticking these two boxes and any third.

All Others Whoever was not included in the above! These included 354 Orthodox not included elsewhere, 53 Radicals not put in other combinations and 4 Orthodox Radicals.

As a result every form could be given a single designation under one of these nine headings, and these are the nine groups used throughout the Census analysis. The numbers and proportions for each of the above were:

Table 56: Groups used for churchmanship analysis

Group	Number of forms	Percentage of total
		%
Broad	4,019	17
Mainstream Evangelical	3,907	16
«Catholic»	3,439	15
Liberal	3,346	14
Low Church	2,890	12
Charismatic Evangelical	2,585	11
Broad Evangelical	1,674	7
Anglo-Catholic	1,345	6
All Others	542	2
Total	23,747	100

Evangelicals

Many ticked just the one box 'Evangelical'. Although clear in distinction from Liberal or «Catholic», used alone it could cause confusion with Broad Evangelicals or Charismatic Evangelicals. A further descriptive word had to be supplied, and after discussion with several church leaders representing quite different traditions, 'Mainstream' was chosen.

Different types of categories used by others were also considered. Robert Towler used the categories of Exemplarists, Conversionists, Theists, Gnostics and Traditionalists,[2] Australians researching in the Combined Churches Survey for Faith and Mission combined 'access' and 'value' eligibility and used the four categories of Conversionism, Devotionalism, Conventionalism and Principalism.[3] Wider categories were possible where more information on the nature of belief was obtained, but we could not use them as we were asking clergy for specific categories relating to the whole of their church, not the variations of belief in their individual church members.

Reg Burrows, in his book *Dare to Contend,* identifies trends and emphases particularly among Anglican evangelists. He distinguishes Old evangelicalism, New evangelicalism and Classic evangelicalism, and works this through via their attitude to the Bible, missionary work, the nature of the church, the world, the role of women and other factors.[4] This employs more detail than we could discern from the Census, and therefore we could not follow his three categories. Another discussion on this subject by David Holloway appears in the book *Restoring the Vision.*[5]

CHURCHMANSHIP STRENGTHS

What results emerged as the essential strengths of each group? The census replies related to a particular *church,* but the table below translates those into *congregational* strengths, whether measured by children, adult churchgoers, or members.

The «Catholics» have relatively few churches, but many more children and adults, and four times proportionately as many members. This follows from the many large churches which are

Table 57: Churchmanship of churches, child and adult churchgoers, and church members 1989

	Broad Evangelical	Mainstream Evangelical	Charismatic Evangelical	Total Evangelical	Low Church
Churches	% 7	% 16	% 11	% 34	% 12
Child churchgoers	9	11	16	36	6
Adult churchgoers	9	7	12	28	6
Members	6	4	6	16	4

	Broad	Liberal	Anglo-Catholic	«Catholic»	All others	Total (= 100%)
Churches	% 17	% 14	% 6	% 15	% 2	38,607
Child churchgoers	8	9	3	37	1	1,221,500
Adult churchgoers	10	11	4	39	2	3,706,900
Members	7	7	3	59	4	7,162,400

Roman Catholic, most of whose priests defined themselves as «Catholic», as might be expected. The Anglo-Catholics, on the other hand, have a higher percentage of churches than of people following this churchmanship.

The Liberals, Broad and Low Church groups all have more churches than their strength in people would suggest. Likewise, the Evangelicals have more churches than people overall (not quite for children) and are especially weak on members. Mainstream Evangelicals are the essential cause for this, and it is the Charismatic Evangelicals who have so many children. Mainstream and Charismatic Evangelicals account for 27% of churches but only 19% of adult churchgoers. Broad and Broad Evangelical churches account for 24% of churches but 19% of adult churchgoers. The average numbers per church in each category are given in Table 58.

The average «Catholic» church has the most children, followed by the average Evangelical, with the Charismatic and Broad Evangelicals having twice as many children as the average Mainstream church. A few of the Mainstream Evangelical churches are FIEC churches which tend to be smaller than average, but on the other hand, proportionately the Mainstream Evangelicals have most children for the number of adults — almost one child for two adults, whereas with the Anglo-Catholics and the Low Church the proportion is 4:1.

Table 58: Child and adult churchgoers and church members per church by churchmanship 1989

	Broad Evangelical	Mainstream Evangelical	Charismatic Evangelical	Total Evangelical	Low Church
Child churchgoers	41	22	46	34	16
Adult churchgoers	123	42	105	79	48
Church members	159	46	101	87	62
Adults per child	3.0	1.9	2.3	2.3	4.0
Members per adult	1.3	1.1	1.0	1.1	1.3

	Broad	Liberal	Anglo-Catholic	«Catholic»	All others	Total (= 100%)
Child churchgoers	15	20	16	78	16	32
Adult churchgoers	56	75	64	250	96	96
Church members	76	93	93	730	371	186
Adults per child	3.7	3.8	4.0	3.2	6.0	3.0
Members per adult	1.4	1.2	1.5	2.9	3.9	1.9

Membership per «Catholic» church is very high compared with the overall figure (which would be only 89 without them). Against this figure Mainstream Evangelicals and the Low Churches are low in membership, and the Others much higher, reflecting the largely Orthodox constituency of this group.

The proportions of churchgoers and members by churchmanship are reflected in the diagram below.

Figure 33: Churchmanship proportions

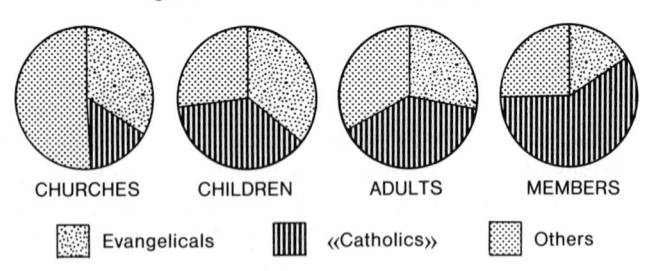

CHURCHES   CHILDREN   ADULTS   MEMBERS

Evangelicals   «Catholics»   Others

Churchmanship growth

The figures in the above diagram relate to 1989. How did the numbers of children and so on change over the four years 1985-1989? The next table gives details.

Table 59: Change in child and adult churchgoers and church members by churchmanship 1985-1989

	Broad Evangelical	Mainstream Evangelical	Charismatic Evangelical	Total Evangelical	Low Church
	%	%	%	%	%
Child churchgoers	−10	−9	+3	−4	−8
Adult churchgoers	−3	+2	+7	+3	−4
Members	−2	+2	+6	+2	−3

	Broad	Liberal	Anglo-Catholic	«Catholic»	All others	Total (= 100%)
	%	%	%	%	%	%
Child churchgoers	−6	−5	−4	−4	+2	−5
Adult churchgoers	−5	−4	−5	−2	+3	−1
Members	−4	−3	−5	+3	+2	+1

Child attenders were declining across all churchmanships except Charismatic Evangelicals (reflecting the House Church growth) and Others (reflecting Orthodox growth). Adult attenders also increased in both these groups but among Mainstream Evangelicals also, making the Total Evangelicals positive. This especially reflects the growth of the FIEC and Baptist Churches in this group. Membership was similar to adult attendance except that the «Catholic» membership was growing, reflecting the increase in the Roman Catholic population.

CHURCHMANSHIP AND DENOMINATION

Adult churchgoers

One of the most fascinating aspects of churchmanship is determining how the different churchmanships are spread across the various denominations. Here, as before, analysis concentrates on adult churchgoers. Full figures for 1985 and 1989 are given for both child churchgoers and church members in the much fuller set of tables in *Prospects for the Nineties*.

The basic numerical data is given in Table 60. This table is important. Although there are more Baptist evangelicals, for example, than Methodists, because the Methodists are a larger church a small percentage of Methodist evangelicals still yields four-fifths the number of Baptist evangelicals!

Table 60: Adult churchgoers by churchmanship

	Methodist	Baptist	URC	Independent	Afro-Caribbean	Pentecostal
Broad Evangelical	93,900	37,400	3,600	31,600	2,700	600
Mainstream Evangelical	16,800	79,200	2,400	64,300	10,500	7,400
Charismatic Evangelical	15,200	43,900	7,300	115,200	46,300	83,300
Total Evangelical	125,900	160,500	13,300	211,100	59,500	91,300
Low Church	76,600	7,100	17,500	8,200	300	600
Broad	96,900	12,400	25,000	19,300	300	400
Liberal	81,900	17,800	54,600	16,900	1,100	200
Anglo-Catholic	500	100	—	17,400	100	—
«Catholic»	5,400	500	1,200	14,700	5,800	200
All Others	8,900	1,000	2,400	5,200	1,400	2,500
Total	396,100	199,400	114,000	292,800	68,500	95,200

The table shows there were just over one million evangelicals in England in 1989, but the largest group is the «Catholic» with 1.4 million. Then come the Liberals and the Broad (though to the latter could be added the Broad Evangelicals which would make their combined group half the size of the «Catholic»).

Table 61 converts actual numbers of adult churchgoers by denomination and churchmanship into percentages.

The Roman Catholics are the largest single church, and 98% of them have «Catholic» churchmanship, the highest percentage of a particular churchmanship applying to a particular denomination, though the Pentecostals are not far behind with 96% being Evangelical. The next group are the Afro-Caribbeans, Others, Baptists and Independents (in that order) who are 72%-87% Evangelical. Next are the URC who are 48% Liberal, and Methodists who are 32% Evangelical, 25% Broad and 21% Liberal. This variation within a particular denomination is repeated by the Anglicans who are even more spread out. They are 26% Evangelical, 20% Liberal, 18% Broad, 13% «Catholic», 12% Anglo-Catholic, 10% Low Church, and 1% Others.

Truly something for everyone, and perhaps a correct feature for the State Church. The figures in Tables 60 and 61 are illustrated in Figure 34.

HOW OUR BELIEFS ARE PRACTISED 163

and denomination 1989

Other Free	Total Free	Anglican	Roman Catholic	Orthodox	Total
24,000	193,800	146,500	★	—	340,300
40,200	220,800	39,500	2,500	—	262,800
3,300	314,500	106,200	3,400	—	424,100
67,500	729,100	292,200	5,900	—	1,027,200
4,800	115,100	118,400	200	★	233,700
3,800	158,100	209,400	2,000	400	369,900
5,000	177,500	223,300	9,100	—	409,900
★	18,100	139,400	3,900	100	161,500
300	28,100	143,800	1,272,200	100	1,444,200
1,600	23,000	17,400	11,300	8,800	60,500
83,000	1,249,000	1,143,900	1,304,600	9,400	3,706,900

★ Fewer than 50 people

Figure 34: Churchmanship by denomination 1989

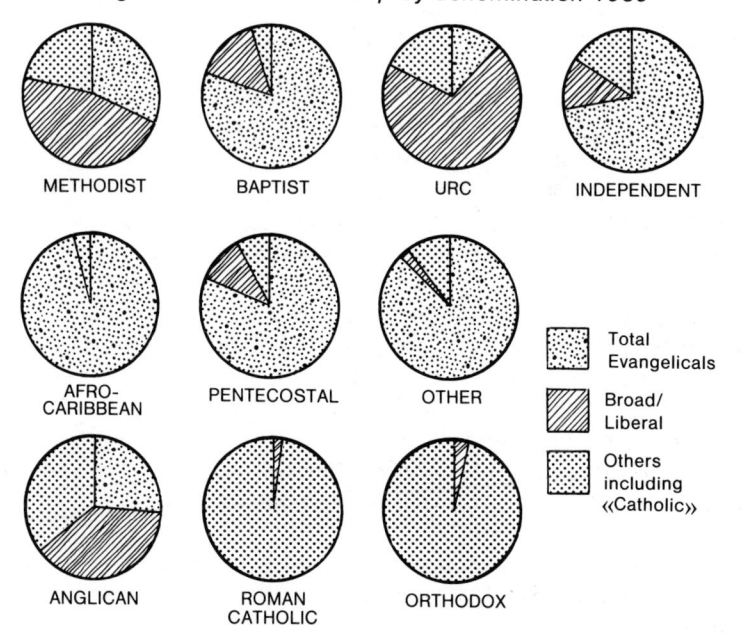

METHODIST　BAPTIST　URC　INDEPENDENT

AFRO-CARIBBEAN　PENTECOSTAL　OTHER

ANGLICAN　ROMAN CATHOLIC　ORTHODOX

- Total Evangelicals
- Broad/Liberal
- Others including «Catholic»

Table 61: Adult churchgoers' churchmanship

	Metho-dist	Baptist	URC	Inde-pendent	Afro-Carib-bean	Pente-costal
	%	%	%	%	%	%
Broad Evangelical	24	19	3	11	4	1
Mainstream Evangelical	4	39	2	22	15	8
Charismatic Evangelical	4	22	7	39	68	87
Total Evangelical	32	80	12	72	87	96
Low Church	19	4	15	3	½	1
Broad	25	6	22	6	½	0
Liberal	21	9	48	6	2	0
Anglo-Catholic	0	0	—	6	0	—
«Catholic»	1	0	1	5	8	0
All Others	2	1	2	2	2	3
Total (= 100%)	396,100	199,400	114,000	292,800	68,500	95,200

Table 62: Change in adult churchgoers by churchmanship

	Metho-dist	Baptist	URC	Inde-pendent	Afro-Carib-bean	Pente-costal
	%	%	%	%	%	%
Broad Evangelical	−7	−12	−5	0	+13	(+20)
Mainstream Evangelical	+2	+5	−11	−1	−14	0
Charismatic Evangelical	−7	+13	+24	+19	+7	+12
Total Evangelical	−5	+2	+7	+9	+3	+11
Low Church	+2	+4	−9	+22	(−25)	(+200)
Broad	−15	−2	−2	+25	(0)	(+100)
Liberal	−5	−2	−11	+17	−8	(0)
Anglo-Catholic	(0)	(0)	—	+17	0	—
«Catholic»	+35	(+25)	(+71)	+47	−8	(−71)
All Others	−1	0	+9	+73	+8	+92
Total	−6	+2	−6	+14	+1	+11

Figures in brackets are less reliable as they are based on small numbers

HOW OUR BELIEFS ARE PRACTISED

by denomination 1989

Other Free	Total Free	Anglican	Roman Catholic	Orthodox	Overall
%	%	%	%	%	%
29	16	13	0	—	9
48	18	4	0	—	7
4	25	9	0	—	12
81	59	26	0	—	28
6	9	10	0	0	6
5	13	18	0	4	10
6	14	20	1	—	11
0	1	12	0	1	4
0	2	13	98	1	39
2	2	1	1	94	2
83,000	1,249,900	1,143,900	1,304,600	9,400	3,706,900

and denomination 1985-1989

Other Free	Total Free	Anglican	Roman Catholic	Orthodox	Overall
%	%	%	%	%	%
−2	−6	+2	(0)	—	−3
−1	+1	+15	−14	—	+2
+3	+13	−6	+36	—	+7
−1	+4	+1	+9	—	+3
+17	+2	−9	(−50)	(0)	−4
+36	−7	−4	+25	(+33)	−5
+9	−4	−3	−4	—	−4
(0)	+16	−7	−11	(0)	−5
(+50)	+26	+2	−2	(0)	−2
+23	+20	−14	−2	+10	+3
+2	+2	−3	−2	+12	−1

Tables 60 and 61 give the figures and proportions as they were in 1989. How had they changed over the previous four years, longer-term trends not being available? The percentages in Table 62 provide the answer.

This table shows where the various changes are happening: for instance, it indicates that among the Anglican Churches the Mainstream Evangelicals are growing (from a much smaller base) and the Anglo-Catholics and Low Churches are declining, and at a slightly faster rate than the Charismatics.

In the Roman Catholic Church the Charismatics, are growing as are the Broad churchgoers, but Mainstream Evangelicals and Anglo-Catholics are declining.

The Methodist Church is experiencing a small growth in its Mainstream Evangelicals and a much larger growth in its «Catholic» attenders, but a steep decline in its Broad churchgoers and a less rapid decline amongst its Liberals, Broad Evangelicals and Charismatics.

Baptists are losing Broad Evangelicals but gaining Charismatics and, less rapidly, Mainstream Evangelicals. The United Reformed Church is also seeing Charismatic gain, but Liberal and Mainstream Evangelical decline.

The Independents are experiencing Charismatic gains, as are the Afro-Caribbeans and Pentecostals. The Independents are also achieving Low Church, Broad, Liberal, Anglo-Catholic and «Catholic» growth.

Broad Evangelicals are struggling, as are Mainstream Evangelicals overall. The first declined slightly from 1985 to 1989, the latter increased marginally. It is the Charismatic Evangelicals' strong growth which is really responsible for Evangelical growth. The Low Church, Broad, Liberal, and Anglo-Catholic churchgoers all dropped 4 or 5% in the same period, real but not disastrous declines.

The substantive growth areas are three:

● The Charismatics across all denominations except the Anglican and Methodists.

● Those of a «Catholic» persuasion, except in the Roman Catholic Church where this particular group is declining.

● The Independent Churches in the non-evangelical churchmanships.

Churches

Table 61 gave percentages of churchmanship by denomination for adult churchgoers; Table 63 gives similar percentages, but this time for churches or congregations.

The broad results from this table are similar to those emerging from Table 61. It is the differences between the figures in these two tables which are of most interest. There are 16 figures which vary by at least four percentage points. The largest is for the Independents.

● 38% of Independent Churches are Mainstream Evangelical but only 22% of their people, because there are many small FIEC and House Church fellowships.

● 16% of URC Churches are Broad Evangelical but only 3% of their people. These small churches have an average congregation of only 13.

● 37% of the URC Churches are Liberal accounting for 48% of their people, with an average congregation of 88.

● 21% of Other Churches are Broad Evangelical representing 29% of their people, with an average congregation of 78.

● 13% of Other Churches are Liberal against 6% of their adult attenders, giving an average congregation of 26.

CHURCHMANSHIP BY REGION

How does churchmanship vary across the country? This is given in Table 64 on the next pages.

This table shows «Catholic» strength in the North West, the North and London, and corresponding weaknesses in Evangelicalism in the North West and the Northern Regions, but not in Greater London where there are fewer Liberals, Low Church and Broad churchgoers. The Evangelicals generally are stronger in the South than the North and the North West in particular (many Methodists there). Charismatics are weak in the North West especially. The Low Church and Broad churchgoers are evenly spread across the country as are the Liberals (though strongest in the South East [North]) and Anglo-Catholics (though strongest in the West Midlands). Because of the close correspondence between «Catholic» and Roman Catholics, naturally where one is strong the other is also.

Table 63: Churches/congregations' churchmanship

	Methodist	Baptist	URC	Independent	Afro-Caribbean	Pentecostal
	%	%	%	%	%	%
Broad Evangelical	22	19	16	4	4	1
Mainstream Evangelical	7	42	4	38	20	11
Charismatic Evangelical	4	23	4	37	67	83
Total Evangelical	33	84	24	79	91	95
Low Church	24	5	17	4	1	1
Broad	23	5	19	4	1	1
Liberal	16	5	37	6	2	0
Anglo-Catholic	0	0	—	2	0	—
«Catholic»	1	0	0	3	1	0
All Others	3	1	3	2	4	3
Total	6,740	2,339	1,681	4,123	949	1,002

Table 64: Adult churchgoers' churchmanship

	North	Yorks/Humberside	North West	East Midlands	West Midlands
	%	%	%	%	%
Broad Evangelical	8	9	8	12	8
Mainstream Evangelical	6	6	5	6	5
Charismatic Evangelical	8	11	6	13	10
Total Evangelical	22	26	19	31	23
Low Church	6	8	7	8	5
Broad	10	13	7	12	10
Liberal	9	12	8	13	12
Anglo-Catholic	3	4	2	5	7
«Catholic»	48	35	56	29	42
All Others	2	2	1	2	1
Total (= 100%)	248,700	336,800	607,000	255,300	410,200

by denomination 1989

Other Free	Total Free	Anglican	Roman Catholic	Orthodox	Overall
%	%	%	%	%	%
21	16	9	0	—	7
43	21	2	0	—	16
4	19	7	1	—	11
69	56	18	1	—	34
6	13	13	0	0	12
8	13	23	0	3	17
13	13	18	1	—	14
0	1	12	0	3	6
0	1	14	97	3	15
4	3	2	1	91	2
1,462	18,296	16,373	3,824	114	38,607

by region 1989

East Anglia	South East (North)	South East (Greater London)	South East (South)	South West	Overall
%	%	%	%	%	%
13	9	6	10	14	9
10	9	9	8	8	7
10	15	15	14	11	12
33	33	30	32	33	28
8	6	3	6	8	6
13	10	4	12	13	10
13	15	8	12	13	11
5	4	3	6	6	4
26	30	48	32	25	39
2	1	4	0	2	2
177,500	339,900	502,500	429,100	399,900	3,706,900

Counties by Churchmanship

The table does not show churchmanship by counties so that you cannot see in which of them the Liberals, say, are strongest. Maps 23, 25, 27, 29, 31, 33, 35, 37, 39 and 41 at the end of the book do this.

It may be helpful if the large amount of visual information in these maps is summarised in overview tabular form as follows in Table 65.

Table 65: Strength of adult churchgoers' churchmanship 1989

	Where strongest				Strong in			Proportionately strongest county(ies)
	North	Mid-lands	South East	South West	Urban Areas?	Rural Areas?	Mixed Areas?	
Broad Evangelical	Yes			Yes		Yes	Yes	Devon
Mainstream Evangelical	Yes		Yes	Yes		Yes	Yes	Cambridgeshire & Inner London Northeast
Charismatic Evangelical		Yes	Yes	Yes			Yes	Inner London Southeast
Total Evangelical	Yes		Yes	Yes		Yes	Yes	Inner London Southeast & Devon
Low Church	Yes			Yes		Yes	Yes	Lancashire and Isle of Man
Broad	Yes	Yes		Yes		Yes		Cumbria
Liberal	Yes	Yes	Yes	Yes		Yes	Yes	Oxfordshire and Wiltshire
Anglo-Catholic		Yes	Yes	Yes		Yes	Yes	Staffordshire
«Catholic»	Yes				Yes		Yes	Merseyside and Lancashire
All Others	Yes	Yes					Yes	North East London

The table shows the weakness already known from earlier tables — the lack of strength of any group in the cities across the country except those of «Catholic» persuasion. Rural and mixed strength is however common to many groups. The South East has concentrations of particular groups: Anglo-Catholics, Evangelicals and Liberals; the Midlands likewise: Anglo-Catholics, Broad churchgoers, Liberals and Others. The strongholds of different churchmanships go right across the country, and include both urban, rural and mixed areas.

What are the relative strengths of these different churchmanships? Where are they changing? Yet another series of maps (Maps 24, 26, 28, 30, 32, 34, 36, 38, 40, and 42) show these, and, again for simplicity, the implications are summarised in the following table, where a plus sign (+) indicates growth, a zero (0) indicates staticness, and a minus sign (−) indicates decline, and combinations indicates both elements.

Table 66: Change of adult churchgoers churchmanship 1985-1989

	Growing where they are Strong? Average? Weak?			Growth/Decline in Urban Rural Mixed Areas Areas Areas			No. of counties where Growing Static Declining		
Broad Evangelical	No	Partly	No	+/−	−	+/0	18	17	20
Mainstream Evangelical	Yes	Partly	No	+/−	+	+/−	25	17	13
Charismatic Evangelical	Yes	Partly	Yes	+/−	+/0	+	38	12	5
Total Evangelical	Partly	Partly	No	+/0	0	+	22	29	4
Low Church	Partly	Partly	No	−	+/0	−	10	15	30
Broad	No	No	Partly	−/0	0	−	7	21	27
Liberal	No	No	No	−	−	+/−	11	17	27
Anglo-Catholic	Partly	Partly	No	−	+	−	13	11	31
«Catholic»	No	Yes	No	+/−	+/−	0	12	24	19
All Others	No	No	Partly	0	0	0/+	14	33	8

All churchmanships are growing somewhere (on average in 13 counties or one out of every four) but are also declining somewhere too (on average in 21 counties or two in every five). They are static elsewhere. The Evangelical groups are growing in more areas than others, and the Broad and Low Church in fewest. These both, along with the Liberals and Anglo-Catholics, suffered the most widespread decline. Most growth is partial, and clearly depends on factors other than location.

APPLICATION

The importance of belief

Growth undoubtedly depends to some extent on your belief system. Otherwise why should some groups be consistently growing more than others? The importance of what we believe is recognised not only in the religious field. Kate Ludeman,[6] responsible for a training company, focuses on what she calls 'Worth Ethic', saying quite categorically that 'You cannot run an organisation on brain power and muscle power alone. You need the human heart at work.' If that is true for those in secular employment, how much more true must it be for those in religious employment? She suggests three levels of change:

- Your own beliefs, values, and attitudes must shift first. Begin by treating *yourself* as a member of the family!
- Once you have shifted your attitudes, you will relate more effectively to your co-workers and employees. You will free yourself to treat others as you treat yourself.
- Empower people by caring about them. Sometimes when David Cormack[7] concludes one of his seminars he mentions the most important three words we can use with our people: 'If you please'. The most important two words are 'Thank you', and single most important word is 'We'.

The value of belief

The value of *belief is* recognised as *crucial for* consumer *behaviour.* In a major paper at an international conference, R A Westwood[8] suggested actually defining the word 'important' to mean 'the power of a belief to motivate choice behaviour' so that the relationship between belief and behaviour could be assessed. If this is where contemporary research is aimed, how greatly must Christian people act out more what they inherently believe. So often our behaviour is *not* a manifestation of our belief. Far too many believe that what a Newcastle student[9] said is true:

'Christians are: Less free
More unfashionable
More isolated
More emotional
Less sexually fulfilled
More boring
Psychologically weaker
Having fewer interests
Less realistic
Less involved in the 'real world'
Less happy
Less friendly . . .
than me'.

In the fly leaf of a Bible of a young girl who tragically died at the age of 14 was found written:

'You are writing a gospel, a chapter a day
By things that you do and words that you say.
Men read what you write, whether faithless or true,
Say! What is the Gospel according to you?'[10]

Belief is crucial for motivation. Bobby Fischer, once the World Chess Champion, said 'The turning point in my career came when I realised you could win with black'.[11] What was the turning point in your career? What will it be? How do we make England Christian?

Belief is crucial for learning. We need to learn from each other. E D Jones[12] writing of American civilization once suggested that we 'Get religion like a Methodist. Experience it like a Baptist. Be sure of it like a Disciple. Stick to it like a Lutheran. Conciliate it like a Congregationalist. Be proud of it like an Episcopalian. Simplify it like a Quaker. Glorify it like a Jew. Pay for it like a Presbyterian. Work at it like the Salvation Army. Propagate it like a Roman Catholic.' And enjoy it like an Afro-Caribbean. We may smile but there is a truth here.

Belief is crucial for action. We need not just to have faith but to act. Dag Hammarskjold,[13] the first UN General Secretary, wrote 'Somebody placed the shuttle in your hand; somebody who already arranged the threads'. We have at our disposal resources already — how can we use them most effectively and most efficiently? How do we best do the right things and best do things right? Oswald

Chambers[14] once said, 'Jesus Christ demands of the man who trusts Him the same reckless sporting spirit that the natural man exhibits. If a man is going to do something worthwhile, there are times when he has to risk everything on his leap, and in the spiritual domain Jesus Christ demands that you risk everything you hold by common sense and leap into what He says, and immediately you do, you find that what He says fits on as solidly as common sense.' On the lunar surface is entombed a poster with the words 'Only those who risk going too far can possibly find how far they can go'.[15] This assumes one thing however:

Belief is crucial for vision. We need to know where we are going. A mountain may have a zig-zag leading to the top but its ultimate direction is accepted. What is it that you want to accomplish? What are your dreams? What are your prayers? What is your experience? How do you perceive what God says in the Scriptures? What are your gifts? Your skills? What key thing do you want to accomplish? What will be different as a consequence of your work? What will have changed because of your life by the year 2000? What do you truly believe? What is your vision? Where are you going? As Lawrence Peter once said, 'If you don't know where you're going, you'll probably end up somewhere else'. Says the leader of the DAWN strategy movement, James Montgomery, 'Growing denominations have a vision larger than themselves'.[16]

Chapter 7: Summary

- 34% of churches in 1989 were Evangelical (including 7% Broad Evangelicals), 17% Broad and 15% «Catholic».
- These represented respectively 28% (9%), 10% and 39% of adult churchgoers.
- Charismatic Evangelicals are growing fastest, followed by All Other churchmanships and Mainstream Evangelicals.
- The Anglo-Catholics and Broad adult churchgoers declined most between 1985 and 1989.
- There are 1.4 million «Catholic» adults, 1 million Evangelicals and 0.8 million Broad or Liberal churchgoers.
- Methodists are one-third Evangelical, a quarter Low Church, and two-fifths Broad/Liberal.
- Three-eighths of URC Churches are Liberal, a quarter Evangelical, a fifth Broad and nearly a fifth Low Church.
- Over three-quarters of Baptist, Independent, Afro-Caribbean and Pentecostal Churches are Evangelical.
- A quarter of Anglican Churches are Broad, one-sixth Liberal, one-sixth Evangelical, one-seventh «Catholic», one-eighth Low Church and one-eighth Anglo-Catholic.
- Roman Catholic Churches are predominantly «Catholic».
- «Catholics» are strongest in Merseyside and Lancashire, Broad/Liberals in Cumbria, Oxfordshire and Wiltshire, Evangelicals in Inner London and Devon.

8. HOW OLD ARE OUR CHURCHES?

When researching earlier the churches in Newcastle,[1] we discovered that the answers to the simple question, 'In what year was your church or congregation formed?' yielded some interesting answers — and found it was almost possible to summarise the development of Newcastle as a city through looking at when their churches were founded. Because of this experience, a similar question was included in the English Church Census.

Virtually all respondents (99%) found it an easy question to answer. A number could not give a specific year and gave events or times instead and an appropriate date was substituted. Where two dates were given, the earlier one was used, recognising that this might be when the congregation was gathered with the second date the year the church was built. As the dates are grouped into centuries or decades little accuracy is lost by a few dates thus not being quite accurate.

The figures of course refer to surviving churches. There is little knowledge, other than of those which have closed since 1985, of congregations or churches built in earlier years which subsequently closed, so we have no real guidance on the total church building programmes of our forefathers.

Win Arn has suggested that the newer the church the more likely it is to be a growing church, but as we have considered church growth in a previous chapter this idea will not be explored here.[2]

OVERALL RESULTS

The ages for the foundations for all the churches and congregations in England are given below, and illustrated graphically immediately afterwards.

Table 67: Date of foundation of church or congregation

	Before 1500	1500-1799	1800-1849	1850-1874	1875-1899	1900-1924	1925-1949	1950-1974	1975 or later	Total (=100%)
	% 23	% 6	% 12	% 12	% 14	% 9	% 8	% 10	% 6	26,125
Interval in years	1,470	300	50	25	25	25	25	25	14	1,959
Churches per year	6	8	95	185	217	132	131	155	156	20

Figure 35: Year of foundation of churches

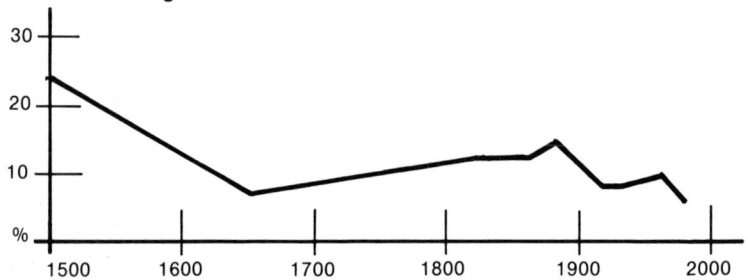

The figures reflect the great church building programme in the second half of the nineteenth century, perhaps partly stimulated by the impact of the 1851 Religious Census, which as well as seeking attendance data, asked for 'sittings' or the number of seats in a church.[3] This showed that if the whole population wished to attend church they could not all get in — there were a million seats short. While this was true nationally, it was especially true in the new urban areas where the shortfall was much greater.

The slight increase after 1950 would include those churches which had to be rebuilt as a result of Second World War damage.

The composition of these churches by denomination is given in Table 68, grossing the results up to the full number of churches in England.

There are no current Roman Catholic Churches from before 1500, since all the Catholic churches were requisitioned by Henry VIII into the Church of England. All churches from before this date are therefore now Anglican, except that the Census included a number of residential schools and colleges, some of which had

Table 68: Date of foundation by church affiliation

Church	Before 1500	1500- 1799	1800- 1849	1850- 1874	1875- 1899
Free	45	1,647	2,927	2,561	3,476
Anglican	8,678	655	1,474	1,637	1,454
Roman Catholic	–	191	344	421	497
Orthodox	–	–	–	–	–
Total	8,723	2,493	4,745	4,619	5,427

	1900- 1924	1925- 1949	1950- 1974	1975 or later	Total	%
Free	1,993	1,830	1,988	1,829	18,296	47
Anglican	839	655	819	162	16,373	43
Roman Catholic	459	765	994	153	3,824	10
Orthodox	–	15	63	36	114	0.3
Total	3,291	3,265	3,864	2,180	38,607	100

ancient beginnings, a number reflected in the 31 Free Churches before 1500.

As the Free Church movement got underway in the sixteenth, seventeenth and eighteenth centuries with the Anabaptists, Methodists and other groups, so the bulk of the churches built were in that category. It was not until the middle of the nineteenth century that all groups began to build churches in the urban industrial areas where so many people had come to live. Roman Catholic emancipation in 1829 allowed them freedom to build churches. They built about 500 in the 1850-1874 period alone.

The numbers of new Anglican Churches have decreased since 1875. The greatest development in building churches has been the Free Churches who collectively have established over half the new churches in each period since 1500. In the twentieth century the Roman Catholics especially have also built many. In the most recent period, since 1975, seven churches (or congregations) in every eight started have been Free Church, reflecting the growth in the Independent sector from the House Church Movement.

Of the churches that remain in England today, some 10,000 were built in the latter half of the nineteenth century. Of these 6,000 are Free Church, 3,100 Anglican and 900 Catholic. As with many of the houses built then, the materials used for construction meant a life of approximately 100 years. Free Churches, especially Methodist chapels, have frequently adapted to the problems of older buildings by closure, but this is less true for Anglican Churches. Older churches were built with much longer lasting materials, but today many are in urgent need of refurbishment. Since 62% of Roman Catholic Churches have been built in this century, they are currently mainly escaping this problem, but it will doubtless come in the next century.

The figures in the previous table can perhaps be more readily appreciated through their representation below.

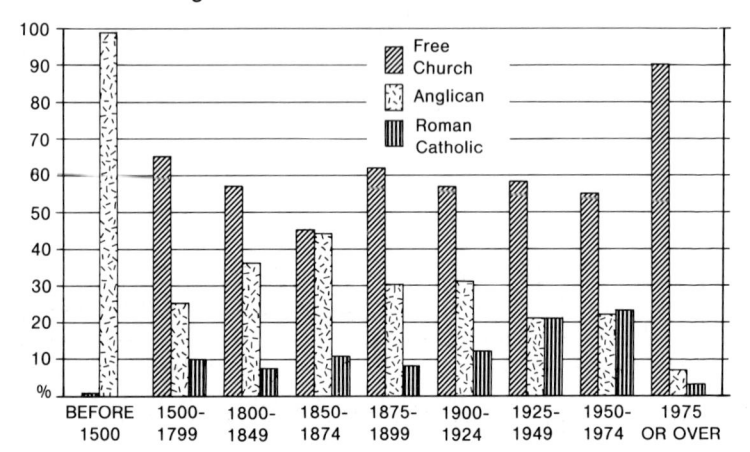

Figure 36: When churches were built

Foundation Dates by Free Church Denomination

How do the overall figures in fact break down by individual Free Church denomination? This detail is given in Table 69.

Table 69: Date of foundation of Free Churches by denomination

	Before 1500	1500-1799	1800-1849	1850-1874	1875-1899	1900-1924	1925-1949	1950-1974	1975 or later	Total (= 100%)
	%	%	%	%	%	%	%	%	%	
Methodist	—	5	22	22	24	13	5	7	2	6,740
Baptist	—	16	25	14	16	8	8	7	6	2,339
URC	—	25	20	14	15	8	8	8	2	1,681
Independent	1	5	7	7	13	10	13	14	30	4,123
Afro-Caribbean	—	—	—	—	—	—	—	57	43	949
Pentecostal	—	—	—	—	—	7	43	25	25	1,002
Other Free	—	16	3	4	39	9	12	11	6	1,462
Total	0	9	16	14	19	11	10	11	10	18,296

This again reflects history with the beginning of Pentecostalism at the turn of the twentieth century, and the immigration of Afro-Caribbeans in the 1950s and 1960s especially and their need to form their own congregations after their rejection by the whites. Although the United Reformed Church was only instituted in 1972, its Congregational and Presbyterian roots of course go back centuries. These dates are presented in graphical form below.

Figure 37: When Free Churches were built by denomination

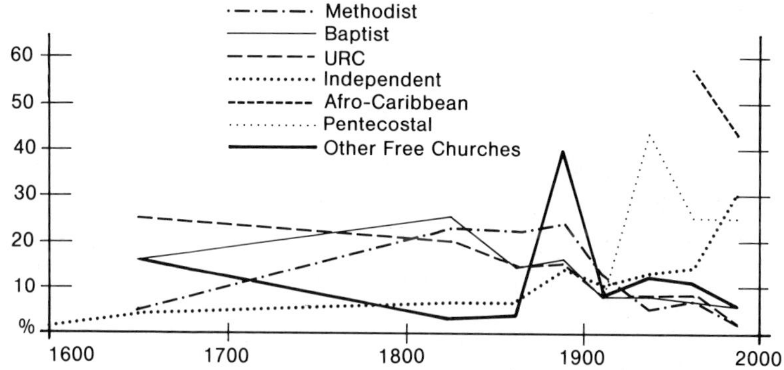

Foundation Dates of Roman Catholic and Orthodox Churches

Tables 70 and 71 give comparable information to that given in Table 69 for Roman Catholic, Orthodox and Anglican churches.

Half the Roman Catholic churches in England have been built since 1925 and three-quarters since 1875. Many of them will therefore still be young and 'fresh'. There were a few Orthodox churches before the Second World War, the bulk having been established in the immediate post-war period. However, they are still starting new congregations — five every two years.

Table 70: Date of foundation of Roman Catholic and Orthodox churches

	Before 1500	1500-1799	1800-1849	1850-1874	1875-1899	1900-1924	1925-1949	1950-1974	1975 or later	Total (= 100%)
	%	%	%	%	%	%	%	%	%	
Roman Catholic	–	5	9	11	13	12	20	26	4	3,824
Orthodox	–	–	–	–	–	–	13	55	32	114

FOUNDATION DATES OF ANGLICAN CHURCHES

Table 71: Date of foundation of later Anglican churches

Before 1500	1500-1799	1800-1849	1850-1874	1875-1899	1900-1924	1925-1949	1950-1974	1975 or later	Total (= 100%)
% 53	% 4	% 9	% 10	% 9	% 5	% 4	% 5	% 1	16,373

This table shows that 53%, or 8,600, Anglican churches now in existence were built over 500 years ago. In some senses the whole problem of Anglicanism today might be summarised by this one figure. The continuation of the past, with an immense number of historic buildings (virtually all listed or worthy of preservation), and all the traditions implicit with a structure which has lasted so long — how can it all be made relevant to the twentieth (and twenty-first) century? So many occupy prime sites at the centre of villages and towns. The land they occupy will be worth a fortune. Some people ask whether the land should be sold to allow modern buildings to be built in similar central places elsewhere. Others feel that even to raise such a question is a cause of offence.

What happens when, inevitably, some are closed? The Redundant Churches Fund was established by law in 1969. This followed recommendations from a committee under Lord Bridges, with the charge of preserving those churches of historical and archaeological interest or architectural quality which are no longer required for regular worship.

Such churches pass into the ownership of the Fund which is financed by the Church and State in partnership. By the end of 1989 some 260 churches had been vested in the Fund. Its annual expenditure was of the order of £2 million, of which 70% was provided by the Department of the Environment and 30% by the Church Commissioners.[4] The Fund thus looks after about one in seven of the churches closed.

Redundant churches not so fortunate to be owned by the Fund are usually sold and are used in a variety of ways. St Mary's at Lichfield, for example, has been turned into a cultural centre. Others have been turned into flats, or businesses. A few have been demolished or are now used as mosques or temples. In the twenty years 1970 to 1990, 1,800 Church of England churches have been closed, but nearly 400 new ones have been opened. Between 1969 and 1981 a total of 302 were opened — an average of 23 per year. Since then the average has dropped to just under 10 per year.[5] Some of these newly opened churches are deliberate church plants by existing congregations.[6]

What of the Anglican churches built before 1500? Details follow.

Table 72: Date of foundation of earlier Anglican churches

Before AD 450	450- 849	850- 1099	1100- 1299	1300- 1499	Total
%	%	%	%	%	%
0.25	3	15	28	7	53

How best should we understand these figures? Ignoring the handful (about 40) started before AD 450 and still in existence today, in the period 450 to 849 nearly 500 churches were started, that is 60 churches every 50 years. Whether that number is high or low, good for the time or not, cannot be stated. The population of the country was not then counted in regular censuses. But the figure can be used as a comparison against later times and thus we get existing churches built for every 50 years—

```
Between  450 and  849, are     60
         850 and 1099, are    500
        1100 and 1299, are  1,200
        1300 and 1499, are    300
        1500 and 1799, are    100*
        1800 and 1849, are  1,500*
        1850 and 1899, are  1,600*
        1900 and 1949, are  1,500*
        1950 and 1989, are  1,000*
```
*Anglican churches only

An astonishing number of churches were built in the twelfth and thirteenth centuries, at a rate unequalled in the centuries immediately before or after. The rate of building is of the same magnitude as in modern times, and as some churches will not have survived, may actually have exceeded the nineteenth and early twentieth peaks.

One has to ask why? The Normans had just conquered England. What did they do? Unite England, defend England, open England, institutionalise England. Viking attacks had been decreasing for some while and the development of castles made such forays more difficult. People moved into the countryside (as we would call it today). The population increased, partly perhaps because immigration was encouraged from Normandy, but also as part of a general European phenomenon. Trade links were being set up, and the landed gentry became rich in their exploitation of it. What trade? Sheep! England could graze thousands — doubtless millions — of sheep. Much grain was also cultivated, giving food for extra mouths, thereby increasing the chances of survival, so helping population growth. This was also aided by a kinder European climate. It was a time of peace, both physically and intellectually. The Renaissance had not yet begun in earnest. Religious changes were still in their infancy, the Lollards a minority. John Hus' ideas would bring change but not yet. So the population increased, expanded across the land, settling in many pleasant valleys, and had leaders wealthy enough to build both castles and churches with farming (or serf!) labour free to help much of the time. The motive for building the churches may have been to provide masses for the dead of rich families but once built others could then also attend. It may have been to replace earlier buildings: many of the 1085 Domesday Book villages would have had a church already. So the Norman invaders effectively consolidated and aided the Christianisation of the land and they did it by planting churches (building them was the only method they knew) wherever a suitable number of people lived. Small congregations, conveniently located within easy walking distance. There was acceptance by the community: they helped build the community, the community helped build them. There was public visibility, and professional leadership. It could be argued that these principles are similar to those used today by the House Church Movement and others starting new churches.

The Black Death then decimated villages, and many ceased to exist, even though their churches still stood! The high population level of the thirteenth century would not be reached again for another three hundred years. The Hundred Years' War with France brought alternative priorities for rich people's money and poor people's labour. Strong religious forces were about to be unleashed — Martin Luther's 95 Theses in 1517 had wide implications. Erasmus had translated the New Testament and Tyndale, although martyred in 1536, was about to produce the foundation for what is regarded as the most beautiful work ever produced in the English language — the 1611 Authorised Version of the Bible — which has had influence beyond words. But with the direct access to Scripture came the rise of the Non-conformists and secret meetings in the woods. The cumulative effect of all this, together with many church buildings still in use, was to reduce drastically the need for more Anglican churches, and so it continued for the next four centuries, when the massive population relocation and redeployment through the Industrial Revolution brought entirely new needs to which the Church responded in due season.

Church building thus had its heyday between 1100 and 1300 under the stabilising influence of the Normans. It was of course during this period that the majority of the country's cathedrals were built. Apart from Coventry, opened in 1962 to replace the one burnt down during the Second World War, Guildford (started in 1936 and consecrated in 1961), and Liverpool (whose foundation stone was laid in 1904 but completed only in 1978), there have been no new Anglican Cathedrals built this century. The other forty older ones are still in use, and many Dioceses still retain their original names. It was also between the eleventh and sixteenth centuries that the 100 Cathedrals in France were built.[7]

Where are the churches built before 1500 and still in existence? These are broadly indicated in Figure 39, which may be compared to the map in Figure 38 showing the location of known Roman churches in the fifth century,[8] with the modern boundaries imposed for ease of comparison.

The largest number of the oldest churches are in East Anglia and Lincolnshire, followed by the South West, especially Devon and Somerset, and then Kent in the South East. The South Midlands and South East (North) and North Yorkshire also have significant numbers.

FOUNDATION DATES BY CHURCHMANSHIP

Thus far we have looked at the age of church buildings by denomination. What of their basic beliefs? When were churches built or congregations started which reflect the various churchmanships?

Table 73 gives the relevant details.

186 'CHRISTIAN' ENGLAND

Figure 38: Church distribution in the fifth century

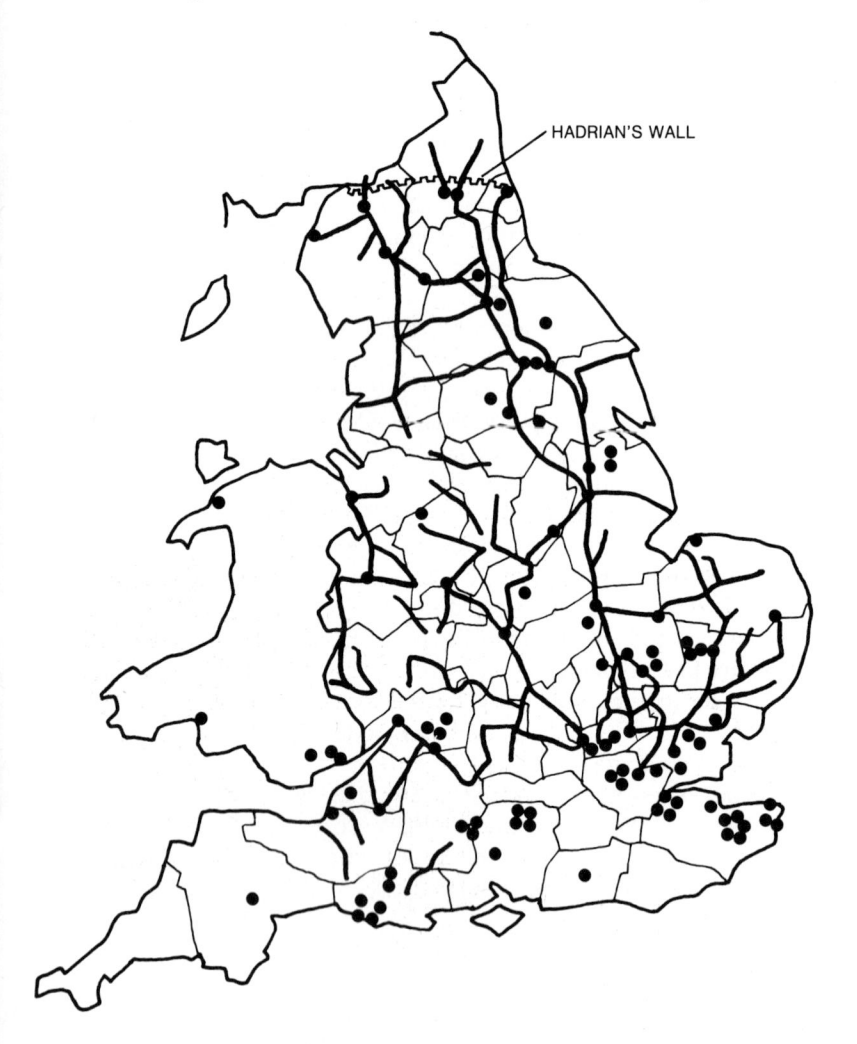

HOW OLD ARE OUR CHURCHES? 187

Figure 39: Distribution of churches built before 1500 and in use in 1989

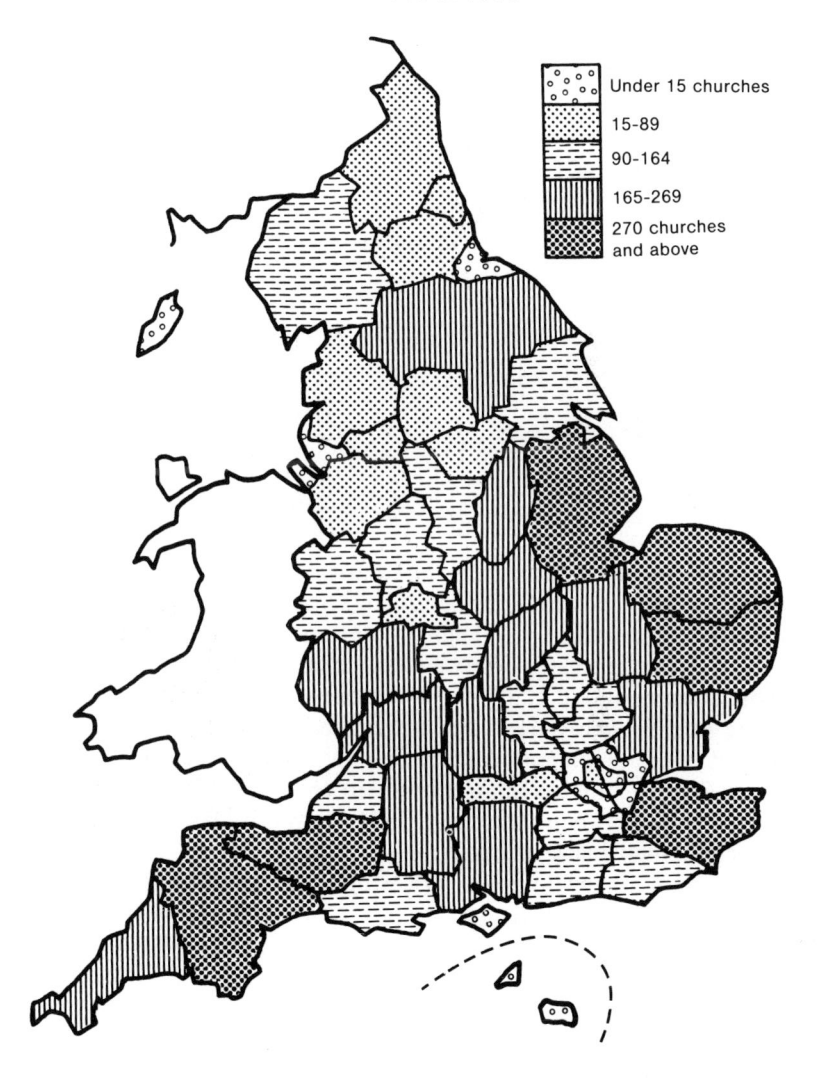

- Under 15 churches
- 15-89
- 90-164
- 165-269
- 270 churches and above

Table 73: Date of foundation of churches/congregations by churchmanship

	Before 1500	1500-1799	1800-1849	1850-1874	1875-1899	1900-1924	1925-1949	1950-1974	1975 or later	Total (=100%)
	%	%	%	%	%	%	%	%	%	
Broad Evangelical	19	7	17	15	19	9	5	6	3	4,190
Mainstream Evangelical	3	6	13	13	22	12	13	11	7	4,344
Charismatic Evangelical	9	3	9	6	10	7	13	16	27	5,107
Total Evangelical	10	5	13	11	17	9	11	11	13	13,641
Low Church	29	7	15	15	15	8	5	5	1	4,441
Broad	44	6	11	11	11	7	4	5	1	6,056
Liberal	32	8	13	11	13	8	6	7	2	5,258
Anglo-Catholic	41	4	9	14	13	8	5	6	0	2,050
«Catholic»	25	4	9	10	12	9	12	16	3	6,205
All Others	25	9	14	8	12	7	4	12	9	956
Overall	23	6	12	12	14	9	8	10	6	38,607

The Evangelicals, especially the Charismatics, have started most new churches since 1975, though many Others have also done so — mostly the Salvation Army. High proportions of all churchmanships except Evangelicals, started before 1500, reflecting the non-evangelical nature of many of the churches in rural areas, where so many of these early buildings are located. More Low Churches started in the nineteenth century than average (45% against 38%). More Other Churches started between 1875 and 1899 (Salvation Army) and between 1950 and 1974 (Seventh-Day Adventists, especially their black churches) than in other periods.

The churchmanship given is of course the current one. Unlike denomination, where changes are rare, churchmanship might well alter during the life of a church, and perhaps several times.

FOUNDATION DATE BY REGION

How has the number of church buildings varied across time over different parts of the country? Table 74 gives some detail.

These figures reflect the settlement in the Midlands and East Anglia before 1500, and in the South West also. They agree with

HOW OLD ARE OUR CHURCHES?

Table 74: Foundation date of churches/congregations by region

	Before 1500	1500-1799	1800-1849	1850-1874	1875-1899
	%	%	%	%	%
North	15	8	10	15	18
Yorks/Humberside	17	8	15	14	15
North West	7	7	16	15	19
East Midlands	33	7	13	10	13
West Midlands	24	5	14	11	13
East Anglia	48	6	7	8	11
South East (North)	30	8	10	9	10
South East (Greater London)	6	4	7	14	17
South East (South)	27	5	9	11	13
South West	32	8	14	11	13
NORTH[1]	18	7	14	13	16
SOUTH	28	6	10	11	12
Overall	23	6	12	12	14

	1900-1924	1925-1949	1950-1974	1975 or later	Total (= 100%)	Median Year
	%	%	%	%		
North	10	9	10	5	2,550	1877
Yorks/Humberside	9	9	9	4	3,827	1868
North West	11	8	12	5	4,039	1882
East Midlands	7	5	8	4	3,911	1838
West Midlands	8	8	11	6	3,868	1866
East Anglia	4	5	6	5	2,769	1600
South East (North)	8	8	11	6	3,943	1856
South East (Greater London)	14	14	12	12	3,549	1904
South East (South)	9	8	11	7	4,297	1870
South West	6	6	6	4	5,854	1836
NORTH[1]	9	8	10	5	17,602	1871
SOUTH	8	8	10	7	21,005	1859
Overall	9	8	10	6	38,607	1864

[1] Defined as in Table 28

Figure 39 as one might expect. To get a broad view of the above table it is worth looking at the median year for each region, that is, the year by which time half the existing churches in that region had been built. This is the date given in the final column. Of the ten regions, six have a median date between 1856 and 1882. Two others, East Midlands and South West have a slightly earlier year, 1838 and 1836 respectively, testifying to their earlier developments.

Two regions are quite different. East Anglia has the earliest median date due to the extraordinary number of very early churches built there and still in use today. Over half the churches (including all denominations) in both Norfolk and Suffolk were built before 1500. Over a thousand churches in those two counties were built over five centuries ago — and in fact 800 of them were built more than seven centuries ago (that is, before AD 1300).

The other exceptional county is Greater London whose late development is demonstrated partly by its having so few very old churches (some would have been destroyed by the Great Fire of 1666), but much more by the explosion of new churches in Inner London through the Afro-Caribbeans, Pentecostals and House Church Movement.

The age of churches thus yields more than might be casually considered. It reveals part of the ancient strategy of the Normans, the impact of the Industrial Revolution, and the desire to plant new churches in recent years. When a farmer was asked why foxgloves re-appear in fallow ground, he replied, 'The seeds of the past are there to create the future'.[9]

Chapter 8: Summary

- Almost a quarter of all churches in England were built more than 500 years ago.
- 33% have been built this century, and 38% in the nineteenth century.
- Over half the Anglican churches were built before 1500, 4,600 in the aftermath of the Norman conquest between 1100 and 1299.
- Forty churches can trace their origins to before AD 450.
- One Baptist church in six is over 300 years old.
- Reflecting their Congregation and Presbyterian origins, a quarter of URC churches were built before 1800.
- 9,000 Free Churches were built in the nineteenth century, and half as many Anglican churches.
- Five churches in every eight built this century have been Roman Catholic, 1,150 of them since the end of the Second World War.
- Over 2,000 churches/congregations have been started in the fourteen years 1975-1989.
- Twice as many of the oldest churches in the land are south of the line joining the Wash and the Severn as are north of it.

9. GIVING TO THE THIRD WORLD

The final question on the form asked 'Which of the following types of Third World Community Aid do you think your church would most wish to support?' Eight alternatives were given — six specific positives, the inevitable 'other, please specify' and a negative: 'We prefer not to give support to this type of work'. Although very few ticked the 'other' or 'negative' box (3% between them) they are sufficiently important to be retained initially.

The six positives were:

Description on questionnaire	*Abbreviation used in this chapter*
1) Types of activity, such as water supply irrigation, medical projects, etc.	Projects
2) Specific geographical areas, such as particular countries or districts in which you take a special interest.	Countries
3) Aid to named communities, such as particular villages or tribal groups.	Communities
4) Aid to named individuals, such as sponsored children.	Individuals
5) Aid to be administered through local churches overseas.	Via churches
6) Evangelism and other missionary work.	Missionaries

Obviously in practice some of these can overlap, and those completing the form were allowed to choose up to three. Many more couldn't count this time — it was the end of the form after all! — and 1½% of respondents ticked four or more boxes. These were all amended to the most appropriate group of three. The most popular combination (19%) was categories (1), (2), (5) and (6). We deleted the (2) in this case.

A full list of categories is given in *Prospects for the Nineties* in the Notes and Definitions Section. Where the name of an organisation (such as Christian Aid, Cafod, Tear Fund, Church Missionary Society) was given, as it sometimes was under 'other' categories appropriate to the work of that organisation were allocated. The main type of 'other' was churches sending money for distribution to their headquarters which sometimes used it for Home Mission, or where money was specially used to help buy Third World commodities.

There were no obvious combinations of categories which could helpfully be used as there were with the churchmanship question. In the following tables therefore the percentages do not add up to 100%, but generally to between 165% and 200%. This is the total of the actual numbers ticking particular boxes — on average nearly two boxes each. In this way the strength of the individual categories can be better assessed. The question was not retrospective, so all answers relate to 1989.

This question also generated a fair amount of correspondence. Some objected to its inclusion at all since it did not seem relevant to church attendance. This is so, but such support reflects attitudes to the wider world, a key and growing interest. Others objected to the wording and examples used, for instance, sponsored children for Individuals, as not everyone accepts this is a beneficial means of helping the Third World. But it was only an example; at least some churches — perhaps many ticking this category — support particular adults because they said so ('Mr Smith with ABC Society'), so the idea conveyed seems to have been correctly understood by most.

OVERALL RESULTS

These are given in Table 75; the second percentage column reduces the actual response to a 100% percentage total since some will wish to use these, as for example, in Figure 40.

Table 76 shows when the various churches supporting the different categories held their services. Each column totals to 100%.

The churches either not supporting Third World Aid or giving in other ways tended to have single services on a Sunday much more frequently than other churches. This suggests they are smaller churches, perhaps, declining churches, less able to give scarce

GIVING TO THE THIRD WORLD 193

Table 75: Type of Third World aid given by churches

	As given on the forms	Reduced to sum to 100%
	%	%
Missionaries	54	29
Projects	42	23
Via Churches	38	21
Countries	19	10
Individuals	17	9
Communities	12	6
No support	2	2
Other	1	
Total	185	100

Figure 40: Third World support

- Missionaries
- Projects
- Via Churches
- Communities and Individuals
- Countries
- No Support

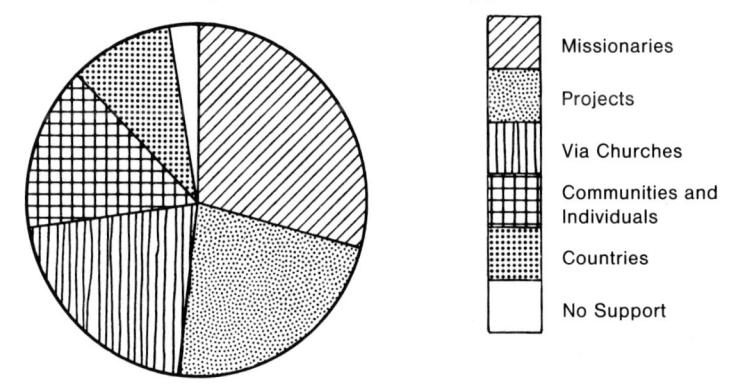

Table 76: Type of Third World aid by church services 1989

	Missionaries	Projects	Via Churches	Countries
	%	%	%	%
Morning only	31	40	37	43
Morning and Evening	58	49	50	49
Evening only	11	11	13	8

	Individuals	Communities	No support	Other	Total
	%	%	%	%	%
Morning only	35	46	59	60	38
Morning and Evening	56	47	15	17	51
Evening only	9	7	26	23	11

resources to others. How far they are like this because they have no vision to help the Third World or vice versa could be discussed, but the items seem to be clearly linked in the above table. These two categories ('No Support' and 'Other') are not discussed further in this chapter.

Combinations of Third World Support

Which combinations of aid categories were most popular? The following table gives this information with each "Yes" meaning that that category(ies) only is(are) being considered on that line. A maximum of three per line was allowed. 91% of churches gave answers to this question (64% of all churches in England). Allowing for the 3% of 'Other' and 'No Support', Table 77 is based on 88% of answers or 23,536 forms and the percentages are of that figure.

The three most popular category combinations by far are Missionaries via Churches, Missionaries and Projects, and Missionaries by themselves. Third World aid in the eyes of churches supporting them is *primarily focused around expatriates,* some of whom they may well know. This is therefore not giving through a third party. How then will churches be weaned away to give to those whom they don't know? What will happen to church support in the Third World as Protestant missionary numbers decrease?[1] What happens to Third World aid as the missionary's typical stay becomes increasingly short-term? What does this say for the outlook of churchgoers in their twenties and thirties whose interest is more localised anyway? What does this mean for missionary societies and relief and development organisations? How do we involve people in generating support? Part of the answer is that patterns of giving are changing. Live Aid draws many people in. Aid is becoming more professional with much less focus on missionary and church outlets.

THIRD WORLD SUPPORT BY CHURCH ENVIRONMENT

How does giving to Third World Community Aid vary by church's different environments? The basic figures are given in Table 78.

Three groups (city centre and the two types of rural area) commitment to missionaries is especially low. This probably

Table 77: Combinations of types of Third World aid given by churches 1989

Projects	Countries	Com-munities	Individuals	Via Churches	Mis-sionaries	%
Yes						7.2
Yes	Yes					3.4
Yes	Yes	Yes				0.6
Yes	Yes		Yes			0.3
Yes	Yes			Yes		0.7
Yes	Yes				Yes	1.6
Yes		Yes				2.2
Yes		Yes	Yes			0.3
Yes		Yes		Yes		0.5
Yes		Yes			Yes	0.6
Yes			Yes			2.6
Yes			Yes	Yes		0.4
Yes			Yes		Yes	1.5
Yes				Yes		5.8
Yes				Yes	Yes	3.4
Yes					Yes	11.0
	Yes					1.8
	Yes	Yes				0.9
	Yes	Yes	Yes			0.3
	Yes	Yes		Yes		0.2
	Yes	Yes			Yes	0.2
	Yes		Yes			0.9
	Yes		Yes	Yes		0.2
	Yes		Yes		Yes	0.5
	Yes			Yes		2.5
	Yes			Yes	Yes	1.0
	Yes				Yes	4.1
		Yes				1.2
		Yes	Yes			0.9
		Yes	Yes	Yes		0.4
		Yes	Yes		Yes	0.4
		Yes		Yes		1.1
		Yes		Yes	Yes	0.7
		Yes			Yes	1.3
			Yes			1.4
			Yes	Yes		1.4
			Yes	Yes	Yes	2.5
			Yes		Yes	3.2
				Yes		5.9
				Yes	Yes	11.4
					Yes	10.7

Table 78: Types of Third World Aid by church environment 1989

	Missionaries	Projects	Via Churches	Countries	Individuals	Communities	Total
	%	%	%	%	%	%	%
City centre	49	47	38	19	18	16	187
Inner city	58	37	38	22	14	11	180
Council estate	58	38	34	17	20	13	180
Suburban/ urban fringe	57	45	40	21	18	13	194
Separate town	59	43	39	20	19	11	191
Other built-up area	62	39	34	18	20	13	186
Rural: commuter/ dormitory	51	43	39	21	19	13	186
Rural: other area	49	40	37	16	14	10	166
URBAN[1]	57	43	39	20	18	13	190
TOWN[2]	60	42	38	20	19	12	191
RURAL[3]	50	41	38	18	16	11	174
Overall	54	42	38	19	17	12	182

[1] Defined as the first four categories   [2] The fifth and sixth categories
[3] The last two categories

reflects that churchgoers in these areas know far fewer missionaries in the rural context because fewer missionaries come from or go back to those areas. The city centre churches will tend to have many student members and therefore a higher turnover. This means there is little likelihood of continuity of contact if a missionary only returns every four years.

Missionary support is the only one to vary significantly across the different environments. If rural churches give less, perhaps because they have less to give, where do they tend to give their support? If they were strong in other areas this might be a guide to alternative giving. But in fact every other category showing a percentage in Table 78 is lower for rural churches — the implication is that rather than other categories replacing missionaries, the lack of missionaries to stimulate support simply reduces giving slightly.

Two things must be noted however. The first is that this discussion relates to giving by churches. Giving by individuals is different, and is stimulated in different ways. Secondly although the key focus of much church giving is associated with missionaries, nevertheless many churches do support via the other categories.

THIRD WORLD SUPPORT BY CHURCHMANSHIP

The second caveat above is supported when we look at the variations in giving overseas by the churchmanship of churches. This is highlighted in the next table which is illustrated in the following diagram.

Table 79: Types of Third World aid by churchmanship 1989

	Missionaries	Projects	Via Churches	Countries	Individuals	Communities	Total
	%	%	%	%	%	%	%
Broad Evangelical	69	40	41	16	19	8	195
Mainstream Evangelical	85	30	31	13	17	5	183
Charismatic Evangelical	82	27	36	22	23	7	199
Total Evangelical	76	31	35	17	19	7	187
Low Church	50	40	37	15	16	9	173
Broad	42	45	40	20	16	12	180
Liberal	38	51	44	22	17	16	191
Anglo-Catholic	40	41	39	24	17	16	181
«Catholic»	37	56	36	21	15	19	186
All Others	40	37	37	17	12	11	165
Overall	54	42	38	19	17	12	182

Figure 41: Third World support by churchmanship

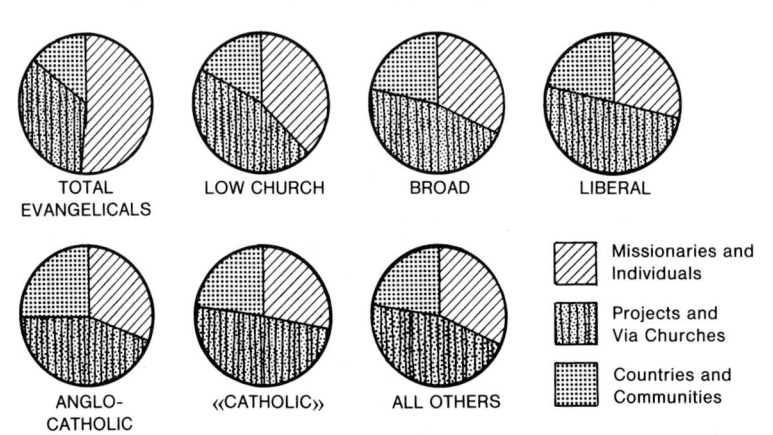

The main variation with churchmanship is seen in the relationship between evangelical giving to the Third World for missionaries and individuals (the latter especially comes from the House Churches, which frequently give to particular people known to them who may well not be missionaries).

Other churchmanships all support missionaries less (all except the Low Church much less). Projects are specially supported by Liberal and «Catholic» Churches, and rather less by Others. Via Churches does not vary greatly with churchmanship, even with Evangelicals. Four in every nine (44%) Liberal Churches give to Third World using a local church overseas. Countries are supported by a quarter of Anglo-Catholic Churches, and almost as high a proportion of Liberal Churches. Individuals are relatively poorly supported by the Other Churches. «Catholic» Churches are much more likely than others to support particular communities, or groups. Evangelicals and Low Church are less likely to do so. The comments in this paragraph might be taken to support Bible Society's suggestion that '60% of churchgoers and 43% of clergy in England and Wales consider giving to meet people's physical needs overwhelmingly more important than meeting their spiritual needs'.[2]

What sort of churchmanship are you? How much do you conform to the above pattern? Why? What strengths does it have? What weaknesses? Should you change in some way? If so, what is the first step you must take to begin that process?

THIRD WORLD SUPPORT BY REGION

Does this type of giving to the Third World vary across the country? The answer is given in the following table, and, as can be seen, the variations are insignificant.

A church's willingness to give to the Third World does not vary by the part of the country it is located in, so the general conclusions reached apply nationally.

Table 80: Types of Third World aid by region 1989

	Mis-sionaries	Pro-jects	Via Churches	Countries	Indi-viduals	Com-munities	Total
	%	%	%	%	%	%	%
North	52	44	39	17	16	12	180
Yorks/Humberside	53	44	40	18	15	11	181
North West	56	46	38	17	19	11	187
East Midlands	53	40	36	16	16	9	170
West Midlands	53	41	37	21	17	12	181
East Anglia	49	40	35	17	16	11	168
South East (North)	54	42	36	20	19	13	184
South East (Greater London)	59	40	37	21	17	12	186
South East (South)	55	42	40	21	20	14	192
South West	55	41	39	22	17	12	186
NORTH[1]	54	43	38	18	17	11	181
SOUTH	54	41	38	20	17	13	183
Overall	54	42	38	19	17	12	182

[1] Defined as in Table 28

Third World Aid

It is in fact by churchmanship that giving varies. This is the most significant factor. The Census asked no question on amounts given, so it is not possible to compare intention with practice.

The Christian public likes to ensure today that its money is spent on identifiable people for projects than on less specific things — hence a greater support for projects and people than for general programmes. David Barrett suggests that the 32% of the Christians in the world use 62% of its resources, and spend 97% of the consequent wealth on themselves.[3] Membership rolls in the UK have been falling faster than ministerial decline or church building closures, so the pressures on the faithful few will increase. A new generation needs to be taught afresh an up-to-date theology of stewardship, whereby those who follow Him who had no place to lay His head, place their earnings, their houses, their time, ambitions and opportunities afresh into His hands. That in effect means a reworked theology of the Kingdom of God.

Chapter 9: Summary

- Churches preferred mostly to support missionary and other work of evangelism in the Third World (29%).
- This was followed by support for project activities (23%) and giving via local churches (21%).
- Broad, Liberal and «Catholic» Churches especially favoured project activities.
- Evangelical and Low Churches preferred supporting missionary work.
- Figures varied little by either region or church environment.

10. TOWARDS A CHRISTIAN ENGLAND

Where are we? The English Church Census has given a photograph of church-going on October 15th 1989. It has shown the strengths of that church attendance by denomination, by churchmanship and by church environment both collectively and as it varies across the country. It has looked at all this detail by adult churchgoers, children in church and church members. Where have we come from? The Census has enabled general trends to be noted since details were requested for 1985 and the overall figures may be compared with the previous Census results for 1975 and 1979 wherever similar data was collected. Some of those trends are positive, some negative.

Where are we going? What do the trends suggest for the future? 'We are now what we have been becoming,' Spencer Bower once said.[1] That is true, but the interesting corollary is 'What will we become?' as the year 2000 approaches. If we dare think of England as Christian we need to know the answer *assuming present trends continue*. That always has to be the proviso. If revival comes or the Lord returns (or both!) the outcome will be somewhat different. So this chapter looks cautiously ahead. If we don't like what we see, then now is the time to take action to prevent the anticipated from happening. Do you feel depressed, overwhelmed at the task? Mary Wang, the Chinese church leader, quoted Pastor Wang once: 'When I am down, I look up to God, and when I look up, I am always blessed.'[2]

NOMINAL CHRISTIANITY

One aspect not so far examined is the number of nominal Christians, here defined as 'church members who do not regularly attend church'. Some thus included would have been regular attenders now prevented from going by physical infirmity; this number is unknown. A proxy for these nominal numbers can be obtained by subtracting the number of churchgoers from the number of church members. Overall the figure is 3.5 million or 9% of the adult population. This is *in addition* to the 10% of churchgoers, making those positively connected with the church in England 19% of the adult population.

Unfortunately for this purpose the Roman Catholic Church includes young children in their membership figure which few Anglican or Free Churches do, so these need to be left out. Also the Free Churches overall have more churchgoers than church members and it is not possible to have negative nominal members! If the figures are adjusted for these two features[3] they are as given in the next table, using Census definitions, not total church community figures.

Table 81: Estimated number of nominal members 1989

Category	Free Churches	Anglican	Roman Catholic	Total	% of adult population
Adult churchgoers	1,249,000	1,143,900	1,304,600	3,706,900	10
Adult members	1,174,200	1,559,000	3,609,500	6,574,800	17[4]
Nominal adult members	95,000	415,100	2,304,900	2,815,000	7

In addition to adults there are the children who go to church (and the child Catholic Church members). These amount together to 1,481,700 children, 17% of the child population. The total number of people, both children and adults, is 8,056,500 which was 17% of the total English population in 1989. By 1990 this had decreased to 16%. It will be instructive to estimate similar figures for Wales and Scotland, from their similar Censuses; these follow and are then represented diagrammatically from an update of a table for 1980.[5]

This contains a new category — that of Notional Christians, who are 'Those who would say they are Christian but are neither church members nor regular churchgoers'. The diagram shows that change in the British religious scene is relatively slow — a percentage point or two over a decade. This is slower than was thought a few years ago. The percentage of people connected with the church in Great Britain is 18% (1% + 9% + 8% in the fourth line). The English

Table 82: Churchgoers and members in Great Britain as a percentage of relevant population 1990

	England	Wales	Scotland	Total Great Britain
	%	%	%	%
Adult churchgoers	9.4	12.5	15.3	10.1
Adult members	15.9	20.5	38.8	18.2
Children connected with church	16.1	25.1	24.0	17.3
All ages connected with church	15.9	21.5	36.0	18.0
Nominal members	6.5	9.0	20.7	7.9

Figure 42: Religious structure of population in Great Britain 1990
Figures in brackets give 1980 percentages

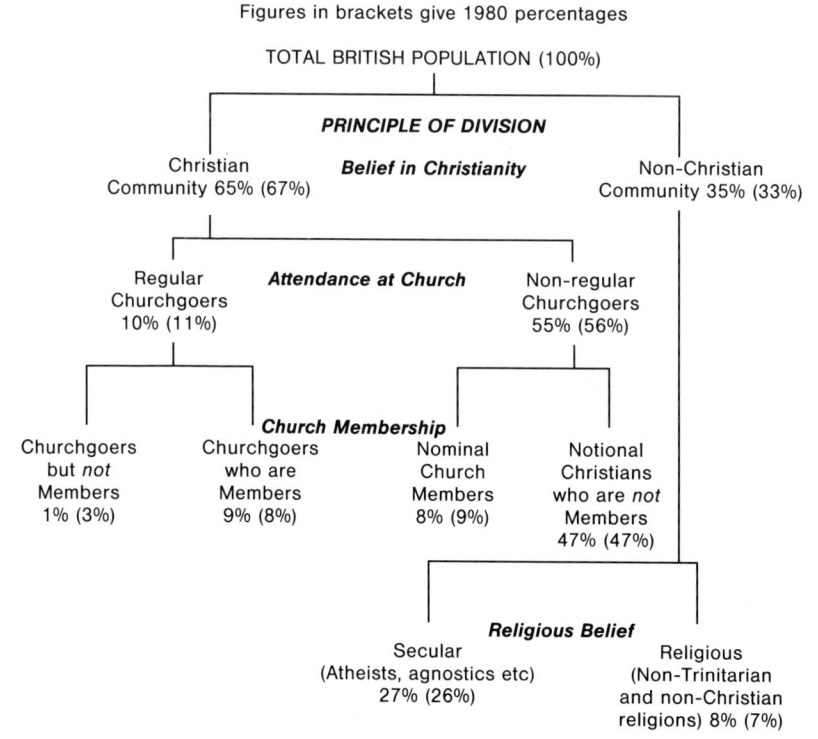

TOTAL BRITISH POPULATION (100%)

PRINCIPLE OF DIVISION
Belief in Christianity

Christian Community 65% (67%) — Non-Christian Community 35% (33%)

Attendance at Church

Regular Churchgoers 10% (11%) — Non-regular Churchgoers 55% (56%)

Church Membership

Churchgoers but *not* Members 1% (3%) — Churchgoers who are Members 9% (8%) — Nominal Church Members 8% (9%) — Notional Christians who are *not* Members 47% (47%)

Religious Belief

Secular (Atheists, agnostics etc) 27% (26%) — Religious (Non-Trinitarian and non-Christian religions) 8% (7%)

percentage of 17% in Table 81 rises to this 18% for Great Britain because of higher numbers of church people in Wales and Scotland. That 18% was 20% ten years ago — but three changes are locked into that drop of 2%. They are all important, and are:

- Nominal church members have dropped from 9% of the population to 8% — a decline of over half a million people, of whom at least two-thirds will simply have died. It is difficult to estimate the number of church members dying as it has been assumed that the ages and genders of church members (which are not known) are the same as those of churchgoers (which are). The proportions of deaths are probably higher, in fact, as church members are likely to be older than churchgoers. Even so, the percentage dying does not account for all the decline, suggesting a lapse in faith among some church members, that is, they are renouncing their *membership* (however occasional their attendance may have been at this stage). As already mentioned some research suggests that this might well be an especial problem among Roman Catholic members. Frank Field, the Labour MP for Birkenhead, said at a Diocesan Communication Officers' Conference in Cambridge: 'An organisation in decline controls the membership',[6] and we are seeing some evidence of this in some churches.

- Numbers of churchgoers who are also members have increased from 8% of the population in 1980 to 9% in 1990. This suggests a greater uniformity and cohesion, and greater emphasis on membership and its implications (that is, regular church-going is expected). Perhaps some churches are encouraging membership more, knowing the commitment this often brings. Some attempts at this (for example, in the Salvation Army) are known to be successful. Does it work rather better on older people than young? Alas, that is not known.

- The percentage of churchgoers who are *not* members has dropped from 3% of the population in 1980 to 1% in 1990. Given the apparent fluidity of opinions, the ease of transport, the desire for lack of specific commitments, especially among the younger people, such a large drop was not to be expected. While some of this 1% will undoubtedly be new people, not yet Christian maybe, certainly not yet involved within a church, the decline is still great. However, the 1% still represents more than half a million people and perhaps a fifth of these might be those who went forward at the Billy Graham or other campaigns. But why the decline? It suggests that people are not willing to 'go and see' what church is like. It suggests the church is becoming more marginalised — acceptable to insiders, but with fewer wanting to join. How then do we make our churches sufficiently attractive for people to choose to attend them rather than do other things?

Figure 42 also shows that the percentage of Notional Christians in the population has remained the same. The overall 'pool' has not declined; no equivalent of dry weather to lower the level. The dam is as full as ever it was.

The number of people associated outside basic Trinitarian Christianity has increased — from 7% to 8%. The *UK Christian Handbook* shows that the growth points here are the increases in two particular non-trinitarian churches (the Jehovah's Witnesses and the Mormons) and the increasing numbers of Muslims.

The percentage of those identifying themselves as 'secular' has also increased by 1% to 27% of the population. This is a relatively small increase and shows that underneath the surface there is a large amount of latent religiosity (to give it no narrower a meaning). This continues what is already known about implicit religion in this country, and the high percentage in Western Europe generally of those connected, however remotely, with a Christian church. Despite all that is said, the majority of people still believe in God.

What does all this imply for the future? It suggests that **Christianity is becoming a more active religion.** Nominal Christianity is losing ground, church membership is gaining ground, even if church attendance has been decreasing and will continue to do so. If you are going to be a Christian you will need to express it in some positive form of life-style. The issue is becoming more specific, more black and white; the grey is slowly receding. That means that Christians will have a more definite image, with the clout to bring pressure. Christianity is therefore likely to become more political, suggesting solutions to injustice, poverty and violence. It means that Christians will probably be more willing than previously to 'Stand up and be counted', as the British Council of Churches Report of that title urged back in 1972. The activity relates to one's individual expression of Christian concern, rather than an expansion in the size of numbers going to church.

It also suggests that ***Christianity is becoming a more closed religion.*** The variety of viewpoints within Christianity could slowly decrease. In the Church of England which of all churches stands for so many things, it is only the «Catholic» and Mainstream Evangelical groups which are growing. Whatever else is true about these two groups they both stand for something. 'In most of the political issues of our day, in the fight for instance, for the institution of the family, Evangelical and Catholic are side by side,' writes the prominent MEP for Cambridge, Sir Frederick Catherwood.[7] That implies that churchgoers will increasingly move into one or other camp. It is interesting that the Census shows that even in the four groups so closely identified with evangelicalism (the Pentecostals, Afro-Caribbeans, Baptists and Independents) *all* have some who see themselves as «Catholic» (the Afro-Caribbeans and Independents especially).

It also suggests that ***Christianity will need to become a more attractive religion.*** Most people are not attracted to active, closed groups, which can often function like pressure groups. If Christianity is to increase it will be by people joining us not because they have to, but because they want to. We must show love not just for one another but for those outside too. Bridges *must* be built into the non-Christian world. Unless we can get alongside people, befriend them at their time of need, how can they know the reality of Christ's love? Our arms are His arms today, our legs are His legs, our mouth His mouth. This means becoming more holistic, more involved with the real world, more dedicated to social issues, more concerned to see justice truly done, more willing to play a part to change society. The lessons from the success of Ichthus could be copied throughout Britain. We have to become accessible by non-churchgoers.

The figures do not suggest we are likely to lose much of our God-consciousness. They show other religions and groups such as the Jehovah's Witnesses and Mormons becoming more popular. The figures suggest that secularisation will increase, but slowly. They do not suggest immediate cataclysmic change but rather a continuing window of opportunity. How well will we take it?

FUTURE ATTENDANCE BY DENOMINATION

How many people will be going to church in the year 2000 in England? Forecasting 11 years ahead is not easy, especially when the earliest comparable figures are 1975. People don't normally take 14 years knowledge and jump 11 ahead! The 1975 data also is only available by denomination and county, and only adults and members. Churchmanship and environment only date from 1985, and extrapolating 11 years ahead on the basis of only four would be totally foolish were it not possible to constrain these guestimates by the results of the larger look forecast. *Prospects for the Nineties* does give some future projections for children and members but we will limit ourselves here to adult churchgoers and church buildings or congregations.

If present trends continue the number of churches is set to increase very slightly — up 1% to 39,000, virtually the same number as in 1979. The distribution of those churches will be different however as Table 83 shows.

Table 83: Number of churches/congregations 1979-2000

	1979	Change	1989	Change	2000
Methodist	7,650	−900	6,750	−850	5,900
Baptist	2,200	+150	2,350	+100	2,450
URC	1,850	−150	1,700	−150	1,550
Independent	3,450	+650	4,100	+1,450	5,550
Afro-Caribbean	800	+150	950	+50	1,000
Pentecostal	950	+50	1,000	+100	1,100
Other Free	1,450	0	1,450	+50	1,500
Total Free	18,350	−50	18,300	+750	19,050
Anglican	16,950	−550	16,400	−800	15,600
Roman Catholic	3,650	+150	3,800	+400	4,200
Orthodox	100	0	100	+50	150
Total	39,050	−450	38,600	+400	39,000

Although there is initially no change in the total number of churches and congregations between the beginning and end of the last twenty years of the twentieth century, the number of Methodist and Anglican Churches have considerably decreased — between them they have lost (net) 3,000 buildings in this period. Both are building new churches, however, and the figures are net figures. In 1989 the Church of England, for the first time this century, opened more new churches than it closed redundant ones.

The URC will have closed 300 in 1979-2000 if present trends continue, but the Baptist, Afro-Caribbean, Pentecostals and Orthodox will all have opened fairly modest numbers. The Roman Catholics look set to open another church for every ten they hold in 1989. The really massive change is the 2,100 new churches or congregations to be opened by the Independents between 1979 and 2000. Two-thirds of this number are projected as new congregations for the 1990s. That's a substantial projection.

Those churches reflect growth in the Independent sector, which by 2000 looks to become the third largest 'denominational' group after the Anglican and Roman Catholic. Change in attendance is shown below, and although negative, it is but an extrapolation of present trends. The outcome predicted is not inevitable, and the Decade of Evangelism in the 1990s could well cause significant variations from these projections — and we hope it does.

Table 84: Number of adult churchgoers by denomination 1979-2000

	1979	Change	1989	Change	2000
		%		%	
Methodist	447,000	−11	396,100	−11	352,000
Baptist	203,000	−2	199,400	+3	205,000
URC	139,000	−18	114,000	−20	91,000
Independent	206,000	+42	292,800	+36	397,000
Afro-Caribbean	66,000	+4	68,500	+2	70,000
Pentecostal	88,000	+8	95,200	+25	119,000
Other Free	98,000	−15	83,000	−12	73,000
Total Free	1,247,000	0	1,249,000	+5	1,307,000
Anglican	1,256,000	−9	1,143,900	−11	1,017,000
Roman Catholic	1,515,000	−14	1,304,600	−15	1,112,000
Orthodox	7,000	+34	9,400	+28	12,000
Total	4,025,000	−8	3,706,900	−7	3,448,000

Some of the larger downward trends in this table are due to demographic factors.[8] The Methodists, URC and Anglicans all have substantial proportions of their members aged over 65 — respectively 30%, 30% and 23%. Of the net 44,000 drop in Methodist churchgoers in the eleven years 1989-2000, 37,000 (84%) are likely to be simply because of the death of those over 65. 11,000 of the URC's decline of 23,000 (48%) are likely to be through death, and likewise of the Anglican decline of 127,000, 82,000 or 64% will probably be by death of its older people. These are substantial numbers and proportions to lose in this way. By comparison of the projected drop in 193,000 Roman Catholics, only 65,000 or 34% will be through death of the elderly. The overall picture of decline by deaths is given below.

Table 85: Churchgoing by age and gender 1989-2000

Age of church-goers	1989 Attendance (thousands) M	W	T	Assumed average age	Percentage likely to die 1989-2000 M	W	Residual 2000 attendance of 1989 attenders (thousands) M	W	T	Percentage change 1989-2000
					%	%				%
15-19	137	183	320	17	0.9	0.3	136	182	318	−1
20-29	183	275	458	25	0.9	0.5	181	274	455	−1
30-44	320	503	823	37	2.2	1.5	313	495	808	−2
45-64	458	641	1,099	55	15	8.7	389	585	974	−11
65 & over	366	641	1,007	72	33	30	245	449	694	−31
Total	1,464	2,243	3,707				1,264	1,985	3,249	−12

M = Men   W = Women   T = Total

This table shows a net drop of 12% churchgoers in the final decade of the century simply through death. 458,000 churchgoers are likely to die between 1989 and 2000, but the net decline projected is only 259,000 or 7%. In other words these figures, which seem depressing, actually contain an *increase* of 199,000 (458,000 less 259,000) or a growth of 5%. The increase of 199,000 churchgoers is in the context of a population increase of 1.4 million over the same period.

This analysis shows that the church *is* winning people, and is expected to continue to do so in the eleven years 1989-2000. The figures will not show as an increase, however, until the numbers joining exceed those dying. The church as a whole has many elderly people, a much higher proportion than in the population as a whole (19% against 15%). So our vision for an enlarging church is happening.

FUTURE ATTENDANCE BY CHURCH ENVIRONMENT

It is worth looking briefly at how churchgoers are likely to change by the environment of their church, given in the table below. It must be remembered there are four years between 1985 and 1989, but eleven years between 1989 and 2000.

Table 86: Adult churchgoers by environment 1985-2000

	1985	Change	1989	Change	2000
		%		%	
City centre	211,600	−5	200,300	−16	169,000
Inner city	384,300	−3	372,700	−14	320,000
Council estate	300,600	−1	297,600	−9	272,000
Suburban/ urban fringe	1,291,600	−2	1,270,300	−8	1,171,000
Separate town	580,100	+2	589,300	−1	583,000
Other built-up area	170,400	−1	167,900	−1	166,000
Rural: commuter/ dormitory	404,100	−1	400,500	−4	384,000
Rural: other	412,000	−1	408,300	−6	383,000
Total	3,755,000	−1	3,706,900	−7	3,448,000

The urban areas are expected to decline much faster than churchgoing in other areas, especially the city centre and inner city. Not only are these two areas the weakest areas now, but that weakness is likely to be exacerbated in the 1990s.

In contrast the separate towns and other built-up areas will blossom relatively, even if absolutely declining. Presumably new churches will continue to be started in these areas, especially as when people move they are often much more willing to experiment, and those alive to such willingness may well see extra numbers coming.

Likewise the rural areas will do better than average even if still declining. The more remote areas suffer more than the commuter belts, which with people relocating often gives an impulse to go and see when given a friendly welcome.

FUTURE ATTENDANCE BY CHURCHMANSHIP

Detail for the same years for churchmanship is given below: again please remember the first two-year points span four years and the second two eleven.

Compared with the overall change, Mainstream Evangelicals, the Low Church and Others are about average. Broad Evangelicals, Broad churchgoers and «Catholics» are somewhat worse than average, and since many of these are Anglicans and Methodists, the figures reflect the high numbers of their people likely to die in the next decade.

Table 87: Adult churchgoers by churchmanship 1985-2000

	1985	Change	1989	Change	2000
		%		%	
Broad Evangelical	349,100	−3	340,300	−10	305,000
Mainstream Evangelical	256,500	+2	262,800	−5	249,000
Charismatic Evangelical	394,800	+7	424,700	+17	497,000
Total Evangelical	1,000,400	+3	1,027,200	+2	1,051,000
Low Church	243,500	−4	233,700	−7	218,000
Broad	389,800	−5	369,900	−11	328,000
Liberal	426,500	−4	409,900	−12	361,000
Anglo-Catholic	169,600	−5	161,500	−14	139,000
«Catholic»	1,466,300	−2	1,444,200	−10	1,294,000
All Others	58,900	+3	60,500	−6	57,000
Total	3,755,000	−1	3,706,900	−7	3,448,000

It is the Liberals and Anglo-Catholics which seem likely to fare worst, with the largest declines, and with strong Methodist, Anglican and URC components the death factor is again relevant. It is the Charismatic Evangelicals alone which are expected to grow and to grow substantially.

This table shows the changing nature of English Christianity. Charismatic Evangelicals were 11% of the total in 1985, but by the year 2000 their proportion will have increased to 14%. The Liberals on the other hand were also 11% of the 1985 total, but will drop to 10% by 2000, a small but real change. Gradually therefore our belief systems are being reflected in the nature of our church attendance, but the changes are slow and will not pass away in the next generation — or even three or four generations at the present pace of change.

WHAT THEN OF THE FUTURE?

Where does this all bring us? Changing beliefs, declining religion in our cities and dying churchpeople. What kinds of people will we need in our churches as we look ahead soberly but realistically?

Quality Leaders

The Census has *not* looked at styles of leadership, nor their involvement with laity, nor laity v clergy, or length of service or other such factors. But indubitably church attendance in some way relates to leadership, though, as with television, 'there is no necessary relationship between appreciation scores and audience size'.[9] After Archbishop Robin Eames had finished speaking at Synod in July 1989 he got a standing ovation; the question he had posed was 'How far does the churchman provide prophetic leadership which his own people may not want to hear?'[10] The answer is probably 'not far', but it needs to be farther if the church in England is to move from the trends which currently grip it. 'Christian leaders have the arduous task of responding to personal struggles, family conflicts, national calamities, and international tension with an articulate faith in God's real presence,' wrote Henri Nouven.[11] Napoleon said, 'A leader is a dealer in hope'.

Willing Pioneers

If you place a frog in a kettle of boiling water it will quickly jump out, as it is aware that its environment is dangerous. If you place a frog in a kettle full of room temperature water and slowly increase that temperature until it is boiling, the frog will stay in the water until it boils to death. How far will the Christian community be like the frog? If it is not to be, we need pioneers. How else will the urban wasteland be won? We might rejoice in the growth of the church in parts of Inner London, but the cities of the north are just as needy. South Yorkshire is a metropolitan county area also but it has the lowest percentage of churchgoers in the country. We need risk-takers, people willing enough to take a new approach and risk all. Who will help plant and/or develop more living churches in these crucial areas?

Bullseye Prioritisers

One September day in San Antonio, Texas, the temperature stood at 99°F (37°C), and a ten-month old baby girl was accidentally locked inside a parked car by her aunt. Frantically the mother and aunt ran round the car in near hysteria while a neighbour tried to unlock the door with a coat hanger. Soon the infant was turning purple and had foam on her mouth. It was a life-or-death situation when Fred, a banger driver, arrived on the scene. He grabbed a hammer and smashed the back window and set the girl free. Was he thanked? 'The lady was mad at me because I broke the window. I just thought — what's most important — the baby or the window?'[12] What's most important for the church? People criticise the efficiency of the church when it does not give 'adequate answers to the problems of our society, nor to the problems of family life, nor to man's spiritual needs'.[13] Are these our priorities? If not, what should our priorities be? We are in a life-or-death situation. What is most important — the quality of our worship, the accessibility of service times, the relevance of the teaching, the enjoyment of the experience, or the dynamism of our evangelism? What's your bullseye priority?

Change Motivators

In management trainer James Belasco's book[14] on change, he says, 'My experience tells me that organisations (churches) are like elephants — they both learn through conditioning. Trainers shackle young elephants with heavy chains to deeply embedded stakes. In that way, the elephant learns to stay in its place. Older elephants never try to leave even though they have the strength to pull the stake and move beyond. Their conditioning limits their movement with only a small metal bracelet around their foot — attached to nothing. Like powerful elephants, many individuals and companies (churches) are bound by conditioning restraints. Success ties you to the past. "We've always done it this way." Yet when the circus tent catches fire — and the elephant sees the flames with its own eyes and smells the smoke with its own nostrils — it forgets its old conditioning and charges. Your task — set fire to the tent so your people see the flames with their own eyes and smell the smoke with their own nostrils — without burning the tent down.'

Committed Visionaries

Someone once said, 'It's not your commitment that counts, but commitment to your commitment'. Don Posterski, then Acting General Director of Inter Varsity, Canada, said: 'The church doesn't travel on the Trans-Canada Highway: we have been pushed back to the secondary roads. We are relating to a culture where the church has been marginalised and many Christians are feeling intimidated.'[15] It may take some while to build the bridge from the secondary road back to the Highway, but let's be committed to it.

Our vision needs to be clear. It must focus on the end result. We need to know roughly how long it will take us — ten years from now, or 'By the year 2000'. A vision 'illustrates meaning and purpose, the values behind your work, and why you do it'.[16] It originates as you dare to believe what God has called you to attempt to do. What is your vision?

But any vision has to be fulfilled through a leader. Henri Nouven concludes his book with the words: 'I'll leave you with the image of the leader with outstretched hands, who chooses a life of downward mobility. It is the image of the praying leader, the vulnerable leader, and the trusting leader. May that image fill your hearts with hope, courage and confidence as you anticipate the next century.'[17]

CONCLUSION

'The place God calls you to is the place where your deep gladness and the world's deep hunger meet.'[18] Although this book is about churchgoing in England, ultimately Christianity is not about church attendance. Nor is Christianity about our worship, however high that may be on the agenda. Nor is Christianity about service, urgent as the needs may be, and our willingness to help meet them. In the final analysis, the heart of Christianity is obedience. In the 1930s the popular preacher Campbell Morgan said, 'Obedience is the one thing needful'. Sixty years later, it still is. What does God want you — not your church, not your assistant, but you — to do? Will you obey the Christ who calls, 'Follow me'? And help make England, Christian England?

Chapter 10: Summary

- 8% of the British population in 1990 were nominal adult church members, a reduction from 9% in 1980.
- The Christian Community decreased from 67% to 65% in the same period.
- This drop is mainly in those attending church who are not members — down from 3% to 1%.
- The figures suggest Christianity is becoming both more active and more closed. It needs to become more attractive.
- The number of churches/congregations is not expected to change greatly between 1989 and 2000.
- But the number of adult churchgoers is expected to decline a further 250,000.
- This is because 450,000 are expected to die, but only 200,000 newly join the church.
- The change is likely to be greatest in the city centre and inner city areas, and least in the separate towns.
- The change is likely to occur across all groups except Charismatic Evangelicals.
- Proportionately Anglo-Catholics will lose most (−14%), but the «Catholics» will lose the largest number (170,000).
- Leaders, pioneers and visionaries will be of the essence in the 1990s.

NOTES

Chapter 1
1. Peter Brierley, *Mission to London*, Phase 1 and Phase 2 MARC Europe, London, 1984 and 1985.
2. Phil Back, *Mission England*, MARC Europe, London, 1985.
3. *UK Christian Handbook*, 1987/88 Edition, MARC Europe, London, 1986, Page 139.
4. Confusing with the Swedenborgian churches of the same name but very different ethos.
5. *UK Christian Handbook*, 1989/90 Edition, MARC Europe, London, 1988, Pages 160, 161.
6. *Ibid*, Page 161.
7. *Faith in the City*, Church Information Office, London, 1986.
8. Rev Ian Bunting, *The Places to Train*, MARC Europe, London, 1989.
9. *Op cit* (item 5) Page 144.
10. Peter Brierley, *Vision Building*, Hodder & Stoughton and MARC Europe, London, 1989, Page 53.
11. *Op cit* (item 5) Pages 151 and 14.
12. *Op cit* (item 10) Page 57.
13. *Op cit* (item 5) Page 529 for 1980-1987. 1990 figures are linear projections.
14. *Prospects for the Eighties*, Bible Society, Swindon, 1980.
15. *Prospects for the Eighties*, Volume 2, MARC Europe, London, 1983.
16. Peter Brierley and Byron Evans, *Prospects for Wales*, Bible Society and MARC Europe, London, 1983.
17. Peter Brierley and Fergus MacDonald, *Prospects for Scotland*, National Bible Society of Scotland and MARC Europe, London, 1985.
18. Quoted by the Bishop of Pontefract at a Church Army dinner on July 29th, 1987.
19. Peter Brierley (compiler and editor) *Prospects for the Nineties*, MARC Europe, London, 1991.
20. Alan R Tippett, *Church Growth and the Word of God*, Eerdmans,

Grand Rapids, Michigan, 1970.
21 The similarity of figures masks a difference in the counting of children which the official figures include (on a slightly different definition) and which the Census figures given here do not. The Census child figures include Sunday School attendance.

Chapter 2

1 Derek Williams, *Christian NewsWorld* magazine article, 'Who dares, thinks,' August 1990, Page 5.
2 Horace Mann, *Religious Worship in England and Wales,* the Report of the 1851 Census, George Routledge, London 1854.
3 This figure of 11%, while concurring with previously published figures, is in fact a revision comprised of two compensating influences. The figure of 11% emerged from the 1979 Census and was first published in *Prospects for the Eighties*. That Census did not, however, distinguish twicers, and the 11% strictly related to attend*ances* and not to attend*ers*. An estimate at the time of 20% of twicers reduced the 11% figure to 9% which has been quoted and used in several publications since. In assessing the results of the 1989 Census however it was discovered that somehow Roman Catholic mass attendance in 1979 was inaccurately reported, and the total should have been nearer 1.5 million rather than the 1.3 million published in *Prospects for the Eighties*. This has been corrected in *Prospects for the Nineties*, and would have made the percentage of church attend*ances* 13% not 11%. The two amendments together fortuitously keep the corrected figure the same as that published.
4 The 1975 and 1979 figures are revisions of those which initially appeared in *Prospects for the Eighties*.
5 Phil Back, *Where are they now?*, a survey of Mission England respondents. MARC Monograph No 21, 1989.
6 *Lifestyle Survey*, Board of Social Responsibility, Church of Scotland, 1987.
7 Personal conversation with Dr Kemi Ajayi, April 1990.
8 *Christian NewsWorld*, May 1990, Page 15.
9 *Assemblies Address Book*, Christian Team Publications, 1990.
10 Dr Andrew Walker, *Restoring the Kingdom*, Hodder & Stoughton, London, 1985.
11 *UK Christian Handbook,* 1989/90 Edition, MARC Europe, London 1988.
12 Peter Kaldor, *Who Goes Where? Who Doesn't Care?* reporting on church attendance in Australia, Lancer Books, 1987.

13 Robert J Wybrow, *Britain speaks out 1937-87*, Macmillan, London, 1989. Pages 49, 54 and 68.
14 George Gallup, in a Gallup Poll, reported in *Christian NewsWorld*, August 1990, Page 33.
15 Philippa King (editor), *La France Chrétienne*, MARC Europe, London, 1989.
16 *Finnish Christian Handbook*, SKSK and MARC Europe, Helsinki, 1989. Pages 3 and 17.
17 *Danish Christian Handbook*, Scandinavia and MARC Europe, Copenhagen, 1989. Page 19. Attendance estimated.
18 *Norwegian Christian Handbook*, Lunde Forlag and MARC Europe, Oslo, 1990, Page 17. Attendance estimated.
19 *Op cit* (item 11) Pages 144 and 151.
20 *French-speaking Switzerland Christian Handbook*, MARC Europe, London, 1990. Page 12. Attendance estimated.
21 *Op cit* (item 15) Pages 25 and 28.
22 Mary Lawson (editor), *Compendio Christiano Español* (Spanish Christian Handbook) MARC Europe, 1991.
23 Mary Lawson (editor), *Austrian Christian Handbook,* MARC Europe, 1991.
24 *Op cit* (item 12), reviewed by Phyllis Tibbs for Zadok Institute for Christianity and Society Series 1 Paper Number S33, September 1987.
25 *Op cit* (item 14) Church attendance figures only; community my estimate.
26 Peter Brierley, *Church Membership in South Africa,* MARC Monograph No 13, 1988, Pages 10 and 3.

Chapter 3

1 *Retail Directory of UK*, 1989. 1987 figure for UK is 42,873; figure for England is estimated.
2 *Britain 1990: An Official Handbook*, HMSO, Norwich, 1989.
3 Obtained by phoning relevant publicity department. Woolworth's figure is for 1989, W H Smith's for 1988.
4 Michael J C Wicks (editor), *Devon in the Religious Census 1851*, Michael Wickes, 1990, Page 11.
5 Susan Simmonds, Thesis: *A Public Service: Churches in Aberdeen*, 1976.
6 Ian McAuley, *Guide to Ethnic London*, Michael Haas, London, 1987.
7 Based partly on detailed notes provided by Dr Kemi Ajayi, English Church Census Administrator at MARC Europe.

Chapter 4

1. See for example Chris Shaw, 'The sex ratio at birth in England and Wales' in *Population Trends*, OPCS, London, No 57, Autumn 1989, Page 26.
2. Peter Brierley, *Vision Building*, Hodder & Stoughton and MARC Europe, London, 1989, Page 53.
3. Jim Smith, *Manhunt*, 'Reaching men for God', Kingsway, 1985.
4. *Children and the Church*, MARC Monograph No 16, 1989, Page 28.
5. C Höhn, *Determinants of Fertility Trends*, Ordina, 1983, Page 26.
6. Leslie Francis, *Religion in the Primary School*, Collins, 1987, Page 202.
7. See for example, *Christ in the Community*, Diocese of Rochester, 1990, Page 19.
8. Peter Kaldor, *Religious Musical Chairs*, Report No 5 from the 1986 Joint Church Census, Uniting Church Board of Mission, Sydney, and summarised in Lausanne Link No 4, September 1990, Page 1.
9. Sissons, Peter L, *The Social Significance of Church Membership in the Borough of Falkirk*, Report to Hope Trust and Church Ministry Department, Church of Scotland, 1973.
10. *Together into the Future*, Proposed Pastoral Project of the Archdiocese of Glasgow, St Peter's Pastoral and Retreat Centre, 1985, Section 3.
11. George Barna, *The Church Today*, 'Insightful Statistics and Commentary', Barna Research Group, Glendale, California, 1990, Page 22.
12. *Men 2000*, Mintel Publications, London, 1989, Page S.4.
13. Peter Kaldor, *Who Goes Where? Who Doesn't Care?*, Lancer Books, Australia, 1987.
14. Dr Reginald Bibby, *Christian Week*, quoted in MARC Canada *Communique*, No 2, 1990, Page 1.
15. Philip J Hughes and 'Tricia Blombery', *Patterns of Faith in Australian Churches*, Christian Research Association, Melbourne, Australia, 1990, Page 99.
16. Tony Castle, *The Hodder Book of Christian Quotations*, Hodder & Stoughton, London, 1982, Page 168.
17. Adapted from Lyle Schaller, 'The New Baby Boom', *Church Management — the Clergy Journal*, February 1990, Page 42.
18. Dr James F Engel and Jerry D Jones, *Baby Boomers and the Future of World Missions*, Management Development Associates, 1989, Page 4.
19. *Op cit* (item 11) Page 27.

20 *Ibid.*
21 *Op cit* (item 11) Page 28.
22 David Newton, 'Age Concern', *Church Growth Digest*, Volume 11 No 3, Spring 1990, British Church Growth Association, London, Page 6.
23 *Op cit* (item 15) Page 103.
24 John Haskey, 'The ethnic minority population of Great Britain' article in *Population Trends*, OPCS, London, No 60, Summer 1990, Page 36, giving estimates by ethnic group and country of birth.
25 *UK Christian Handbook*, 1987/88 Edition, MARC Euorope, London, Page 135.
26 As reported in Item 24.
27 *Young People in the 80s*, HMSO, Norwich, 1984, Table 2.43, Page 86.
28 Thomas W Laquer, *Religion and Respectability: Sunday Schools and Working Class Culture 1780-1850*, Yale University Press, 1976, and quoted in Item 4 Page 22.
29 *The Daily Telegraph*, August 24th, 1990.
30 Mrs Monica Hill, 'Where have all the children gone?', in *Church Growth Digest*, London, Volume 11, issue 2, Winter 1989, Page 6.
31 'Tricia Blombery, *Tomorrow's Church Today*, Christian Research Association, Melbourne, Australia, 1989, Page 9.
32 Quoted in Caughey Gauntlett, *Today in Darkest Britain*, MARC, Monarch, Eastbourne, 1990, Page 81.
33 *The Daily Telegraph*, August 21st 1990.
34 John Harris, *Homeless Youth, the Facts and a Christian Response*, Zadok Institute for Christianity and Society, Australia, Series paper S43, September 1989, Page 3.
35 Mick Byrne, 'The Marilyn Project', article in *Survey*, Market Research Society, Autumn 1990, Page 12.
36 *Children beyond Reach* (Working title) was to be published in mid-1991 by the Church of England Board of Education at time of writing.

Chapter 5

1 Peter Brierley, *Prospects for the Nineties*, MARC Europe, London, 1991.
2 *The Daily Telegraph*, July 2nd, 1990.
3 *More than one Church*, MARC Monograph No 27, reporting on a survey of 600 churches in East Anglia, 1989.
4 The Rt Rev Peter Nott, Bishop of Norwich, *Moving Forward: A Strategy for the Diocese of Norwich*, 1989.

5 David Lee, 'Faith in the Country', *Today* magazine, February 1990, Page 23.
6 See for example Ray Bakke, *The Urban Christian*, MARC Europe, London, 1987.
7 Colin Marchant, *Signs in the City*, Hodder & Stoughton, London, 1985, Pages 128 and 129.
8 Mrs Marjorie Idle, *Joy in the City*, Kingsway, 1988.
9 *Faith in the City*, Church Information Office, London, 1985, Page xv.
10 *Ibid*, Page 377.
11 *Ibid*, Pages 119 and 133.
12 Clare Jones and Bob Armitage, 'Population change within area types: England and Wales 1971-1988, *Population Trends*, OPCS, London, No 60, Summer 1990, Page 25.
13 *Op cit* (item 9) Page 37.
14 *Op cit* (item 7) Pages 47, 48.
15 The Rt Rev David Sheppard, *Built as a City*, Hodder & Stoughton, London, 1974.
16 The Rt Rev David Sheppard, *Bias to the Poor*, Hodder & Stoughton, London, 1982.
17 *Op cit* (item 15) Page 447.
18 Dr Greg Smith, *Christianity in the Inner City*, MARC Monograph No 17, Page 59.
19 Estimated by taking one-third of the number of civil parishes in non-metropolitan counties in England.
20 Loren Seibold, 'Small town, small church', *Ministry*, January 1990, Page 10.
21 Quoted in Ed Dayton's *Whatever happened to commitment?*, Zondervan, 1984, Page 166.

Chapter 6

1 *The Daily Telegraph*, August 6th, 1990.
2 Peter Kaldor, *Where the River Flows*, Lancer, 1988, Page 23.
3 *Leadership* magazine, Summer, 1988.
4 'Size and Growth' in *Prospects for Wales*, Bible Society and MARC Europe, London, 1983, Page 20.
5 *Ibid*, Page 28.
6 Peter Brierley and Fergus MacDonald, *Prospects for Scotland*, National Bible Society of Scotland and MARC Europe, London, 1985, Page 61.
7 *More than One Church*, MARC Monograph No 27, 1989, Page 17.

8 In working out these figures a representative number for each group has been used. This has not been the mid-point as is customary, but, because intermediate groups showed concentrations at the beginning of each group, a figure of about 10% over the minimum was used instead. Thus the representatative numbers are respectively 1, 12, 30, 55, 110, 165, 220, 330, 440, and 550 (when an over 500 group was included).
9 *Op cit* (items 4 and 6 respectively).
10 Dr Neil Summerton, *Christian (Open) Brethren in the British Isles in Numerical Context*, presented to a Christian Brethren Conference, July 1990.
11 Private Survey, 1989/90.
12 Met Castillo, 'Church Growth in the Philippines', *Global Church Growth*, April-June 1990, Page 13.
13 The Rt Rev George Carey, addressing Second Day Conference on Church Planting in Church of England, Holy Trinity Church, Brompton, May 1988, and reported in *Church Growth Digest*, Winter 1988/89, Year 10 No 2.
14 Kenneth Boyack 'A new period of evangelization for US Roman Catholics' in *Global Church Growth*, April-June 1990, Page 7.
15 The Rev Tom Houston, 'Church Growth and Decline', in *UK Protestant Christian Handbook Part 2: Home*, Evangelical Alliance, London, 1977, Page 6.
16 Peter Kaldor, *Who Goes Where? Who Doesn't Care?*, Lancer Books, Australia, 1987.
17 Lyle E Schaller, 'The New Baby Boom' in *Church Management – The Clergy Journal*, February 1990, Page 43.
18 *The Missionary Shape of the Congregation*, Methodist Home Mission Division, 1988.
19 *Christ in the Community*, Diocese of Rochester, 1990, Page 80.
20 George Barna, *Church Growth: Practical Steps that work*, Barna Research Group Report, Glendale, California, 1989, Page 6.
21 *What happened at Mission '89?*, MARC Monograph No 31, October 1989, Page 3.
22 *Nairobi Church Survey*, Daystar University College, Nairobi, Kenya, 1989, Page 55.
23 George Barna, *Successful Churches: What they have in common*, Barna Research, 1990, Chapter 2.
24 Ephesians 4:13, Heinz W Cassirer, *God's New Covenant*, William Eerdmans, Grand Rapids, Michigan, 1989.
25 *Op cit* (item 20).
26 *Op cit* (item 13).

27 Dr David Burnett, 'Structures and Relationships of Societies and Local (UK) Churches, Appendix 3' in *Vision 2000*, Evangelical Missionary Alliance, 1988, Page 31.
28 *Op cit* (item 19), Page 84.
29 *Leadership '89*, Research report by MARC Europe, London, 1989.
30 Bob Jackson, *Church of England Newspaper*, January 26th, 1990.
31 See for example, George Barna, *The Church Today*, Insightful Statistics and Commentaries, Barna Research Group, Glendale, California, 1990, Pages 41 and 55.
32 George Barna, *How to find your Church,* 1989, page 117.
33 David Hersh, 'Upon taking a small church' in *Leadership*, Spring Quarter, 1990, Page 79.
34 Catherine Butcher, 'Help for your Housegroup', *Today* magazine, June 1990, Page 5.
35 Magazine of the International Christian Chamber of Commerce, April 1990, Page 9.
36 Taken from Rowland Croucher's World Vision of Australia *Grid*, Autumn 1987, and used with permission.

Chapter 7

1 Analysed in Dr Robert Towler, *The Need for Certainty: A Sociological Study of Conventional Religion*, Routledge and Kegan Paul, London, 1984.
2 *Ibid.*
3 The Rev Philip J Hughes and Mrs 'Tricia Blombery, *Patterns of Faith in Australian Churches*, Christian Research Association, Melbourne, Australia, 1990, Page 14.
4 Reg Burrows, *Dare to Contend!*, Jude Publications, Newcastle upon Tyne, 1990, Pages, 112, 113.
5 The Rev Melvin Tinker (editor), *Restoring the Vision*, MARC, Eastbourne 1990. The first article is the Rev David Holloway's 'What is an Anglican evangelical?'
6 Dr Kate Ludeman, 'From Work Ethic to Worth Ethic' in *Executive Excellence* magazine, November 1989, Page 7.
7 Dr David Cormack, *Making the Most of your Team*, MARC Europe one-day seminar handout.
8 R A Westwood, Research Bureau (Research International) paper on 'The use of models, to investigate the "importance" of belief' at *ESOMAR Seminar* on 'Development in Consumer Psychology', Maidenhead, May 1973.
9 J S Bloice-Smith, *Negative Attitudes to Christianity* research report, and quoted in LandMARC, High Summer, 1990, Page 2.

10 Via Rev Stanley Davies, Evangelical Missionary Alliance, 1989.
11 Quoted in Sylvester Jacob, *Born Black*, Hodder and Soughton, London, 1977, Page 33.
12 E D Jones (editor D J Boorstin), *American Civilization*, Thames and Hudson, London, 1972, Page 60.
13 Dag Hammarksjöld, *Markings*, Faber, London 1966, Page 122.
14 Oswald Chambers quoted by Isobel Kuhn, *Second Mile People*, Overseas Missionary Fellowship, Tunbridge Wells, 1982, Pages 73/74.
15 Quoted in *Urchin Review*, 1985/86, Page 1.
16 James Montgomery 'The DAWN Strategy', *Global Church Growth*, April-June 1990, Page 1.

Chapter 8

1 David Longley and Mervyn Spearing (editors), *Tyne and Wear Christian Directory*, MARC Europe, 1986, Page 33.
2 Dr Win Arn, *Church Growth Newsletter*, No 21, 1988.
3 Horace Mann, *Religious Worship in England and Wales*, George Routledge, London, 1854.
4 Redundant Churches Fund, *Churches in Retirement*, a gazetteer, HMSO, London, 1990, Page 1.
5 *UK Christian Handbook*, 1989/90 Edition, MARC Europe, London, Page 155.
6 For a discussion on the known numbers of these see George Lings, 'Reclaiming the Allotments: recent church planting in the Church of England', *Church Growth Digest*, Year 10 No 1 Autumn 1988, Page 3.
7 Nicoles Poulain, 'A faith captured in stone', in *Readers Digest*, edited by Julie Akhurst Hall, September 1990, Page 144.
8 Charles Thomas, *Celtic Britain: Fifth and Sixth Centuries*, Thames and Hudson, London, 1986.
9 BBC 2 programme, 1987.

Chapter 9

1 Peter Brierley, *Vision Building*, Hodder & Stoughton and MARC Europe, London, 1989, Page 77.
2 Canon Bill Andrew, *Bible Sunday Sermon Outline*, Bible Society 1989.
3 *UK Christian Handbook*, 1989/90 Edition, MARC Europe, London, Page 13.

Chapter 10

1. Rev Spencer Bower speaking at the Annual Conference of the Evangelical Missionary Alliance at High Leigh, Hoddesdon, November 1973.
2. Mrs Mary Wang and G and E England, *Stephen, the Chinese Pastor*, Hodder & Stoughton, London, 1973, Page 170.
3. The same nominal membership proportion in the Methodist, URC and Other Churches (where attendance is less than membership) is assumed to apply to the four remaining Free Church denominations.
4. This figure agrees with that given in the *UK Christian Handbook* 1989/90 Edition when allowance is made for the different definition. In the Handbook Roman Catholic mass attendance is used as a proxy for membership.
5. The derivation of the numbers here are discussed in *Vision Building*, Hodder & Stoughton, London, 1989, Chapter 2.
6. Frank Field, MP, at the Diocesan Communication Officers Conference, Cambridge, July 1990.
7. Sir Frederick Catherwood on 'Nationalism' in *Christian Arena*, Vol 43 No 3, September 1990, UCCF, Leicester, Page 5.
8. *Op cit* (item 5) Page 52f.
9. Bob Hulk's describing Results of Research by Peter Meneer, in *Journal of the Market Research Society*, July 1987 in the IBA magazine, *Sky Waves*, Summer, 1990, Page 12.
10. Quoted by Dr Brian Mawhinney, MP for Peterborough, speaking at Diocesan Communication Officers' Conference, Cambridge, July 1990.
11. Henri Nouven, *In the Name of Jesus*, Crossroad, New York, 1989, Page 67.
12. Quoted by Ray Tiemann, *Leadership* magazine, Summer 1990, Page 49.
13. Robert J Wybrow, *Britain speaks out 1937-87*, a social history as seen through Gallup data, Macmillan, London, 1989, Page 125.
14. Dr James A Belasco, *Teaching the Elephant to Dance*, 1990, quoted in *Executive Excellence*, July 1990, Page 2.
15. Don Posterski, *Reinventing Evangelism*, Inter Varsity Press, Canada, 1989, and quoted in MARC Canada Communique, No 2, 1990, Page 3.
16. Jesse Stoner-Zemel, 'Realizing your vision' in *Executive Excellence*, July 1990, Page 16.
17. *Op cit* (item 10) Page 73.

18 Rev Richard Nelson Bolles, reported in *Leadership*, Summer 1990, Page 19.

Appendix

1 Peter Brierley, *Prospects for the Nineties*, MARC Europe, London 1991.
2 Figures from the *UK Christian Handbook*, 1989/90 Edition, MARC Europe, London, 1988, Page 151.

APPENDIX

THE CENSUS PROGRAMME

These notes explain who supported the study and how it was undertaken. It is written for the general reader: those wanting more detailed explanations should consult the 'Methodology Notes and Definitions' section in the volume containing all the detailed tables, *Prospects for the Nineties.*[1]

Who supported the Census?

Our initial costings suggested that the Census would cost about £160,000, though the final estimate, including overheads, added a further 10% to that figure. Generous grants from World Vision of Britain and the Evangelical Alliance enabled the work to be started. However, the Census was widely supported by leading church figures, many of whom joined the Council of Reference for the Census.

- The Rev Joel Edwards, General Secretary of the Afro-Caribbean Evangelical Alliance, said, 'The Church Census provides us with an excellent opportunity to profile the diversity and richness of the church of Christ in this country'.
- Rev Dr Donald English, currently President for the second time of the Methodist Conference wrote, 'The Methodist Church has been keen to keep accurate statistics right from the time John Wesley kept a list of communicants on his journey to Georgia. We still see the great value of not missing anyone and of facing the facts about our growth or decline so that we may do something about it'.
- John Noble, the leader of the House Church group 'Team Spirit', stated, 'Accurate information is rapidly becoming a new currency. Can we Christians afford to do without it?'

Council of Reference for the English Church Census 1989

The complete list of the Council of Reference is:

Rt Rev Edmund Banyard	Moderator of General Assembly 1988/89, United Reformed Church
Dr Eileen Barker	Reader in Sociology with special reference to the study of religion, London School of Economics and Political Science
Rev Prebendary Richard Bewes	Rector, All Souls Church, Langham Place, London
Sir John Boreham	Former Head of the Government Statistical Service
The Viscountess Brentford	
Rev Clive Calver	General Director, Evangelical Alliance
Rev Joel Edwards	General Secretary, Afro-Caribbean Evangelical Alliance
Rev Dr Donald English	General Secretary, Methodist Church Home Mission Division
Rev Bernard Green	General Secretary, Baptist Union of Great Britain
Dr Michael Hornsby-Smith	Senior Lecturer in Sociology, University of Surrey
Rev David Jackman	Senior Minister, Above Bar Church, Southampton
Mr John Noble	Team Leader, Team Spirit
Commissioner Harry Read	British Commissioner, Salvation Army
Rev Gavin Reid	Secretary, Fellowship for Parish Evangelism and Divisional Director for Evangelism, Church Pastoral Aid Society

Mr Alan Rogers	Head of BBC TV Continuing Education and Training
Mr Peter Searle	Director-General, Mental Health Foundation, formerly Executive Director, World Vision of Britain
Dr Neil Summerton	Elder of Cholmley Evangelical Church
Rt Rev Michael Turnbull	Bishop of Rochester
Mr Basil Varnam	General Administrator, Assemblies of God in Great Britain and Ireland
Father Peter Verity	Director, Catholic Media Office
Rev David Winter	Officer for Evangelism, Diocese of Oxford, and former Head of Religious Broadcasting, BBC

Such support before the Census was most encouraging. In the event we had hundreds of letters accompanying the returned forms which clearly showed a much wider body of support. The Church Secretary of South Milton Keynes Christian Fellowship, Stephen Potter, for example, said that Netherfield Chapel was 'very pleased to help out in this and are encouraged that MARC Europe is collecting accurate figures. We look forward to seeing the results'. Many sent additional material, such as the history of the Society of Friends at Ross, accompanied by a charming letter from Constance Richardson there. Small acts of thoughtfulness yield great encouragement.

Finding all the Churches

The addresses of every church in England, from cathedral to mission hall and village chapel to house church, had to be discovered. We wrote to churches throughout the country asking for details of fellowships which might otherwise be omitted from published lists. 38,607 churches were eventually tracked down. Even so, we have since discovered through correspondence that some of the newer, independent, churches have been missed. Since this is the group that is growing fastest, it is perhaps not surprising that not all could included.

How many have been omitted? This is impossible to know, but a detailed count by the Chairman of the Methodist Church for Cornwall District gave over 30 small fellowships unintentionally left out. If repeated equally over the whole country this would add considerably to the number of Independent, Afro-Caribbean, Pentecostal and Other Free Churches. However, the number in Cornwall not included is probably larger than elsewhere. Even so, we could still be perhaps 800 churches short. They would almost all be churches in the Independent group. We have not included any estimates for these, but if their congregational size was the same as for Independent Churches included this would mean an extra 40,000 people in church on October 15th, 1989 or a further 0.1% of the adult population.

Ascertaining Addresses of Ministers

The main church directories were used initially, and then the denominational press to update them. Some ministers look after more than one church, so that 38,600 churches were managed by nearly 23,000 ministers, an average of eight churches for every five ministers. (This number excludes curates, assistants, etc normally included in total clergy figures.)

Testing out the Form

The form itself, reproduced in *Prospects for the Nineties*, was piloted twice among a mixed group of 200 churches each time. Special thanks are due to church leaders in Aspatria, Barnstaple, Colchester, Derby and parts of London who thus completed the questionnaire twice; they greatly helped in the choice of question wording and also guided in an important difference between the 1989 and 1979 Census.

In 1979 the questionnaire asked for the number attending on average over a particular month (November 1979). In 1989 a single Sunday was chosen. This was partly because on methodological grounds there is no viable distinction, partly because it gave a fuller and quicker response in the pilot testing of it, partly because it was easier to publicise, and partly because October 1989 had five Sundays which would have confused figures for an average month.

October 15th was the third Sunday in the month — chosen because churches often hold Family Services, or Guide Parades, or other such events at the beginning of the month. It also did not clash with most half-term holidays.

Some indicated that the Sunday chosen was not typical for them. Some had a Christening service and/or 'mourning party' that Sunday afternoon which increased their numbers uncharacteristically — some churches excluded such numbers, but others included them. In the absence of any other information it has been assumed that these balance out on average, although there is no real reason to suspect they would. One Baptist Church took their count the Sunday before (and another the Sunday after) because their young people were all away at a camp that weekend. The Roman Catholics had their usual official count of numbers on October 29th and it was suggested to the priest-in-charge that he might wish to use the one count for both Sundays, which many did.

No Sunday can ever be typical but the middle of October is outside the holiday period, and outside special days, such as Harvest or Christmas. Letters were sent to many asking people to pray that this Sunday would be normal as far as the weather was concerned, since the Census fell within the same time of the year as the disastrous hurricane of 1987. And unlike the stormy day when the 1851 Religious Census was taken October 15th was a fine day throughout the country.

Who should be included?

The Census was intended to cover all Christian denominations, including all Free, Protestant, Anglican, Roman Catholic and Orthodox Churches, that is, all those accepting the Trinitarian formula of belief in God the Father, God the Son, and God the Holy Spirit on one Essence. This excluded the Jehovah's Witnesses, Mormons, Christian Scientists, Christadelphinians, Swedenborgians, Jews, Muslims, Hindus and other non-Trinitarian or non-Christian groups. Collectively the group of religious people thus excluded represented a notional 7% of the population of the United Kingdom in 1980 and 8% in 1990. We do not know how many of these people regularly attend for worship but collectively they probably do not amount to more than 1% of the population.[2]

We separately identified and counted churches with two or more places of worship in distinct communities, such as linked Church of England parishes where the parish churches were still in use. In team ministries each congregation counted as a unit, unless they all met unitedly together, when they were treated as a single congregation.

Why not just a Sample?

Could the Census have involved just a sample of churches? Statisticians say that a representative sample gives just as accurate a result as going to an entire population. While this is true, it was not the course we followed.

Selecting an accurate sample implies an accurate framework. In our case this meant that all the churches in the country had to be identified. In itself this was a major expense, and the saving from using only a part of the base would have been relatively trivial. Some denominations are so small in some counties that a 100% coverage would still have been required for them. Going to every church has the advantage also that no one can claim that their church is not included. *Every* church was potentially involved, and the results can therefore be used confidently by all leaders.

What is a Church?

The Census study raised the question of what counts as a church. Do Roman Catholics going to mass on Saturday evening instead of Sunday count as a church? Are the Seventh-Day Adventists worshipping on a Saturday allowed? What of those meeting to study the Bible mid-week? What of boarding children in their school chapel or a university or prison chaplaincies holding services? Those in military bases? What of those at a service in a church opened only once a year?

For the purpose of the Census we counted a church if it was 'a body of people meeting on a Sunday in the same premises primarily for public worship at regular intervals'. For at least 90% of those identified, this 'body of people' may be equated uniquely to 'the same premises', and frequently the word 'church', with its normal meaning of building, is used instead in this book. For those for whom this equation is not true, the word 'congregation' is appropriate, but it is not possible to identify positively any respondent with one or the other since the relevant questions were not asked.

The key elements of the definition of church are:

'*a body of people*', that is, a congregation is the basic unit rather than a building. So where a church building is used by more than one group, each separate group counted as a unit. This covers the frequent situation in rural areas where an Anglican Parish Church may well be used also for the celebration of Roman Catholic mass. On the other hand, where a church had united into one congregation, for instance recognised by both the Methodists and United Reformed Church (URC), it was not counted as two congregations, unless separate services, with essentially different groups of people, were held. Morning service attendance was counted separately from afternoon/evening attendance.

'*on a Sunday*' meant that those groups meeting for prayer and/or Bible Study mid-week were excluded. But a modification from Sunday to Saturday was allowed for the Seventh-Day Adventists and Roman Catholic evening services.

'*primarily for public worship*'. Public worship was taken to mean where ordinary members of the public would be allowed to attend, if necessary with notice. Thus religious communities holding services not open to the public, or closed groups such as prisons, were not included. Schools, colleges, university chaplaincies, military bases, religious orders and others that advertise service times were taken to be open to the public, and therefore included. Prisons, hospitals and services in old people's homes were generally excluded on these grounds. A few hospitals whose services were known to be open to the passing public were included. It was not particularly difficult to identify religious services in schools, colleges and universities, but hospital services tend to rotate around denominations, making it difficult to track down the person responsible. Prison services are not always open to the public, and services in residential care facilities proved almost impossible to identify comprehensively. Many of the people in these groups might still be on the registers of their local churches, creating a situation where some might be counted twice. We excluded them to err on the side of caution.

'*at regular intervals*' allowed for the situation, often in rural areas, where services are not held every week. If a service was held at least monthly numbers were included; those held less regularly were not. This also eliminated special events such as Christian holiday gatherings, conferences, conventions and private chapels used for occasional services such as funerals or festivals. Where a particular congregation had no gathering on Census Sunday they were encouraged to make a return for the most recent Sunday on which there had been a service.

'*in the same premises.*' This was introduced to identify a congregation specifically by its geographical location. Where a group of people have been known to rotate around people's houses Sunday by Sunday they have generally not been included, though exceptions were made for Afro-Caribbean churches.

This definition means that a few worshippers were excluded from the Census count. However, the numbers we do have relate to public worshippers coming to church or chapel in the normally understood sense of 'going to church'.

Publicity for the form

This is described in the first chapter, as are the reactions it generated. On the whole the publicity worked very well and nearly 27,000 forms were returned — an overall response rate of 70%.

Processing the data

A response rate of 70% may be well regarded but what of the other 30% who did not reply? These had to be estimated. Initially this was done on the basis that the size of these churches would be proportionately the same as those which did reply. The form asked for membership, and the membership figures were grossed up by denomination. The total of all the county membership figures thus grossed up were then compared with the published national membership figures or estimates derived from them for 1989.

Usually the grossed up figures were higher than the 'true' membership figures because it was the larger, more efficient churches that tended to reply. The grossed up figures were then reduced proportionately so that their total equalled the national published figure. *The same reduction factor* was also applied to the attendance figures to ensure that the attendance to membership ratio revealed by the Census was maintained. This procedure is as statistically reliable as it can be. The factors applied to the grossed up membership totals averaged −7%, a higher figure than in 1979, partly because of the non-response of some small rural churches, and partly because of the very small response of the Orthodox churches which necessitated special treatment. The final total figures, county data, denomination and churchmanship information are all published in the book *Prospects for the Nineties*.

ALPHABETICAL INDEX

Aberdeen, 73, 74
Abortion, 20
Acceptability of church, 146
Accessability of church, 146
Action in Mission, 19, 41
Active religion, 205
Addresses, 231, 232
Adherents, 33
Adult churchgoers, 30, 35, 51, 58, 82, 93, 108, 110, 111, 142, 159, 160, 161, 209, 214, Map 47
Affinity of church, 146
Affluence, 97
Africans in Britain, 97
Afro-Caribbean Churches
  adult attendance, 37, 38, 39, 41, 47, 54, 57, Maps 11, 12
  age groups, 92, 98
  case study, 74
  child attendance, 53, 54, 87, 92, 102
  church numbers, 64, 65, 112, 180, 207, 208, 232
  churchmanship, 162, 164, 168
  city centre, 112, 113
  congregational size, 47, 48
  decline, 134
  evangelical, 162
  foundation dates, 180, 181
  growth, 20, 39, 123, 124, 132, 134, 144, 148, 149, 190
  membership, 56, 57
  men, 85, 86, 88, 89, 90
  response, 26, 236
  services, 50
  strength, 69, 72, 97, 166, 173, 206
  teenagers, 87
  twenties, 88
  women, 86, 88, 89
Afro-Caribbean Evangelical Alliance, 75
Afro-West Indian Council of Churches, 75
Age of churches, 177
Age of churchgoers, 67, 75, 79, 81, 209
Agnostics, 203
All Saints, Margaret Street, 36
All Souls, Langham Place, 37
Amos, prophet, 74
Anabaptists, 179
Anglican Church
  adult attendance, 35, 36, 47, 53, 57, 151, 211, Maps 19, 20
  age groups, 91, 92
  beliefs, 46, 210
  child attendance, 52, 53, 87, 90, 92, 102, 104
  church numbers, 64, 65, 112, 120, 207
  churchmanship, 163, 165, 169
  city centre, 112, 113, 119
  congregational size, 47, 48, 110, 114, 129, 137, 138, 139
  decline, 89, 134, 140
  elderly, 92
  environment, 113, 114
  foundation dates, 178, 179, 182, 183, 184
  growth, 123, 124, 132, 134, 140, 144, 148, 149, 166
  membership, 55, 56, 57, 208

men, 85, 86, 88, 89
Sunday School, 100, 101
teenagers, 87, 90
women, 86, 88, 89, 90
Anglo-Catholics, 99, 115, 132, 143, 147, 156, 159, 166, 167, 170, 171, 198, 211, Maps 37, 38
Anonymity, 150
Apostolic Church, 41, 42
Arminian, 155
Army, Regular, 104
Arn, Win, 177
Arundel, 147
Aspatria, 232
Assembly of God Churches, 38, 41, 42
Atheists, 203
Attendance frequency, 48
Attractive Christianity, 206
Australia, 33, 59, 87, 91, 92, 103, 127, 146, 158
Austria, 59
Authorised Version, 185
Avon, 66, 69, 122, 144

Baby boomers, 93, 95, 97
Bakke, Rev Dr Ray, 118, 146
Banyard, Rt Rev Edmund, 230
Baptist Churches
  adult attendance, 37, 38, 39, 47, 54, 57, Maps 5, 6
  age groups, 92
  child attendance, 53, 54, 102
  church numbers, 64, 65, 112, 207, 208
  churchmanship, 162, 164, 168
  congregational size, 47, 48
  decline, 37, 38, 40, 134, 143
  evangelical, 161, 162
  foundation date, 180, 181
  growth, 37, 124, 131, 132, 134, 141, 143, 148, 161
  membership, 55, 56, 57
  men, 85, 86, 88, 89
  response, 26
  services, 50
  strength, 68, 72, 166, 173, 206
  suburbs, 112, 113
  teenagers, 87, 97
  women, 86, 88, 89, 90
Baptist Union, 19, 39, 40
Barker, Dr Eileen, 15, 230
Barna, George, 95, 147, 148
Barnstaple, 232
Barrett, Rev Dr David, 199
Bath, 122
Beck, Rev Brian, 38
Bedfordshire, 66, 68
Behaviour, 172
Belasco, James, 213
Belief, 22, 172, 173, 174, 205, 211
Berkshire, 66, 69, 80, 122, 143
Bewes, Rev Preb Richard, 15, 22, 230
Bibby, Reginald, 91
Bible Society, 198
Bible Way Church, 41
Birmingham, 66, 123, 143
Black Death, 116, 184
Black people, 76, 98, 188
Blackstone, Essex, 117
Blombey, Mrs 'Tricia, 103
Bonhoeffer, Dietrich, 125
Boreham, Sir John, 11, 15, 230
Bosch, David, 46
Bower, Rev Spencer, 201
Bowlby, Rt Rev Ronnie, 95
Brentford, Viscountess, 13, 230
Bridge-building, 127, 206
Bridges, Lord, 182
Brighton, 147
Bristol, 69, 122
British Church Growth Association, 102
British Council of Churches, 19, 205
Broad Churches, 50, 99, 115, 132, 156, 157, 159, 162, 166, 167, 170, 171, 210, Maps 33, 34
Broad Evangelicals, 99, 132, 133, 157, 159, 162, 166, 167, 210, Maps 23, 24

ALPHABETICAL INDEX

Brown, Graham, 44
Buckinghamshire, 66, 123, 143
Bunting, Rev Ian, 20
Burnett, Dr David, 149
Burnout, 119
Burrows, Reg, 158
Butcher, Catherine, 151

Cafod, 192
Caister Conference, 149
Calling, your, 152
Calver, Rev Clive, 230
Camberley, Surrey, 127
Cambridgeshire, 65, 66, 69, 121, 124, 129, 143, 144, 206
Canada, 33, 91, 213
Car ownership, 21
Carey, Most Rev Dr George, 9, 145, 149
Cathedrals, 122, 185
Catherwood, Sir Frederick MEP, 206
«Catholic», 50, 99, 115, 133, **156**, 159, 160, 161, 162, 166, 167, 170, 198, 206, 210, Maps 39, 40
Census Sunday, 23, 236
Central heating installations, 21
Chambers, Oswald, 174
Change in the 1980s, 18, 171, 202
Change management, 117, 120, 213
Channel Islands, 23, 39, 65, 66, 67, 71, 80, 123, 143
Charismatic belief, 47
Charismatic Evangelicals, 99, 115, 131, 156, 157, 159, 161, 166, 167, 168, 211, Maps 27, 28
Cheshire, 66, 71, 80, 129
Chicago, USA, 127
Child attendance, 51, 81, 82, 87, 89, 91, 96, 103, 104, 108, 110, 111, 159, 160, 161
China, 103
Chinese churches, UK, 33
Christadelphians, 233
Christian Aid, 192

Christian Brethren (Closed), 42, 44, 45
Christian Brethren (Open), 42, 44, 45, 68, 143/4
Christian Scientists, 233
Church Commissioners, 182
Church Missionary Society, 192
Church of England — *see* Anglican
Church of God of Prophecy, 41
Church of the Nazarene, 42
Church planting — *see* Planting
Church Times, 24, 29
Church Urban Fund, 70
Churches, giving via, 191, 193, 194, 195, 198
Churches of Christ, 41, 43, 44, 45
Churches Together in England, 19
Churchmanship, 114, 115, 132, 135, 142, 155, 157, 185, 188, 197, 210, 211
City centre, 107, 110, 111, 121, 133, 143, 194, 210
City Missions, 33
Classic evangelicalism, 158
Cleveland, 50, 66, 67, 70, 71, 122, 129, 131, 143
Closed religion, 206
Coates, Gerald, 46
Colchester, Essex, 232
Cold War, 97
Colleges — *see* Residential schools
Commitment, 75, 76, 117, 119, 120, 150
Commodities, purchasing, 192
Communities, giving to, 191, 193, 195, 198
Communication revolution, 97
Community, 55, 56, 59, 117, 120, 146, 147, 203
Commuter areas, 65, 107
Congregational Federation, 43, 44, 45
Congregational size, 47
Congregationalism, 173, 181
Conn, Dr Harvie, 118
Cormack, Dr David, 172

Cornerstone, 45
Cornwall, 50, 62, 66, 67, 70, 123, 143, 232
Council Estate, 107, 112, 113, 121
Council of Reference, 15, 23, 230
Countess of Huntingdon's Connexion, 33
Countries, giving to, 191, 193, 195
Covenant Ministries — see Harvestime
Coventry Cathedral, 185
Croatian Catholics, 36
Cromwell, Oliver, 68
Cumbria, 62, 66, 70, 144

Data accuracy, 26
Data collecting, 25
Data problems, 23
Date of foundation, 178, 179
David, King, 25
DAWN strategy, 174
Dayton, Ed, 3
Deaths of churchgoers, 79, 140, 208, 209, 210
Decade of Evangelism, 208
Declining churches, 128, 141, 142, 192
Denmark, 59
Depression, The, 97
Derby, 232
Derbyshire, 66, 69, 143
Devon, 50, 65, 66, 67, 68, 69, 70, 124, 185
Disasters, 21
Disciple, a, 173
Domesday Book, 184
Dormitory areas — see Commuter areas
Dorset, 66, 67, 68, 143
Durham, 66, 123, 124, 143

Eames, Most Rev Robin, 212
East Anglia, 64, 65, 68, 69, 70, 101, 116, 121, 123, 133, 143, 144, 185, 188
East Sussex, 66, 69, 129, 144

Ecumenical, 155
Edwards, Rev Joel, 14, 229, 230
Elderly, 82, 85, 92, 96, 207, 208
Electoral Roll, 55
Elephants, 213
Elim Pentecostal Church, 41, 42
Emmanuel Holiness Church, 41/2, 42
Engel, Dr James, 94
English, Rev Dr Donald, 229, 230
Environment, 107, 108, 109, 110, 111, 112, 113, 114, 133, 136, 137, 142, 194, 196, 209, 210
Ephesus, 152
Erasmus, 184
Ethnic Communities in London, 75
Ethnic London, 74
Essex, 65, 66, 68, 117, 144
Evaluation, 151
Evangelical Alliance, 229
Evangelical Coalition for Urban Ministry, 120
Evangelical Fellowship of Congregational Churches, 43, 44, 45
Evangelicals, 46, 115, 156, 158, 160, 167, 170, 171, 188, 198, 206, Maps 29, 30
Evangelism emphasis, 147, 213
Evening attendance, 49
Evening services, 50, 51, 193
Excellence, 148
Expatriates, 194
Expectations, 116, 149
Ezekiel, prophet, 74

Faith in the City, 19, 117, 119, 145
Faith in the Countryside, 140
Falkirk study, 87
Families, 83, 93, 120, 148, 233
Family Services, 90
Fellowship of Churches of Christ, 41
Fellowship of Independent Evangelical Churches, 42, 44, 45, 46, 144, 148, 159, 161, 167
Fertility, 87

Field, Frank MP, 204
Finland, 59
First United Church of Jesus Christ, 41
Fischer, Bobby, 173
Flower arranging, 93
Forster, Roger, 15, 46, 145, 148
Fragmented Gods, 91
Fragmentation, 76
France, 59, 184, 185
Francis, Rev Dr Leslie, 87
Free Church of England, 36
Free Churches
  adult attendance, 35, 36, 37, 43, 48, 113, Maps 17, 18
  child attendance, 52, 53, 92
  congregational size 47, 48, 110, 137, 138, 139
  decline, 139
  environment, 113, 114
  foundation dates, 179, 180
  growth, 139, 144
  inner city, 113
  membership, 55, 56
  services, 50, 120
  strength, 70, 120
  Sunday School, 100, 101, 102
Free Methodists, 39
Frequency of attendance, 48
Friendly churches, 146
Friendship, 127
Frog in the kettle, 212
Future, the, 201

Galbraith, Jane, 117
Gallup, George, 29
Gallup polls, 58
Gender of churchgoers, 79, 209
German Catholics, 36
Giving – *see* Third World Aid
Glasgow Archdiocese, 88, 147
Gloucestershire, 66, 69, 70, 71, 87, 116, 122
Gospel Standard Strict Baptists, 40
Grace Baptist Assembly, 40

Graham, Dr Billy, 18, 147, 205
Great Fire, 1666, 190
Greater London, 64, 69, 71, 80, 101, 103, 121, 144, 167, 190, 232
  See also Inner London and Outer London
Greater Manchester, 50, 65, 66, 131, 144
Green, Rev Bernard, 15, 230
Greenbelt, 19
Grid, 152
Growth, church, 128, 130, 139, 140, 141, 146, 151, 171, 211
Guildford Cathedral, 185

Hackney, 65
Hammarskjold, Dag, 173
Hampshire, 65, 66, 122
Hannibal, 46
Hansford, Kathryn, 118
Harvestime, 45, 68
Henry VIII, 178
Hereford and Worcester, 66, 80, 123, 124
Hersh, David, 151
Hertfordshire, 65, 66
Hill, Mrs Monica, 102
Hindus, 233
Holloway, Rev David, 158
Home groups, 151
Home Mission, 192
Home ownership, 21
Honest to God, 155
Hornsby-Smith, Dr Michael, 15, 230
Hospital services, 235
House Church Movement
  growth, 37, 38, 44, 45, 46, 161, 190
  history, 18, 45, 149, 184, 198
  part of Independent group, 42, 68, 111, 123, 179
Houston, Rev Tom, 46, 146
Howe, Rev Alan, 127
Humberside, 66, 124, 143, 144
Hundred Years' War, 184
Hungarian Catholics, 36

Hus, Jon, 184
Hutt, Rev D H, 36
Hybels, Rev Bill, 127

Ichthus Fellowship, 45, 50, 68, 123, 145, 147, 150, 206
Idle, Mrs Marjorie, 118/9
Immigrants, 55, 76
Implicit religion, 116
Income, low, 76
Independence, 148
Independent Churches
  adult attendance, 37, 38, 39, 42, 43, 47, 57, 167, Maps 9, 10
  age groups, 91, 92
  child attendance, 53, 54, 92, 102
  church numbers, 64, 65, 112, 207, 208, 232
  churchmanship, 162, 164, 168
  congregational size, 47, 48
  decline, 131, 134
  evangelical, 162
  foundation date, 180, 181
  growth, 38, 88, 111, 123, 124, 131, 132, 134, 141, 143, 146, 147, 148, 149, 166
  membership, 56, 57
  men, 85, 86, 88, 89
  response, 26
  strength, 68, 72, 206
  suburbs, 112, 113
  teenagers, 87, 91
  women, 86, 88, 89
Independent Methodist churches, 39
Independent Old Catholic Apostolic Church, 43
Individuals, giving to, 191, 193, 195, 197, 198
Industrial Revolution, 185, 190
Inner city, 107, 108, 109, 113, 115, 117, 121, 210
Inner London, 66, 69, 143, 144, 190
Inner London Northeast, 65, 66, 69, 71, 123, 145, 212

Inner London Northwest, 50, 70, 71, 131
Inner London Southeast, 50, 68, 69, 70, 118, 119, 129, 131, 143, 144, 145
Inner London Southwest, 65, 69, 123, 144
Institute of Community Studies, 102
Integration, 148
International Christian Chamber of Commerce, 152
International comparisons, 58
Isca, 45
Isle of Man, 50, 62, 65, 66, 67, 70, 123, 129, 143, 145
Isle of Wight, 50, 65, 66, 67, 143
Islington, 65

Jackman, Rev David, 15, 230
Jehovah's Witnesses, 205, 206, 233
Jesus Fellowship, 40
Jews, 173, 233
Jones, Bryn, 46
Jones, E D, 173
Junior Church, 102

Kaldor, Peter, 127, 146
Keep fit, 93
Keld village, North Yorkshire, 116
Kent, 65, 66, 129, 144, 185
Kenya, 147
Kingdom of God, 200
King's Church, 45

Labour Force Survey, 98
Lambeth, 65
Lancashire, 66, 71, 129, 144
Laodicea, 152
Latvian Catholics, 36
Lausanne Congress, 46
Leadership, 148, 149, 212
Learning, cruciality of, 173
Leicestershire, 65, 66, 122
Liberal Catholic Church, 43
Liberals, 99, 115, 132, 156, 159, 162, 166, 167, 170, 171, 198, 211, Maps 35, 36

ALPHABETICAL INDEX

Lichfield, Staffordshire, 182
Lifestyles, 94
Lincolnshire, 62, 66, 123, 145, 185
Lithuanian Catholics, 36
Live Aid, 194
Liverpool Cathedral, 185
Local Ecumenical Projects, 19, 24
Location of church, 146
Lollards, 184
London — *see* Inner London and Outer London
Longley, David, 3, 15, 129
Low Churches, 50, 99, 115, 132, 133, 156, 157, 159, 160, 166, 167, 171, 188, 198, Maps 31, 32
Ludeman, Kate, 172
Luther, Martin, 184
Lutheran Church, 33, 46, 173

McAuley, Ian, 74
McCauley, Pastor Ray, 148
Mainstream Evangelicals, 99, 132, 157, 158, 159, 161, 166, 167, 206, 210, Maps 25, 26
Marchant, Rev Colin, 118, 119
MARILYN Project, 104
Mass attendance — *see* Roman Catholic
Membership, church, 54, 56, 58, 108, 109, 110, 111, 159, 160, 161, 200, 205, 236, Map 48
Men, 79, 82, 83, 84, 85, 86, 89
Merseyside, 65, 66, 70, 71, 120, 131, 143
Methodist Church
  adult attendance, 27, 37, 38, 39, 47, 57, 208, 211, Maps 3, 4
  age groups, 91, 92
  broad, 162
  change, 90, 210
  child attendance, 53, 54, 87, 91, 92, 102
  church numbers, 64, 65, 112, 179, 207, 232
  churchmanship, 162, 164, 168
  decline, 131, 134, 141, 143
  evangelicals, 161, 162
  foundation date, 180, 181
  growth, 131, 132, 134, 141, 147, 166
  liberal, 162
  members, 57
  men, 85, 86, 88, 89
  response, 26
  rural churches, 112
  strength, 67, 72, 167, 173
  twenties, 88
  women, 86, 88, 89
Midlands, 64, 122, 123, 144, 145, 170, 185, 188
Migration, 87, 145
Military bases, 234, 235
Milton Keynes, Bucks, 231
Mintel Survey, 89
Mission centres, 33
Mission 89, 18, 34, 147
Mission England, 18, 34, 40
Mission to London, 18, 34, 40
Missionaries, giving to, 191, 193, 194, 195, 196, 197, 198
Missionary Shape of the Congregation, 19, 56, 146, 147
Montgomery, James, 174
Moravian Church, 33
More than one Church, 133
Morgan, Rev Campbell, 214
MORI polls, 58
Mormons, 205, 206, 233
Morning attendance, 49
Morning services, 50, 51, 193
Morton, Tony, 46
Mosques, 182
Mothers, 93
Mothers' Union, 90, 93
Motivation, 22, 173, 213
Mott, Rev Dr John, 125
Multiple churches, 116
Muslims, 19, 205, 233

Nairobi church survey, 147
Napoleon, 212

National Pastoral Congress, 19
Nationwide Initiative in Evangelism, 19
New Age Movement, 19, 116
New Apostolic Church, 43
New Churches — see House Church Movement
New evangelicalism, 158
New Frontiers, 45, 68
New Life, 45
New Testament Assembly, 41
New Testament Church of God, 41
Newcastle, 172, 177
Newton, David, 96
Nightingale, Florence, 22
Noble, John, 46, 229, 230
Nominal Christians, 20, 57, 201, 202, 203, 204, 205
Non-churchgoers, 31, 65, 95, 96, 121, 127, 203, 204, 206, Maps 1, 2
Non-conformists, 185
Non-Trinitarian churches, 41, 203, 233
Norfolk, 50, 62, 65, 66, 67, 117, 124, 143, 190
Norman churches, 146, 183, 190
North East, 71, 144, 145, 167
North/South, 72, 100, 101, 121, 167
North West, 50, 64, 71, 101, 129, 131, 144, 145, 167
North Yorkshire, 62, 66, 67, 70, 123, 143, 144, 185
Northamptonshire, 66, 69, 80, 129
Northumberland, 65, 66, 68, 80, 123, 124, 143, 144
Norway, 59
Notional Christians, 202, 203, 205
Nott, Rt Rev Peter, 20, 117
Nottinghamshire, 66, 69, 122, 129
Nouwen, Henri, 212, 214

Oakley, Suffolk, 116
Old Baptist Union, 40
Old evangelicalism, 158
Old People's Homes, services, 235
Old Roman Catholic Church, 36
Opinion Polls, 58
Orthodox Church
  age groups, 92
  attendance, 35, 47, 57, 100, 102
  belief, 46
  church numbers, 64, 65, 112, 207, 208
  churchmanship 163, 165, 169
  city centre, 112
  congregation size, 138, 139
  foundation dates, 179, 181
  growth, 89, 90, 143, 145, 161
  members, 56, 57
  men, 85, 86, 88, 89, 90
  response, 26, 237
  strength, 71, 92, 160
  twenties, 88
  women, 86, 88, 89
Orthodox churchmanship, 156
Osborne, Barry, 117
Other built-up areas, 107, 111, 133
Other Free Churches
  adult attendance, 37, 38, 39, 47, 54, 57, 232, Maps 15, 16
  age groups, 91, 92
  child attendance, 53, 54, 102
  church numbers, 207
  churchmanship, 163, 165, 169
  decline, 32, 134, 144
  evangelical, 162
  foundation dates, 180, 181
  growth, 131, 132, 144
  inner city, 112
  membership, 56, 57
  men, 85, 86, 88, 89
  response, 26
  strength, 69, 72, 91, 124, 167, 188
  suburbs, 112, 113
  women, 86, 88, 89, 90
Other Independent churches, 45
Outer Greater London, 62, 66, 68, 129
Outer London Northeast, 50
Outer London Northwest, 70, 71

ALPHABETICAL INDEX

Outer London Southeast, 71, 96, 131, 144
Outer London Southwest, 131, 143
Overseas mission, 94, 95
Oxfordshire, 66, 69, 123

Palau, Luis, 18
Paul, apostle, 116
Pentecostal Churches
  adult attendance, 37, 38, 39, 41, 47, 57, Maps 13, 14
  age groups, 92
  belief, 47, 206
  child attendance, 53, 54, 102
  church numbers, 64, 65, 69, 72, 112, 166, 180, 207, 208, 232
  churchmanship, 162, 164, 168
  congregational size, 47, 48
  decline, 38, 134
  elderly, 92
  evangelical, 162
  foundation dates, 180, 181
  growth, 89, 90, 123, 124, 131, 132, 143, 144, 147, 148, 149, 190
  membership, 55, 56, 57
  men, 85, 86, 88, 89, 90
  response, 26
  services, 50
  twenties, 88
  women, 86, 88, 89
Pergamum, 152
Peter, Lawrence, 174
Philadelphia, 152
Philippines, 144
Pioneer, 45, 68
Pioneers, willing, 212
Planning, 22, 121, 231, 232
Planting churches, 111, 120, 145, 149, 184
Plymouth Brethren No 4, 42
Polish Catholics, 36
Population comparisons, 51, 57, 62, 63, 79, 81, 84, 95, 98, 184
Post Offices, 61
Posterski, Don, 213

Potter, Stephen, 231
Prayer, 149
Pregnancy clinic, 147
Premises, 76
Presbyterian belief, 46
Presbyterian Church in England, 41, 68, 181
Presbyterians, 173
Priorities, 150, 212, 213
Prison services, 234, 235
Projects, giving to, 191, 193, 194, 195
Prospects for the Eighties, 21, 218
Prospects for the Nineties, 24, 50, 111, 125, 156, 161, 192, 207, 218, 229, 232, 237
Protestant Episcopal Reformed Church of England — *see* Protestant Evangelical Church of England
Protestant Evangelical Church of England, 36
Publicity, 236
Pubs, 61, 147

Quakers — *see* Religious Society of Friends
Quality, 148, 211, 213

Radical churches, 156
Randolph, Felicity, 103
Read, Commissioner Harry, 14, 33, 230
Re-dedication, 147
Redundant churches, 182, 207
Redundant Churches Fund, 182
Reformed belief, 46
Reformed churches, 156
Regional comparisons, 62, 64, 72, 80, 100, 101, 122, 131, 142, 167, 168, 188, 189, 198, 199
Reid, Rev Gavin, 230
Relevance, 87, 150, 213
Religious orders, 235
Religious Society of Friends, 33, 69, 156, 173, 231

Renaissance, 184
Renew programme, 32, 147
Renewed churches, 156
Residential schools, 43, 44, 45, 46, 178, 234, 235
Response, 26
Restoring the Kingdom, 46
Retention of churchgoers, 147
Rochester, Kent, 146, 149
Rogers, Alan, 3, 15, 231
Rogers, Rev Tom, 41
Roman Catholic Church
  age groups, 91, 92
  beliefs, 46
  child attendance, 52, 53, 92, 100, 102, 202
  church numbers, 64, 65, 112, 207, 208
  churchmanship, 163, 165, 169
  congregational size, 47, 48, 110, 129, 138, 139, 159
  council estates, 113
  decline, 89, 90, 131, 134, 141, 209
  environment, 113, 114
  foundation dates, 179, 180, 181
  France, in, 58
  growth, 124, 132, 140, 141, 145
  inner city, 112, 114
  mass attendance, 27, 32, 35, 36, 47, 57, 208, 218, Maps 21, 22
  membership, 55, 56, 57, 204, 208
  men, 85, 86, 88, 89, 90
  North West strength, 65, 66
  response, 26, 233, 234
  services, 50
  strength, 50, 71, 72, 90, 120, 162, 166, 167, 173
  teenagers, 87, 90
  twenties, 87, 90
  women, 86, 88, 89, 90
Roman churches, 185
Royal Week, 19
Rural churches, 50, 107, 108, 111, 113, 115, 116, 117, 122, 123, 124, 133, 137, 140, 145, 170, 194, 210, Maps 44, 46
Rural Sunrise, 117
Rushdie, Salman, 19

St Mary's, Camberley, 127
St Mary's, Lichfield, 182
St Peter's, Yately, 127
St Thomas Crookes, Sheffield, 151
Salvation Army, 31, 32, 33, 69, 104, 156, 173, 188, 204
Sample, not a? 234
San Antonio, Texas, 212
Sardis, 152
Satanic Verses, The, 19
Saturday mass, 234, 235
Savage, Rev Bev, 44
Schaller, Lyle, 146
Schools — *see* Residential schools
Scotland, 21, 22, 48, 54, 79, 102, 128, 129, 137, 138, 202, 204
Scottish Lifestyle Survey, 34
Searle, Peter, 3, 15, 231
Secular population, 205, 206
Sellix, Rev Martin, 117
Separate towns — *see* Towns
Seventh-Day Adventists, 14, 33, 47, 54, 69, 121, 188, 234, 235
Sex of churchgoers — *see* Gender
Shaftesbury Society, 33
Shaw, George Bernard, 74
Shaw, Rev Ian, 128
Sheep-stealing, 38
Sheffield, 151
Sheppard, Rt Rev David, 120
Short-term service, 94
Shropshire, 50, 66, 123
Size of congregation, 47, 137, 146
Slovene Catholics, 36
Smith, Greg, 120
Smith, Jim, 79
Smith, W H, 61
Smyrna, 152
Social change, 20
Somerset, 62, 66, 67, 70, 71, 123, 185

Songs of Praise, 20
South African church, 59, 148
South East (North), 64, 123, 144, 167, 170, 185
South East (South), 144, 170, 185
South West, 66, 67, 70, 80, 121, 122, 123, 145, 185, 188
South Yorkshire, 50, 66, 69, 70, 71, 80, 122, 143, 144, 151, 212
Spain, 59, 93
Spirituality of leaders, 149
Spring Harvest, 19
Staffordshire, 50, 66, 70, 80, 122, 145
Static churches, 128, 137, 139, 143
Stewardship, 200
Strategy, 151
Strengths, 72, 158, 170
Suburban/Urban fringe, 107, 108, 110, 113, 114, 115, 121, 133, Maps 43, 45
Suffolk, 65, 66, 68, 69, 70, 116, 124, 143, 190
Summerton, Dr Neil, 44, 144, 231
Sunday School, 87, 93, 100, 218
Surrey, 65, 66, 68, 71, 127
Swedenborgians, 217, 233
Switzerland (French-speaking), 59

Teaching programme, 148, 213
Team Spirit, 45, 68, 229
Tear Fund, 192
Technological advance, 97
Teenagers, 83, 84, 87, 91, 92, 97, 103
Telephone ownership, 21
Theological vision, 116, 149, 200
Third World aid, 191, 193, 194, 195, 196, 197, 198, 199
Thyatira, 152
Tiller, Rev Canon John, 20
Time management, 121
Tower Hamlets, 65
Towler, Dr Robert, 155, 158
Town churches, 50, 107, 108, 111, 112, 114, 115, 120, 121, 133
Tradition of churchgoing, 67
Tridentine Institute, 36
Tunbridge Wells, Kent, 129
Turnbull, Rt Rev Michael, 3, 24, 146, 231
Twenties, people in their, 81, 83, 85, 87, 91, 96, 98, 194
Twicers, 47, 48, 49, 50
Tyndale, William, 184
Tyne and Wear, 66, 70, 80, 103, 122, 123, 143

UK Christian Handbook, 20, 29, 36, 45, 55, 56, 59, 205
Ukrainian Catholics, 36
Unemployment, 97
Union of Evangelical Churches, 42, 44, 45
United Pentecostal Church, 41
United Pentecostal Church of God, 41
United Reformed Church
  adult attendance, 37, 38, 39, 41, 47, 57, 211, Maps 7, 8
  age groups, 92
  child attendance, 53, 54, 87, 102
  church numbers, 64, 65, 112, 167, 181, 207, 208
  churchmanship, 162, 164, 168
  decline, 134
  foundation dates, 180, 181
  growth, 132, 143
  liberal, 162
  members, 57
  men, 85, 86, 88, 89, 90
  response, 26
  strength, 68, 72, 124, 166, 208
  teenagers, 87
  towns, 112
  women, 86, 88, 89
United States, 59
Unity, 75
University services, 234, 235
Urban areas, 70, 71, 103, 117, 119, 122, 133, 144, 210, Maps 43, 45

Urban fringe — *see* Suburban/Urban fringe
Urban Priority Areas, 119
Values, 88, 94, 149
Varnam, Rev Basil, 15, 231
Verity, Father Peter, 231
Viking attacks, 184
Virgo, Terry, 46
Vision, 148, 149, 174, 194, 209, 213, 214
Wales, 21, 22, 48, 54, 79, 102, 128, 137, 138, 202, 204
Wandsworth, London SW18, 65
Wang, Mary, 201
Warwickshire, 66, 71, 144
Weather, 233
Welcoming churches, 146
Wesleyan Holiness Church, 41
Wesleyan Reform Union, 39
West Indians, 76, 97
  See also Afro-Caribbeans
West Midlands, 62, 65, 66, 69, 71, 80, 121, 129, 143, 144, 167
West Sussex, 66, 68, 70, 80, 123
West Yorkshire, 66, 68, 69, 122, 123, 143, 144
Westwood, R A, 172
Willow Creek Church, Chicago, 127
Wilson, Rev Canon Henry, 127
Wiltshire, 66, 69, 123, 124, 144
Wimber, John, 23
Winter, Rev David, 15, 231
Women, 79, 82, 83, 84, 86, 88, 89
Woolworths, 61
World Vision of Britain, 229
World War, First, 97
World War, Second, 97, 178, 181, 185
Worship, attractive, 75, 120, 147, 213, 214, 235
Yately, Surrey, 127
Young Direction, 103
Young, Lord of Darlington, 102
Young People in the 80s, 98
1851 Religious Census, 67, 178, 233

MAP INDEX

MAPS SHOWING STRENGTH AND CHANGE

Map 1   Percentage of adult population not attending church regularly 1979.
Map 2   Percentage of adult population not attending church regularly 1989.
Map 3   Methodist adult churchgoers 1989 as percentage of population.
Map 4   Methodist adult church attendance change 1985-1989.
Map 5   Baptist adult churchgoers 1989 as percentage of population
Map 6   Baptist adult church attendance change 1985-1989.
Map 7   URC adult churchgoers 1989 as percentage of population.
Map 8   URC adult church attendance change 1985-1989.
Map 9   Independent adult churchgoers 1989 as percentage of population.
Map 10 Independent adult church attendance change 1985-1989.
Map 11 Afro-Caribbean adult churchgoers 1989 as percentage of population.
Map 12 Afro-Caribbean adult church attendance change 1985-1989.
Map 13 Pentecostal adult churchgoers 1989 as percentage of population.
Map 14 Pentecostal adult church attendance change 1985-1989.
Map 15 Other Free Church adult churchgoers 1989 as percentage of population.
Map 16 Other Free adult church attendance change 1985-1989.
Map 17 Total Free Church adult churchgoers 1989 as percentage of population.
Map 18 Total Free adult church attendance change 1985-1989.

Map 19 Anglican adult churchgoers 1989 as percentage of population.
Map 20 Anglican adult church attendance change 1985-1989.
Map 21 Roman Catholic adult churchgoers 1989 as percentage of population.
Map 22 Roman Catholic adult church attendance change 1985-1989.
Map 23 Broad Evangelical adult churchgoers 1989 as percentage of population.
Map 24 Broad Evangelical adult church attendance change 1985-1989.
Map 25 Mainstream Evangelical adult churchgoers 1989 as percentage of population.
Map 26 Mainstream Evangelical adult church attendance change 1985-1989.
Map 27 Charismatic Evangelical adult churchgoers 1989 as percentage of population.
Map 28 Charismatic Evangelical adult church attendance change 1985-1989.
Map 29 Total Evangelical adult churchgoers 1989 as percentage of population.
Map 30 Total Evangelical adult church attendance change 1985-1989.
Map 31 Low Church adult churchgoers 1989 as percentage of population.
Map 32 Low Church adult attendance change 1985-1989.
Map 33 Broad adult churchgoers 1989 as percentage of population.
Map 34 Broad adult church attendance change 1985-1989.
Map 35 Liberal adult churchgoers 1989 as percentage of population.
Map 36 Liberal adult church attendance change 1985-1989.
Map 37 Anglo-Catholic adult churchgoers 1989 as percentage of population.
Map 38 Anglo-Catholic adult church attendance change 1985-1989.
Map 39 «Catholic» adult churchgoers 1989 as percentage of population.
Map 40 «Catholic» adult church attendance change 1985-1989.

MAP INDEX 253

Map 41 All Other Churchmanships adult churchgoers 1989 as percentage of population.
Map 42 All Other Churchmanships adult church attendance change 1985-1989.
Map 43 Urban and Suburban adult churchgoers 1989 as percentage of all churchgoers.
Map 44 Rural adult churchgoers 1989 as percentage of all churchgoers.
Map 45 Urban and Suburban adult church attendance change 1985-1989.
Map 46 Rural adult church attendance change 1985-1989.
Map 47 Adult churchgoers by county 1989.
Map 48 Church members by county 1989.

254 'CHRISTIAN' ENGLAND

Figure 43: Counties of England

1. Percentage of adult population not attending church regularly 1979

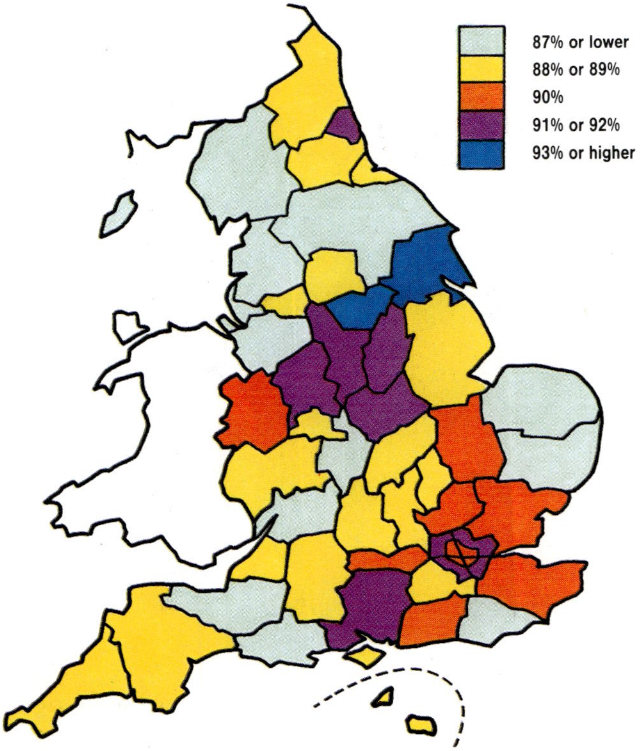

- 87% or lower
- 88% or 89%
- 90%
- 91% or 92%
- 93% or higher

2. Percentage of adult population not attending church regularly 1989

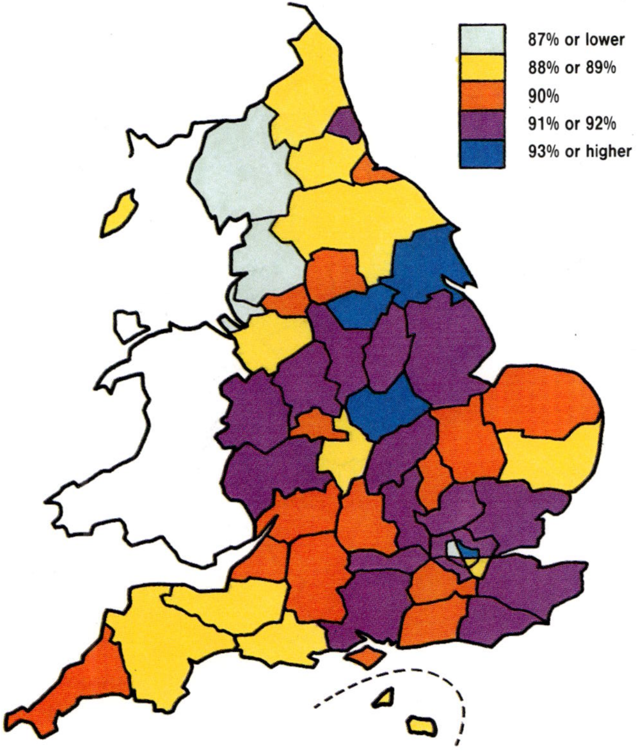

- 87% or lower
- 88% or 89%
- 90%
- 91% or 92%
- 93% or higher

3. Methodist adult churchgoers 1989 as a percentage of the population

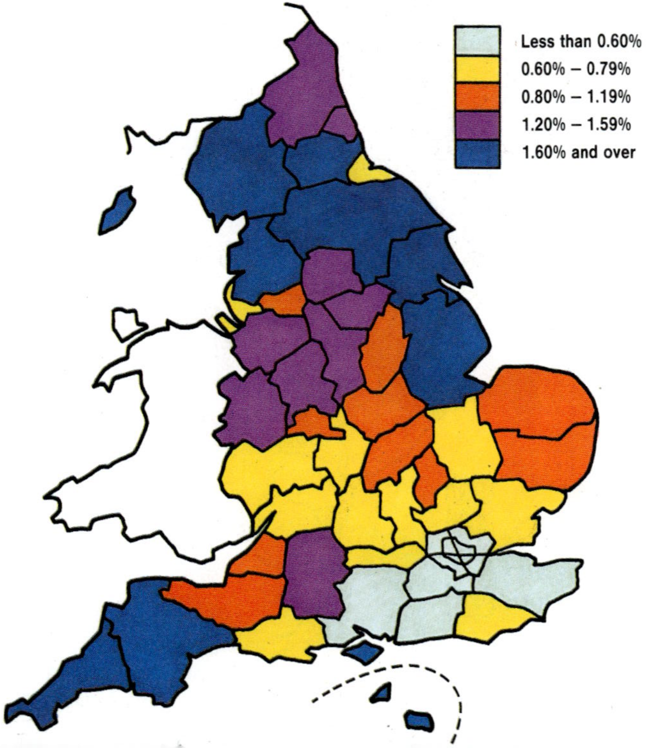

- Less than 0.60%
- 0.60% – 0.79%
- 0.80% – 1.19%
- 1.20% – 1.59%
- 1.60% and over

4. Methodist adult church attendance change 1985-1989

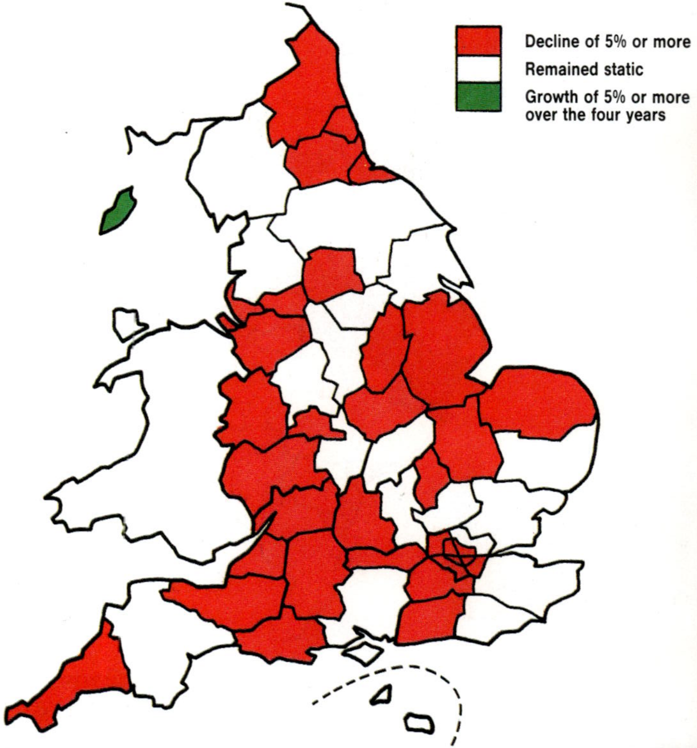

- Decline of 5% or more
- Remained static
- Growth of 5% or more over the four years

5. Baptist adult churchgoers 1989 as a percentage of the population

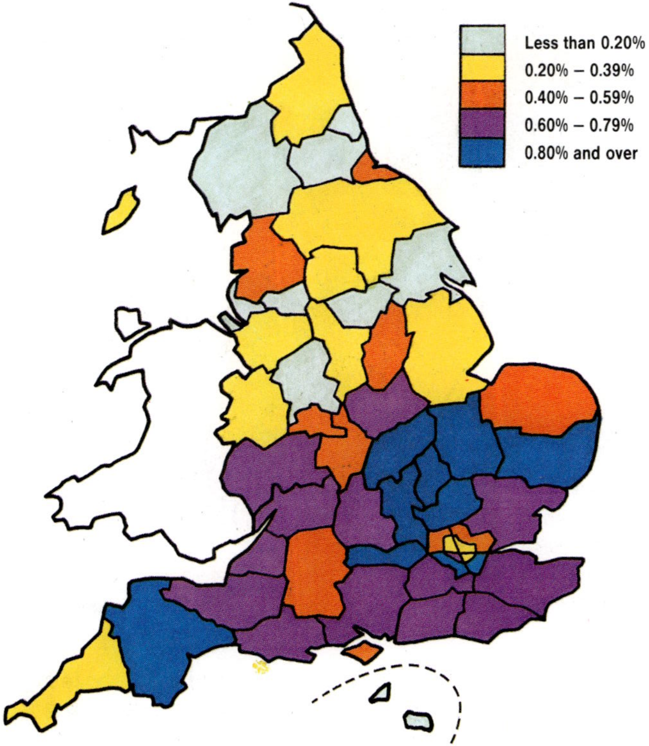

- Less than 0.20%
- 0.20% – 0.39%
- 0.40% – 0.59%
- 0.60% – 0.79%
- 0.80% and over

6. Baptist adult church attendance change 1985–1989

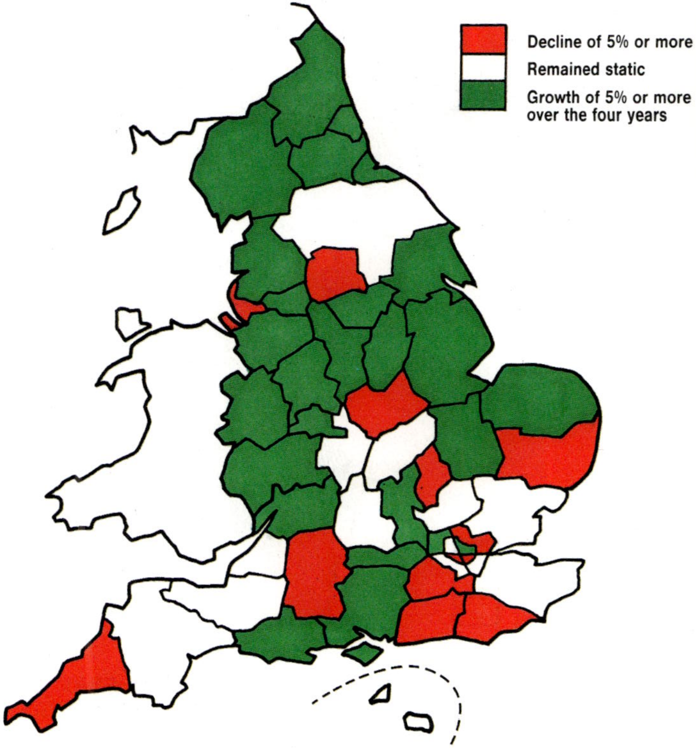

- Decline of 5% or more
- Remained static
- Growth of 5% or more over the four years

7. URC adult churchgoers 1989 as a percentage of the population

- Less than 0.10%
- 0.10% – 0.19%
- 0.20% – 0.29%
- 0.30% – 0.39%
- 0.40% and over

8. URC adult church attendance change 1985-1989

- Decline of 5% or more
- Remained static
- Growth of 5% or more over the four years

9. Independent adult churchgoers 1989 as a percentage of the population

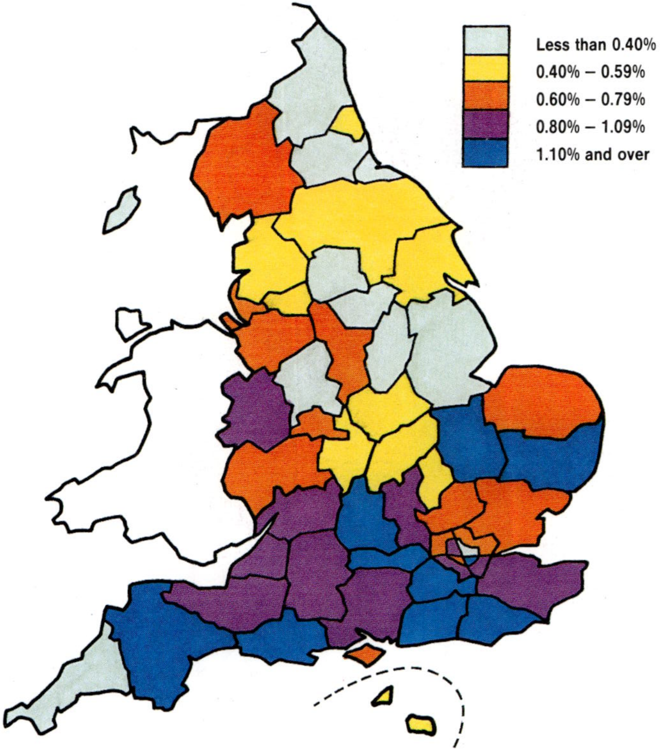

- Less than 0.40%
- 0.40% — 0.59%
- 0.60% — 0.79%
- 0.80% — 1.09%
- 1.10% and over

10. Independent adult church attendance change 1985-1989

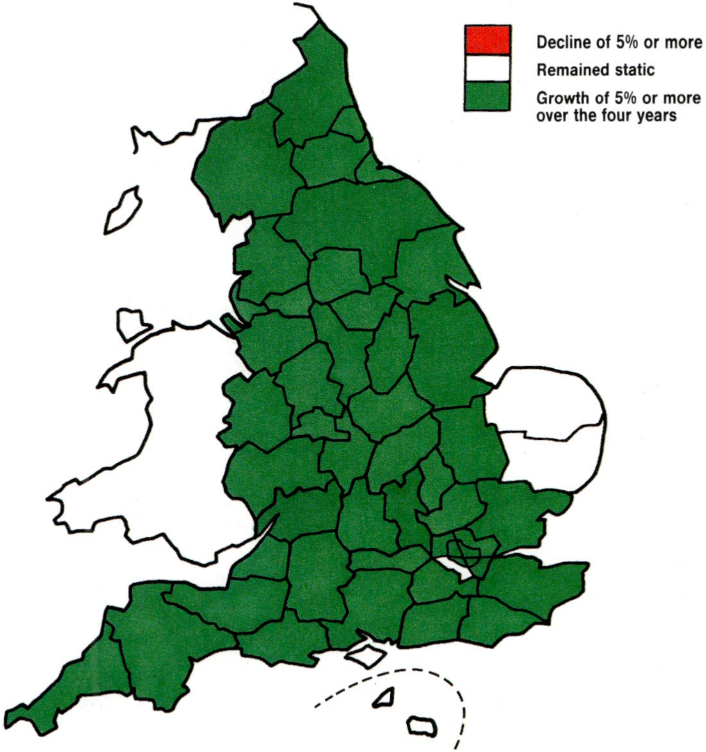

- Decline of 5% or more
- Remained static
- Growth of 5% or more over the four years

11. Afro-Caribbean adult churchgoers 1989 as a percentage of the population

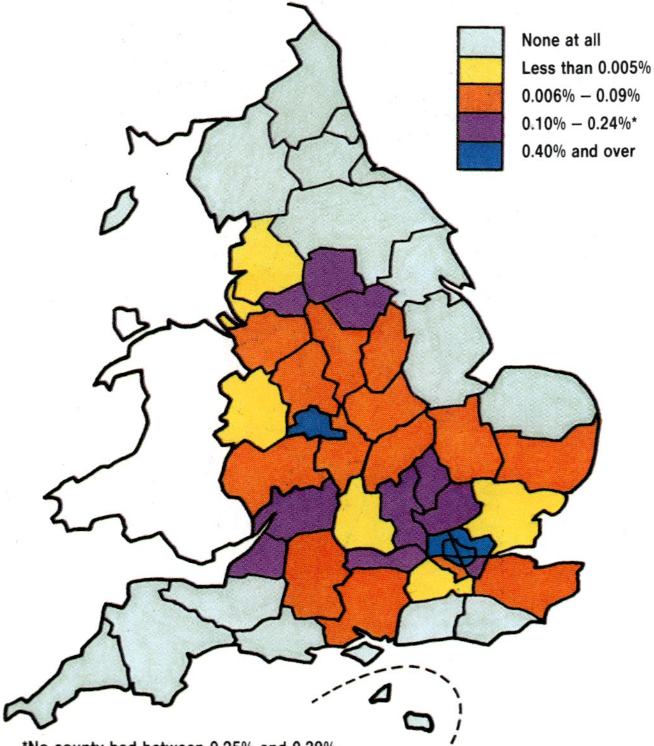

- None at all
- Less than 0.005%
- 0.006% – 0.09%
- 0.10% – 0.24%*
- 0.40% and over

*No county had between 0.25% and 0.39%

12. Afro-Caribbean adult church attendance change 1985-1989

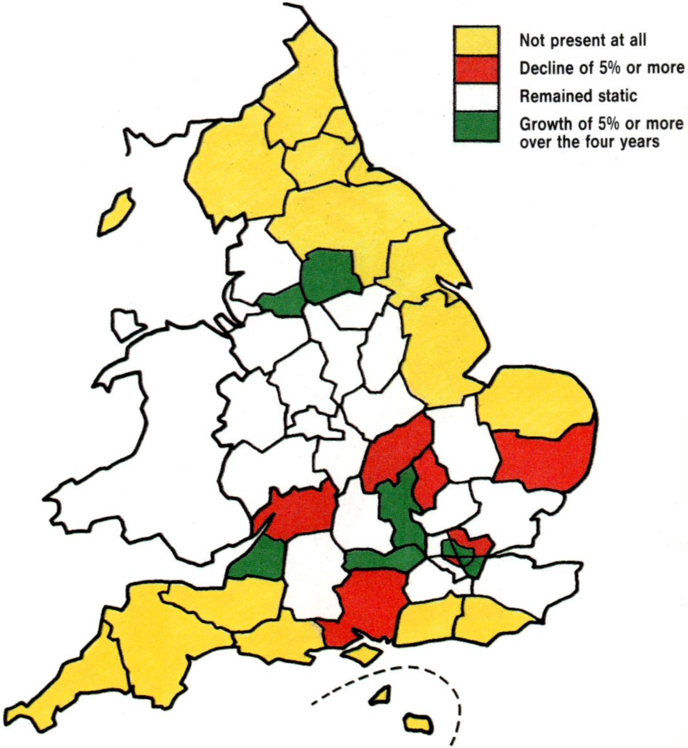

- Not present at all
- Decline of 5% or more
- Remained static
- Growth of 5% or more over the four years

13. Pentecostal adult churchgoers 1989 as a percentage of the population

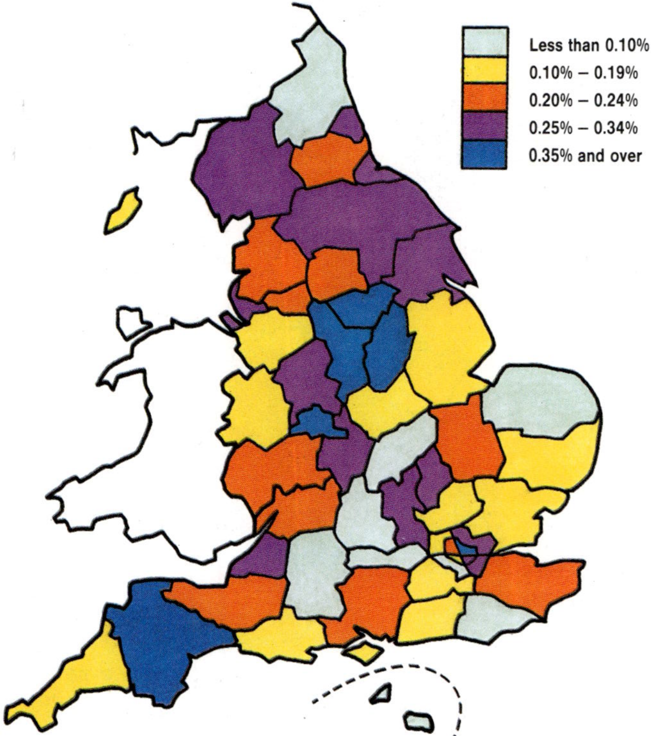

- Less than 0.10%
- 0.10% – 0.19%
- 0.20% – 0.24%
- 0.25% – 0.34%
- 0.35% and over

14. Pentecostal adult church attendance change 1985-1989

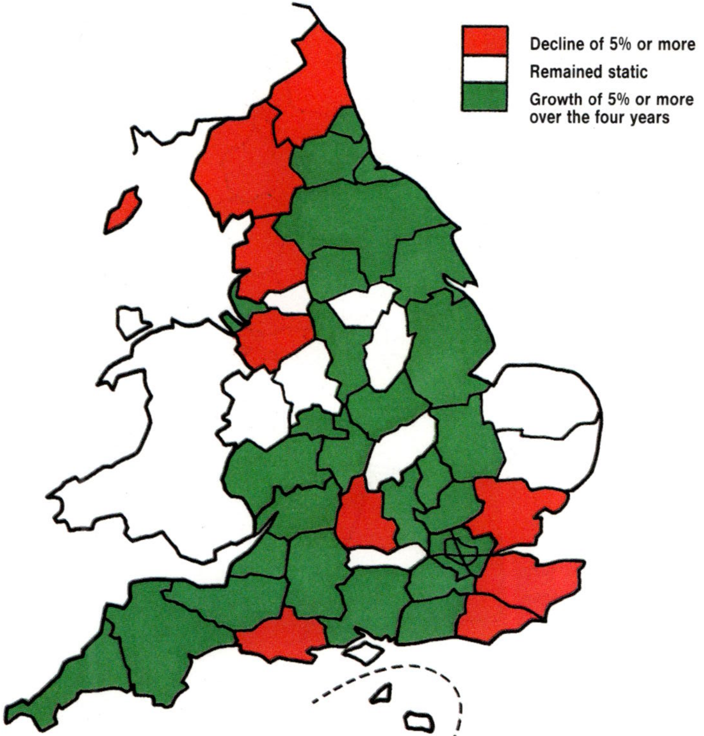

- Decline of 5% or more
- Remained static
- Growth of 5% or more over the four years

15. Other Free Church adult churchgoers 1989 as a percentage of the population

Less than 0.10%
0.10% – 0.14%
0.15% – 0.19%
0.20% – 0.29%
0.30% and over

16. Other Free Church adult attendance change 1985-1989

Decline of 5% or more
Remained static
Growth of 5% or more over the four years

17. Total Free Church adult churchgoers 1989 as a percentage of the population

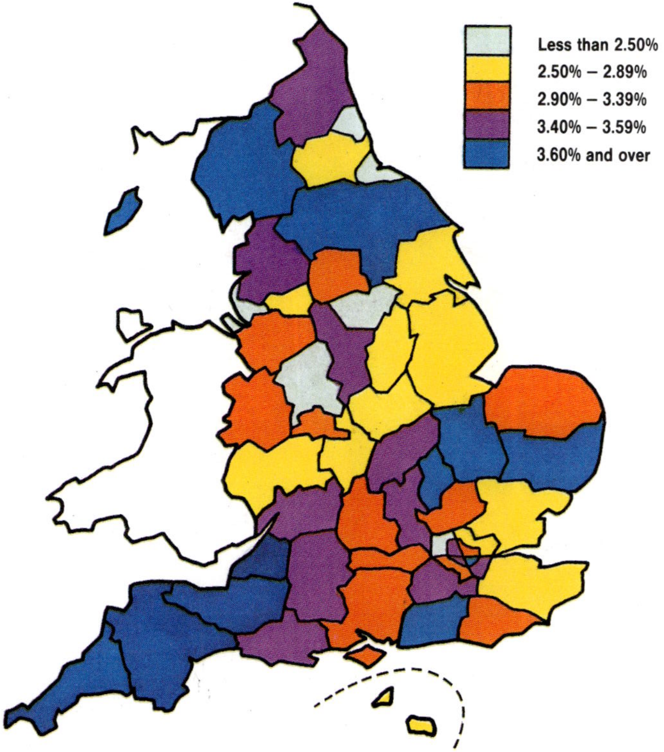

- Less than 2.50%
- 2.50% – 2.89%
- 2.90% – 3.39%
- 3.40% – 3.59%
- 3.60% and over

18. Total Free Church adult attendance change 1985-1989

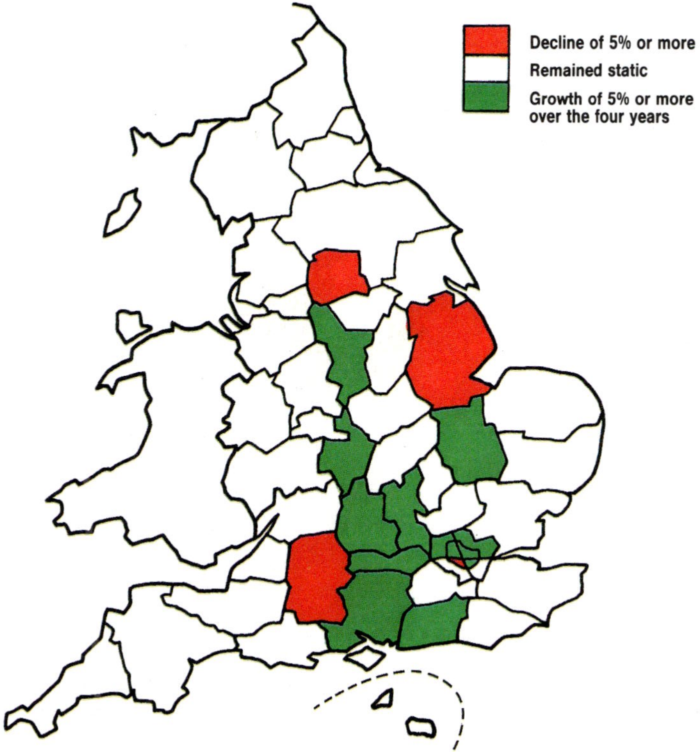

- Decline of 5% or more
- Remained static
- Growth of 5% or more over the four years

19. Anglican adult churchgoers 1989 as a percentage of the population

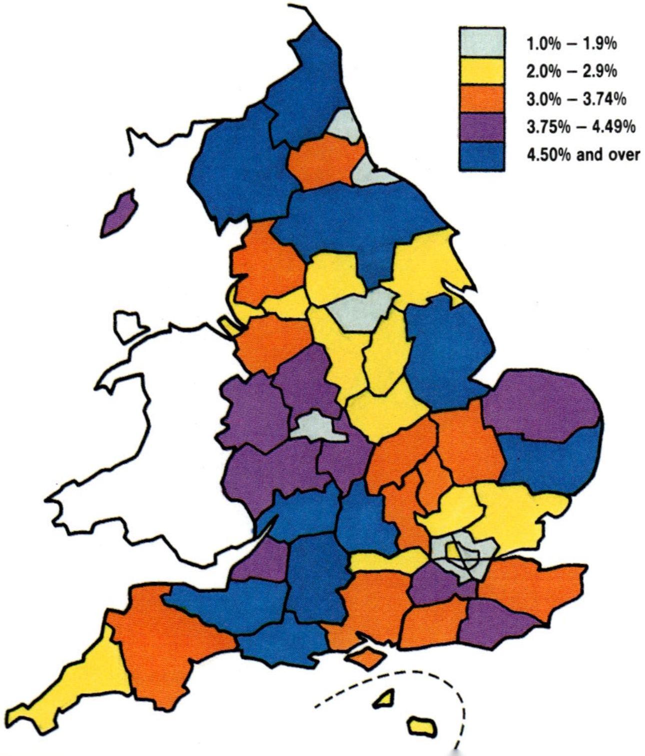

- 1.0% – 1.9%
- 2.0% – 2.9%
- 3.0% – 3.74%
- 3.75% – 4.49%
- 4.50% and over

20. Anglican adult church attendance change 1985-1989

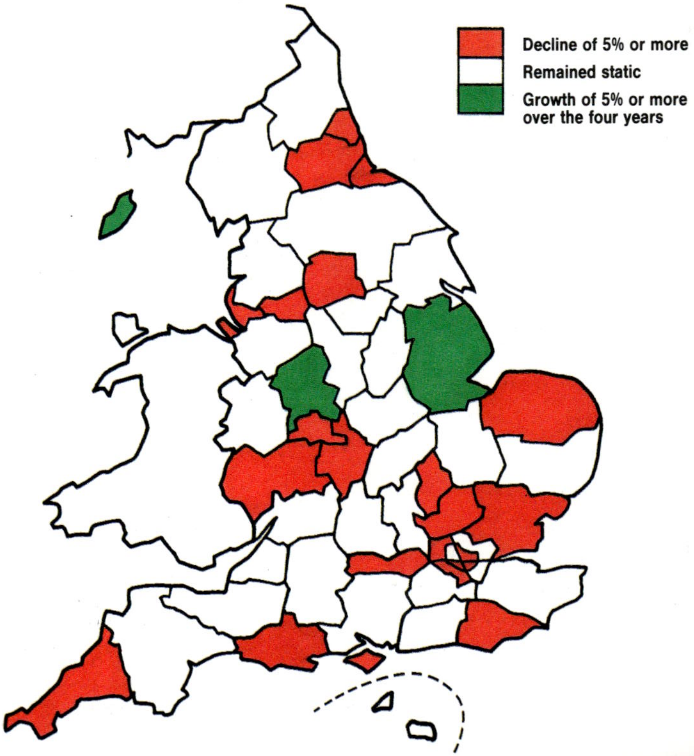

- Decline of 5% or more
- Remained static
- Growth of 5% or more over the four years

21. Roman Catholic adult churchgoers 1989 as a percentage of the population

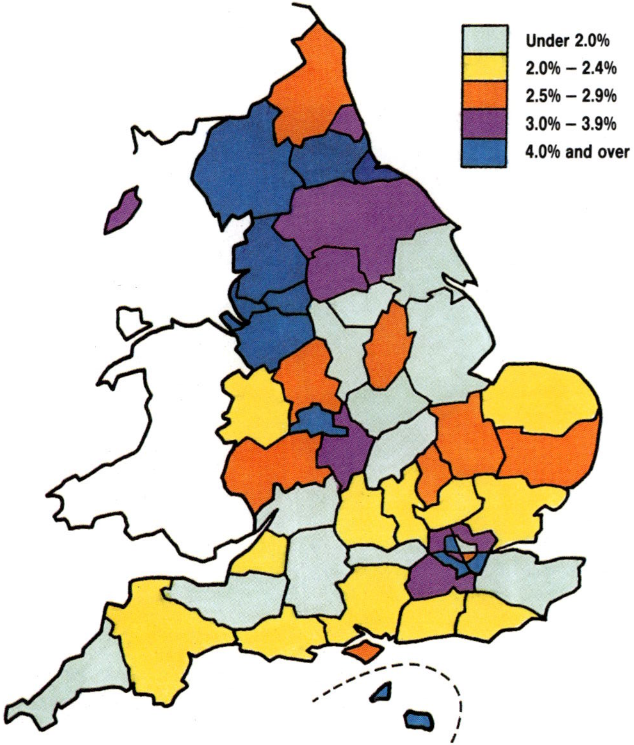

- Under 2.0%
- 2.0% – 2.4%
- 2.5% – 2.9%
- 3.0% – 3.9%
- 4.0% and over

22. Roman Catholic adult church attendance change 1985-1989

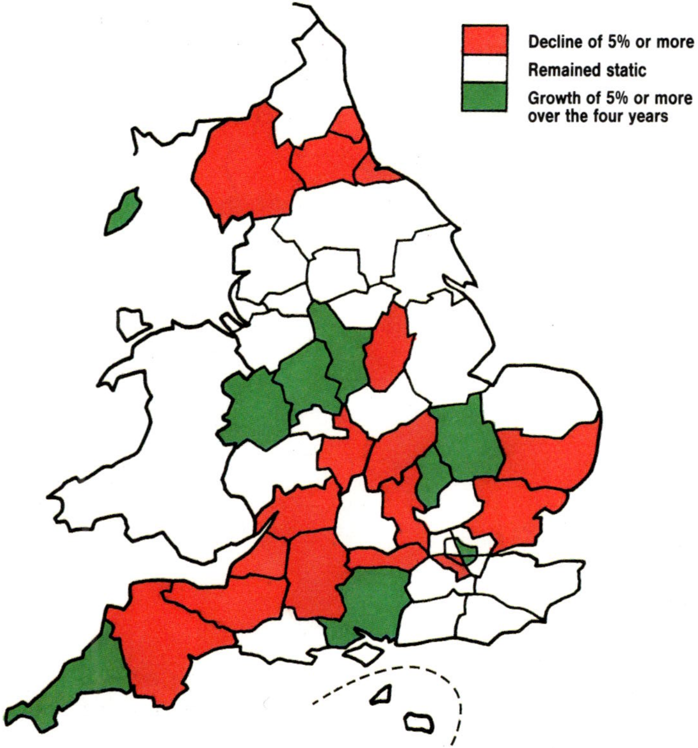

- Decline of 5% or more
- Remained static
- Growth of 5% or more over the four years

23. Broad Evangelical adult churchgoers 1989 as a percentage of the population

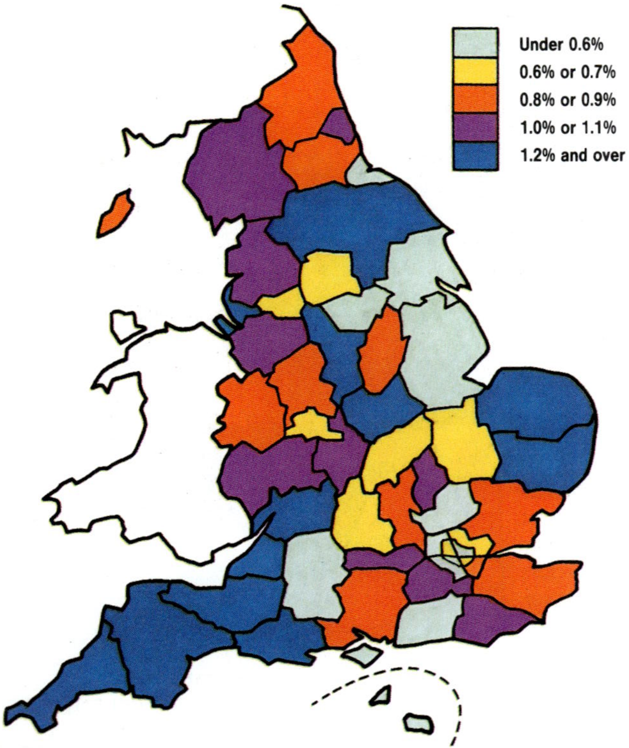

Under 0.5%
0.6% or 0.7%
0.8% or 0.9%
1.0% or 1.1%
1.2% and over

24. Broad Evangelical adult church attendance change 1985-1989

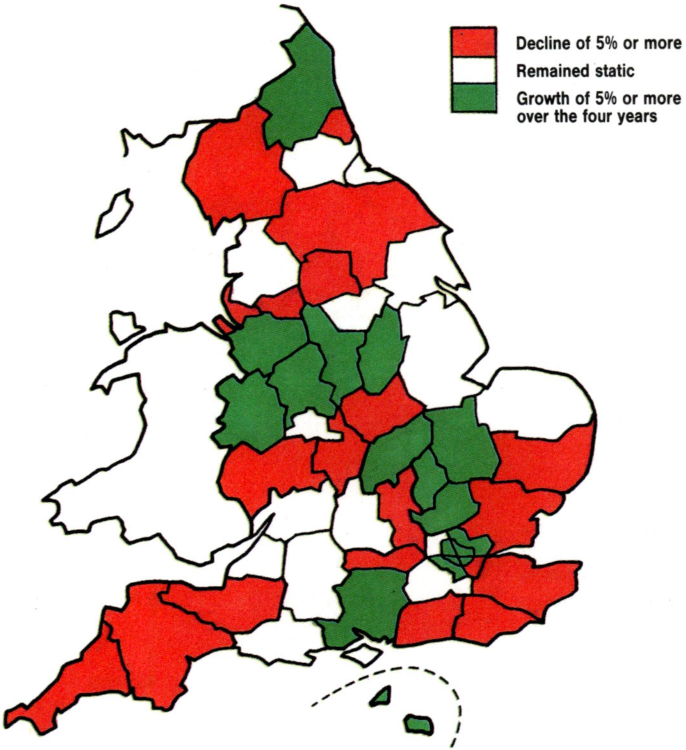

Decline of 5% or more
Remained static
Growth of 5% or more over the four years

25. Mainstream Evangelical adult churchgoers 1989 as a percentage of the population

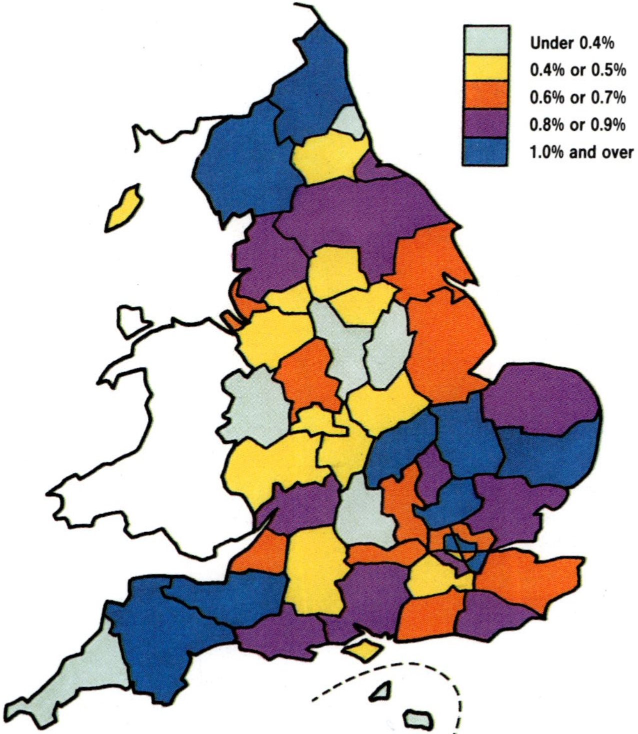

- Under 0.4%
- 0.4% or 0.5%
- 0.6% or 0.7%
- 0.8% or 0.9%
- 1.0% and over

26. Mainstream Evangelical adult church attendance change 1985-1989

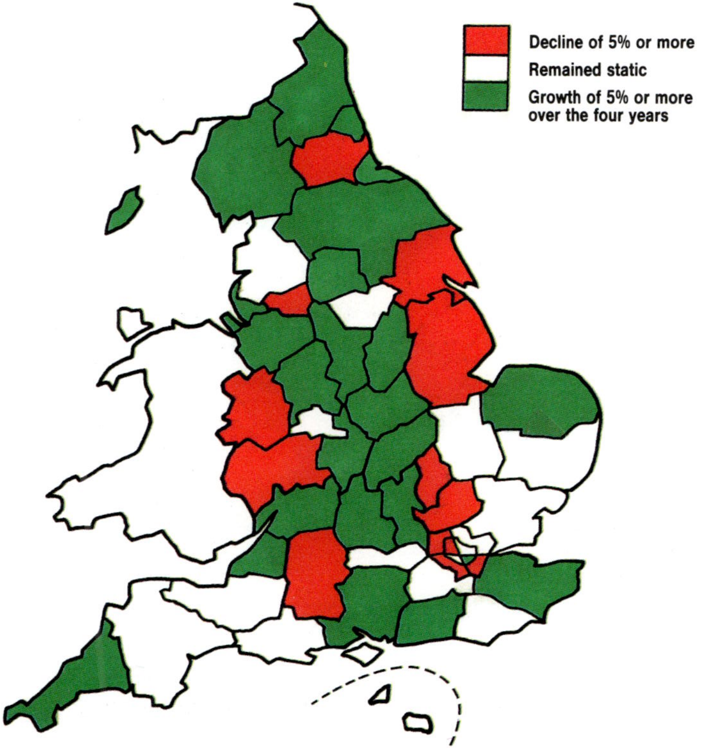

- Decline of 5% or more
- Remained static
- Growth of 5% or more over the four years

27. Charismatic Evangelical adult churchgoers 1989 as a percentage of the population

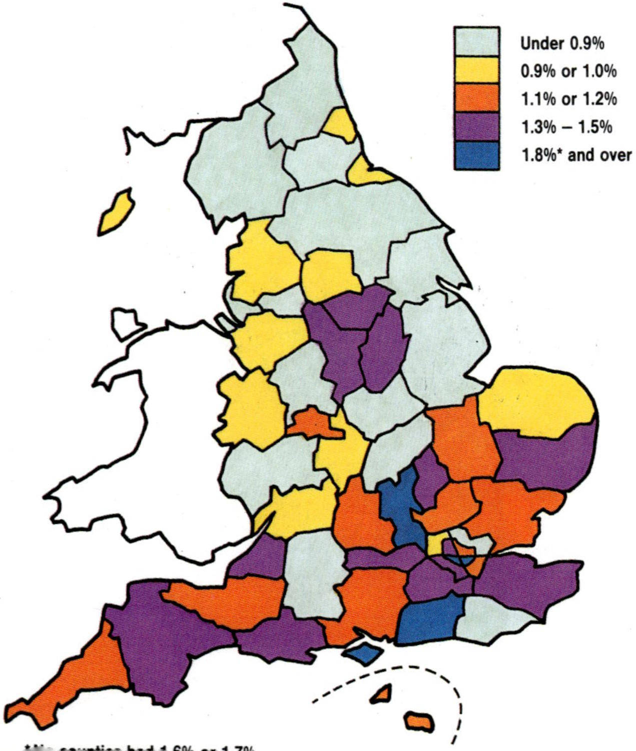

- Under 0.9%
- 0.9% or 1.0%
- 1.1% or 1.2%
- 1.3% – 1.5%
- 1.8%* and over

28. Charismatic Evangelical adult church attendance change 1985-1989

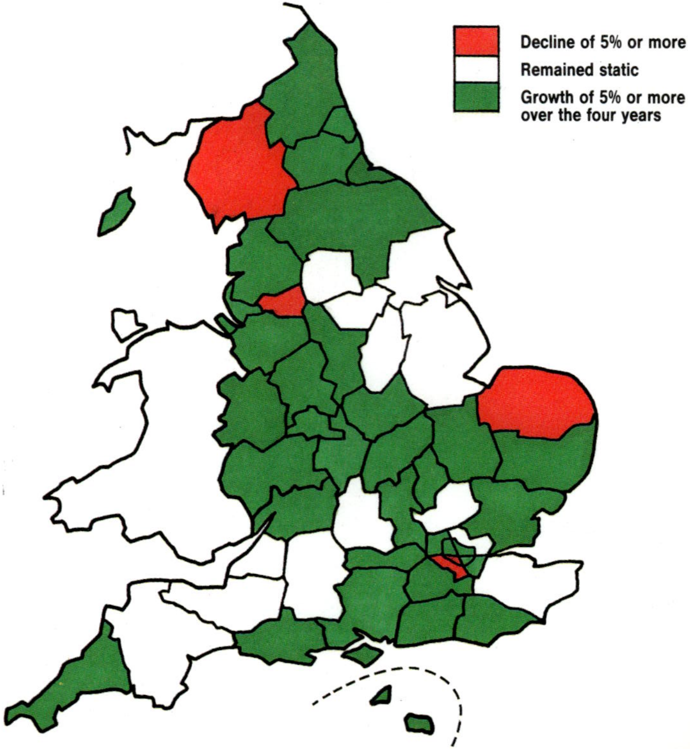

- Decline of 5% or more
- Remained static
- Growth of 5% or more over the four years

29. Total Evangelical adult churchgoers 1989 as a percentage of the population

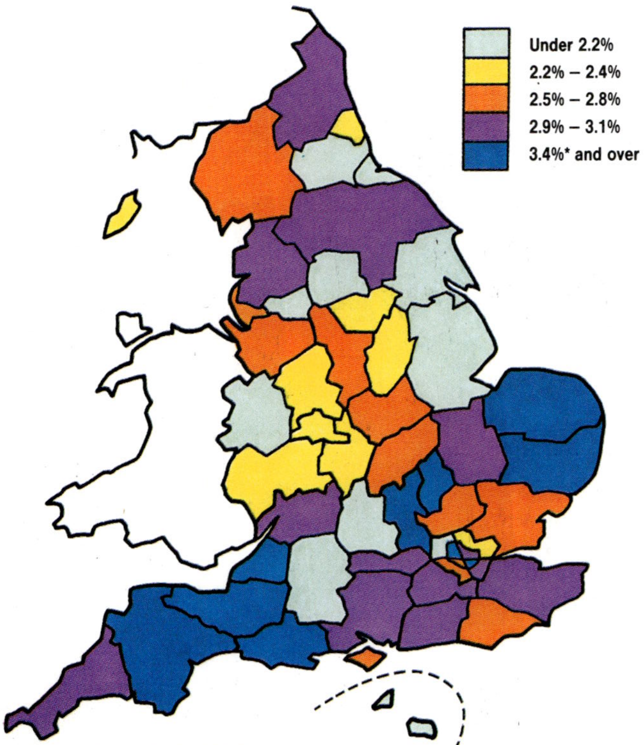

- Under 2.2%
- 2.2% — 2.4%
- 2.5% — 2.8%
- 2.9% — 3.1%
- 3.4%* and over

*No counties had 3.2% or 3.3%

30. Total Evangelical adult church attendance change 1985-1989

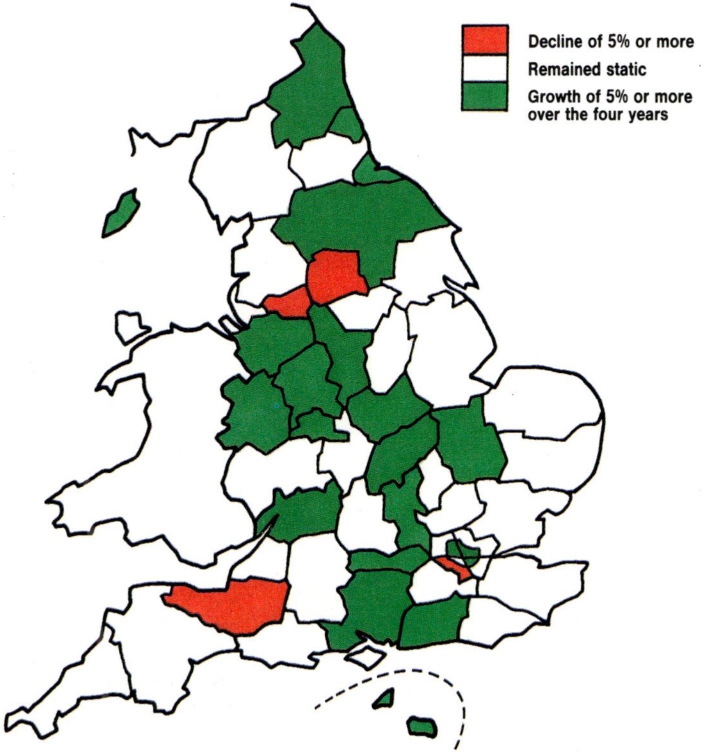

- Decline of 5% or more
- Remained static
- Growth of 5% or more over the four years

31. Low Church adult churchgoers 1989 as a percentage of the population

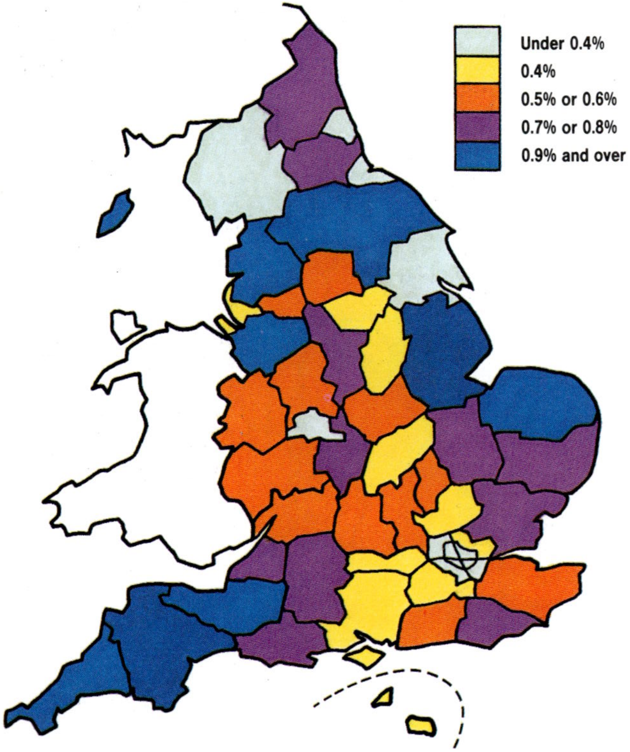

- Under 0.4%
- 0.4%
- 0.5% or 0.6%
- 0.7% or 0.8%
- 0.9% and over

32. Low Church adult church attendance change 1985–1989

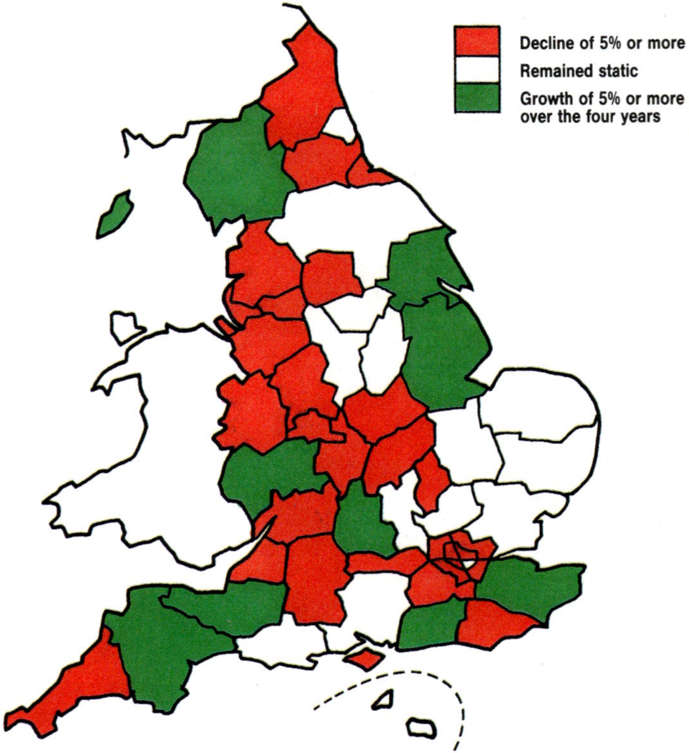

- Decline of 5% or more
- Remained static
- Growth of 5% or more over the four years

33. Broad adult churchgoers 1989 as a percentage of the population

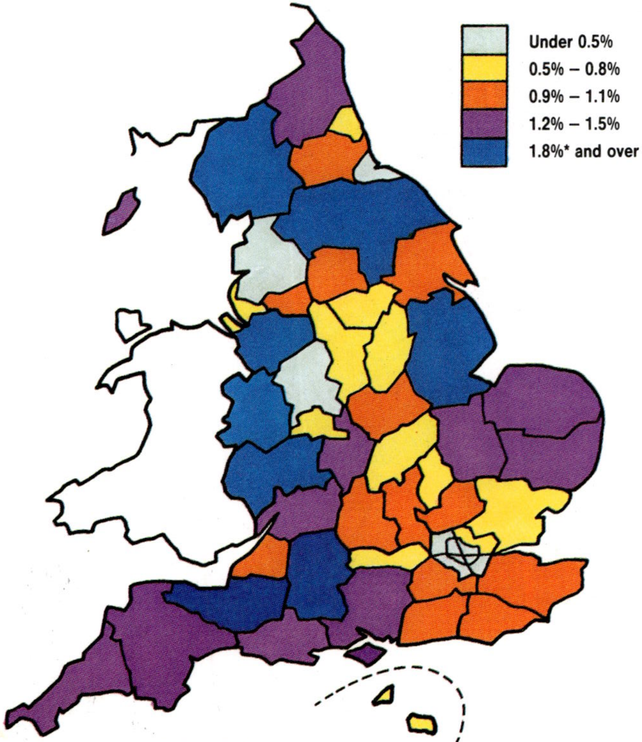

Under 0.5%
0.5% – 0.8%
0.9% – 1.1%
1.2% – 1.5%
1.8%* and over

*No counties had 1.6% or 1.7%

34. Broad adult church attendance change 1985-1989

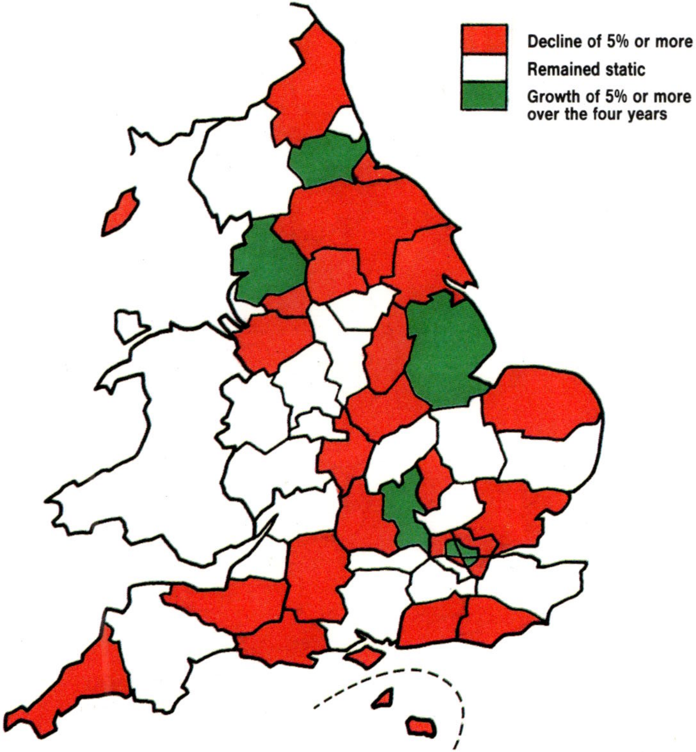

Decline of 5% or more
Remained static
Growth of 5% or more over the four years

35. Liberal adult churchgoers 1989 as a percentage of the population

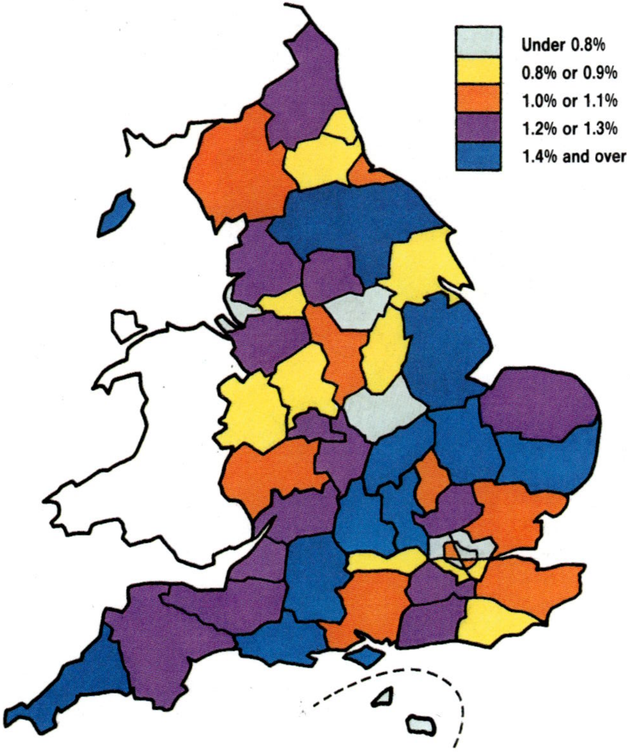

- Under 0.8%
- 0.8% or 0.9%
- 1.0% or 1.1%
- 1.2% or 1.3%
- 1.4% and over

36. Liberal adult church attendance change 1985-1989

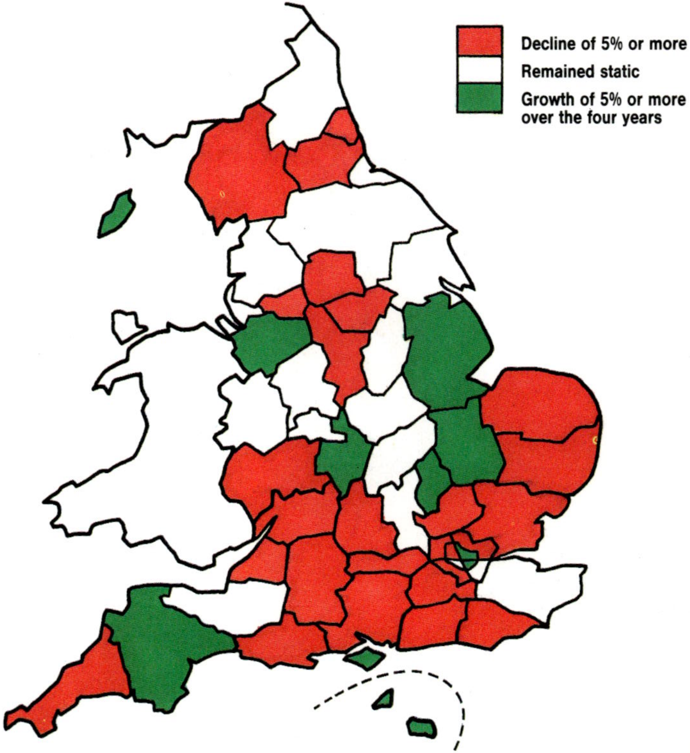

- Decline of 5% or more
- Remained static
- Growth of 5% or more over the four years

37. Anglo-Catholic adult churchgoers 1989 as a percentage of the population

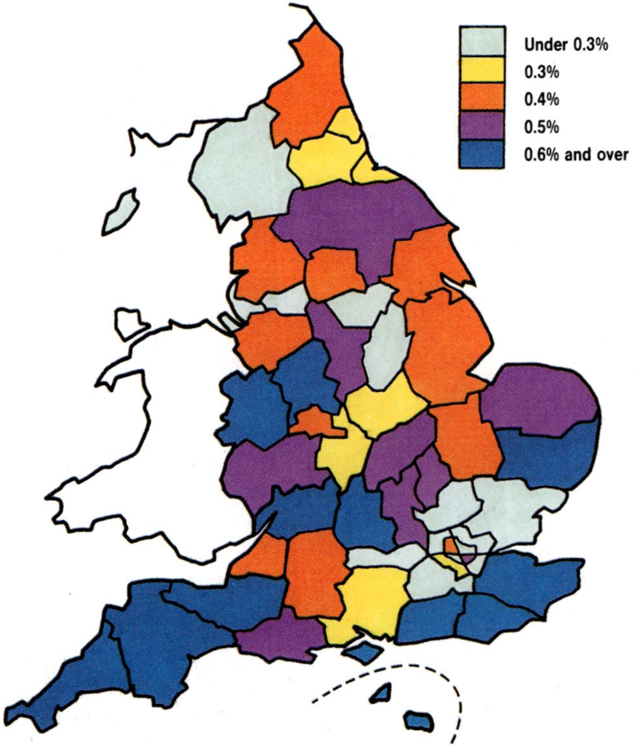

- Under 0.3%
- 0.3%
- 0.4%
- 0.5%
- 0.6% and over

38. Anglo-Catholic adult church attendance change 1985-1989

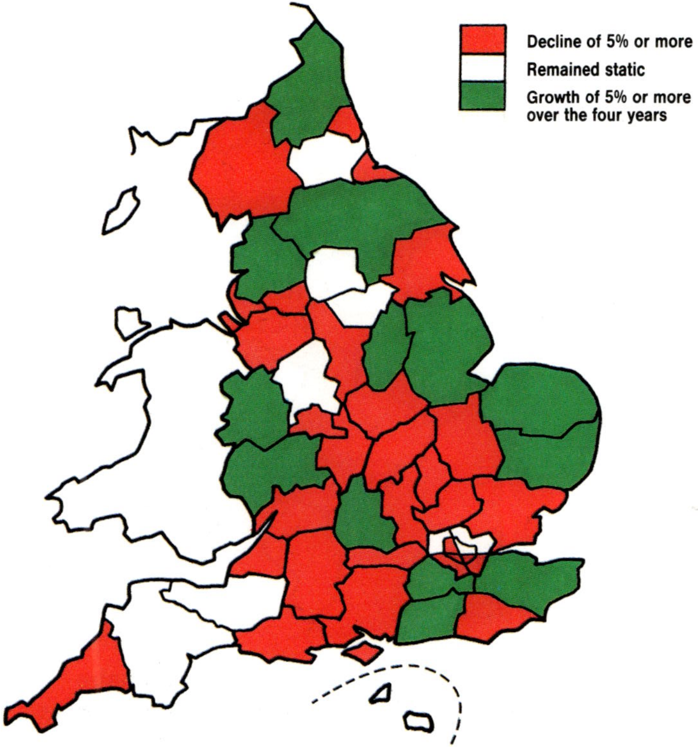

- Decline of 5% or more
- Remained static
- Growth of 5% or more over the four years

39. Catholic Churchmanship adult churchgoers 1989 as a percentage of the population

Under 2.4%
2.4% – 2.7%
2.8% – 3.3%
3.4% – 4.5%
4.6% and over

40. Catholic Churchmanship adult church attendance change 1985-1989

Decline of 5% or more
Remained static
Growth of 5% or more over the four years

41. All Other Churchmanships adult churchgoers 1989 as a percentage of the population

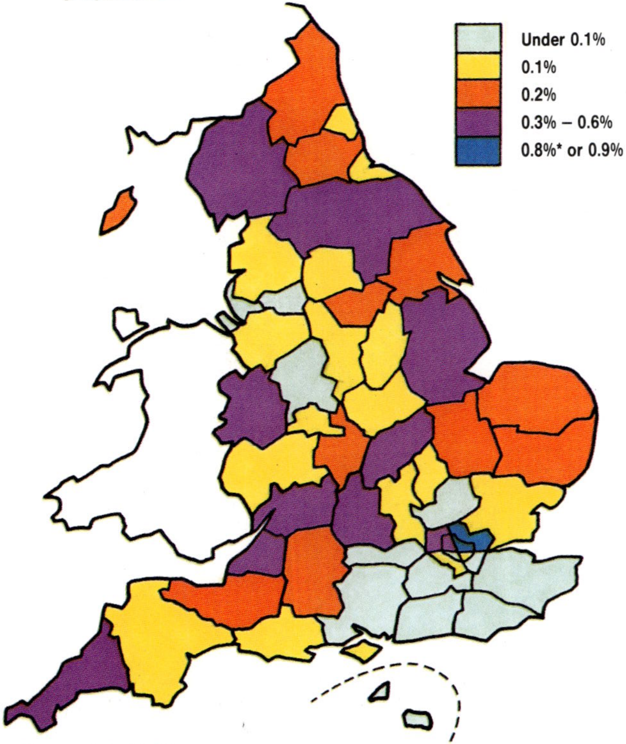

- Under 0.1%
- 0.1%
- 0.2%
- 0.3% – 0.6%
- 0.8%* or 0.9%

*No county had 0.7%

42. All Other Churchmanships adult church attendance change 1985-1989

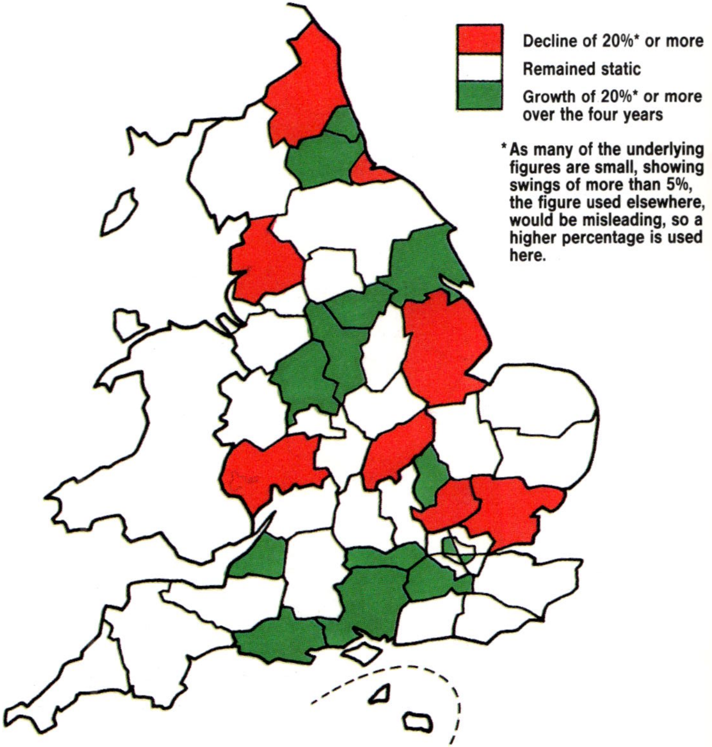

- Decline of 20%* or more
- Remained static
- Growth of 20%* or more over the four years

*As many of the underlying figures are small, showing swings of more than 5%, the figure used elsewhere, would be misleading, so a higher percentage is used here.

43. Urban and Suburban adult churchgoers 1989 as a percentage of all churchgoers

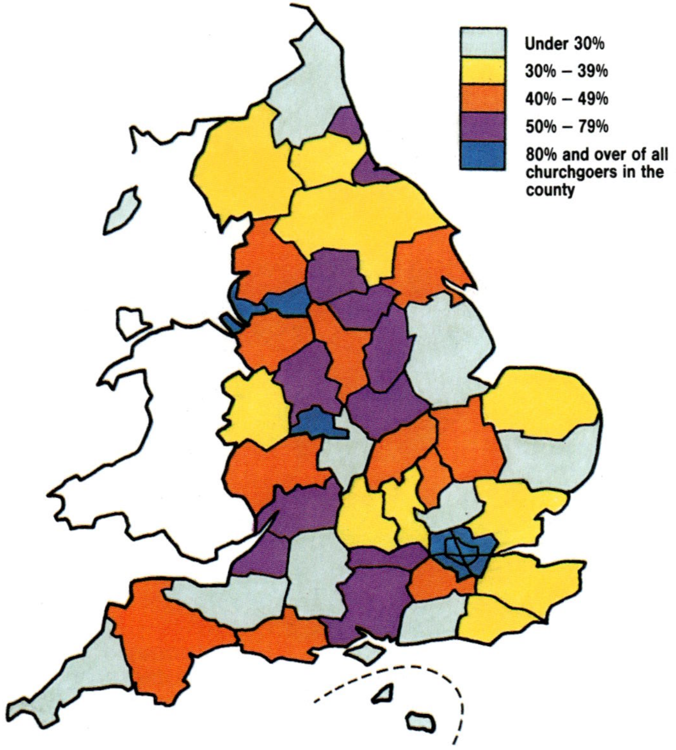

44. Rural adult churchgoers 1989 as a percentage of all churchgoers

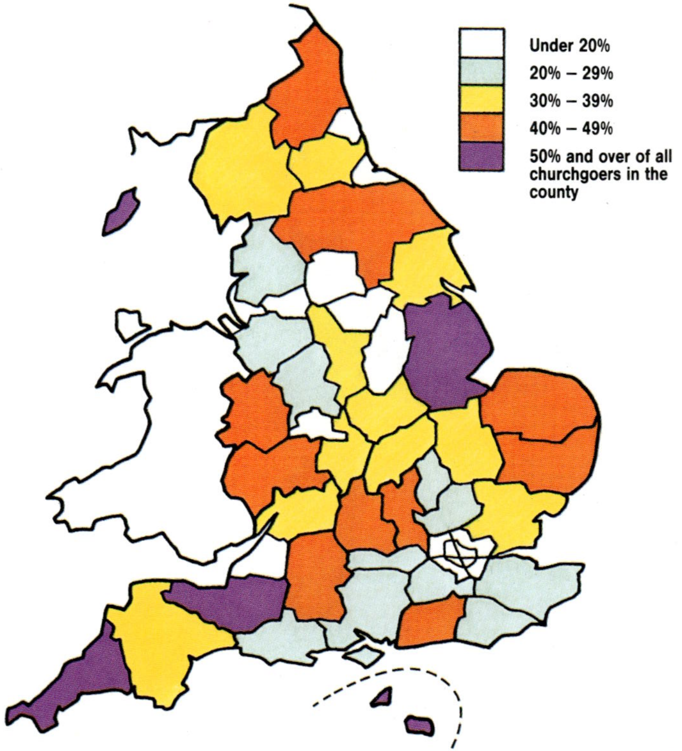

45. Urban and Suburban adult church attendance change 1985-1989

- Decline of 5% or more
- Remained static
- Growth of 5% or more over the four years

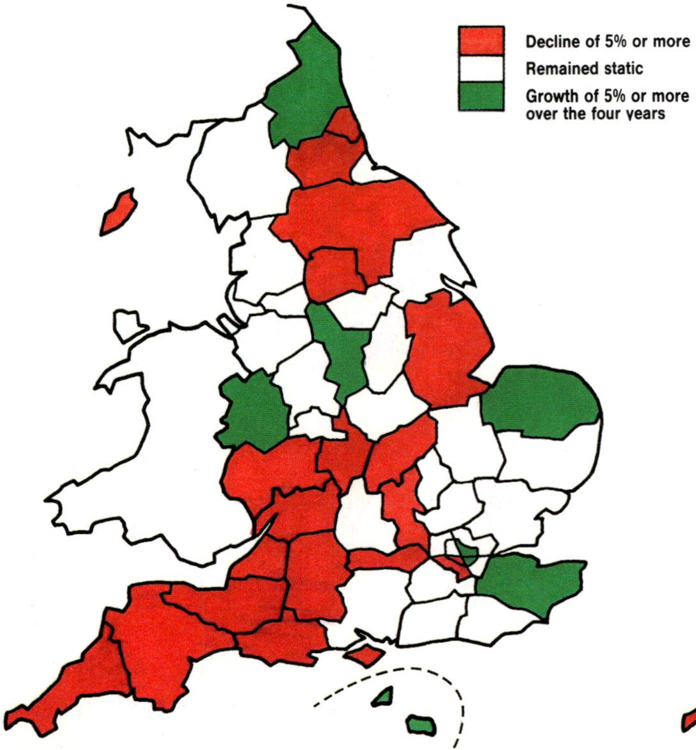

46. Rural adult church attendance change 1985-1989

- Decline of 5% or more
- Remained static
- Growth of 5% or more over the four years

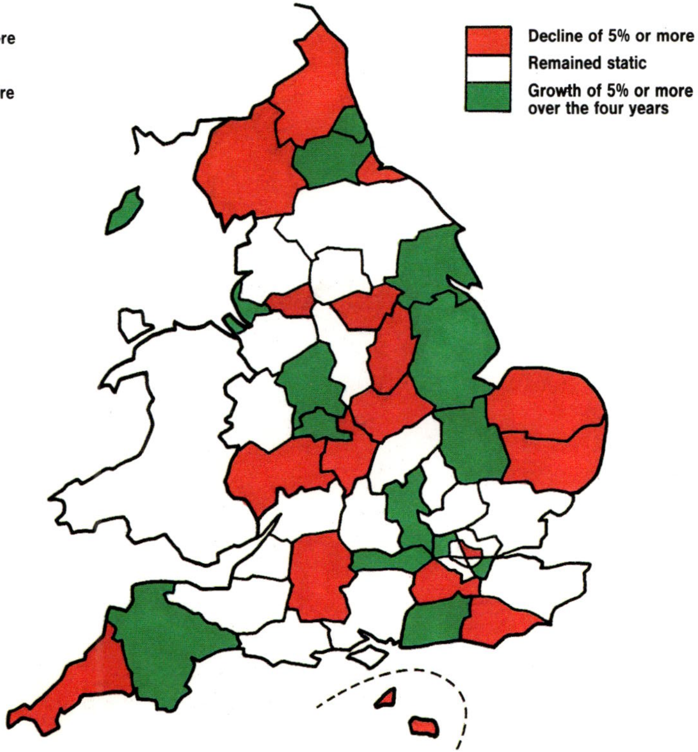

47. Adult churchgoers per county 1989

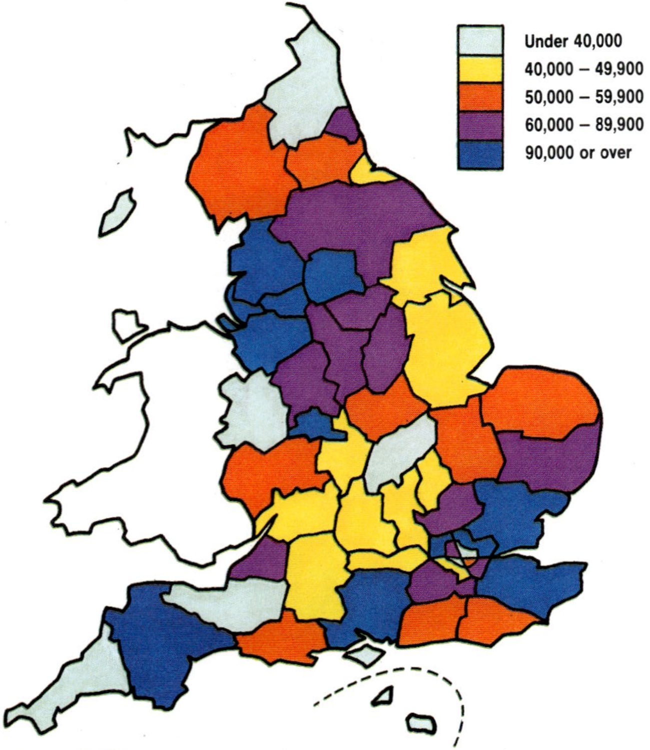

	Under 40,000
	40,000 – 49,900
	50,000 – 59,900
	60,000 – 89,900
	90,000 or over

48. Church members per county 1989

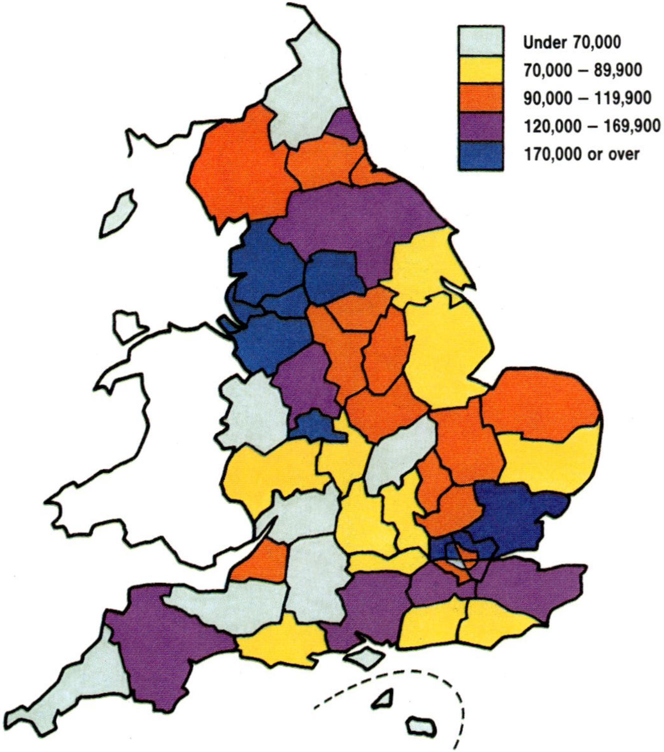

	Under 70,000
	70,000 – 89,900
	90,000 – 119,900
	120,000 – 169,900
	170,000 or over